Social justice and neoliberalism

D1569226

Social justice and neoliberalism

Global perspectives

Edited by Adrian Smith,
Alison Stenning and Katie Willis

ZED BOOKS
London & New York

Social Justice and Neoliberalism: Global Perspectives was first published in 2008
by Zed Books Ltd, 7 Cynthia Street, London N1 9JF, UK
and Room 400, 175 Fifth Avenue, New York, NY 10010, USA

www.zedbooks.co.uk

Designed and typeset in Monotype Garamond
by illuminati, www.illuminatibooks.co.uk
Cover designed by Andrew Corbett
Printed and bound in the EU by Biddles Ltd, King's Lynn

Distributed in the USA exclusively by Palgrave Macmillan, a division
of St Martin's Press, LLC, 175 Fifth Avenue, New York, 10010, USA

A catalogue record for this book is available from the British Library
Library of Congress Cataloging in Publication Data available

ISBN   978 1 84277 919 4 Hb
ISBN   978 1 84277 920 0 Pb

Contents

Figures and tables

Acknowledgements

This book arose out of a set of sessions held at the 2006 Annual Conference of the Royal Geographical Society (with the Institute of British Geographers) in London. We are very grateful to all the presenters in these sessions, several of whom – for a variety of reasons – we were not able to include in this collection. We are also very grateful to our discussants at the conference, Wendy Larner from the University of Bristol and Roger Lee from Queen Mary, University of London. Both provided stimulating feedback and discussion of the range of issues examined through these conference sessions. We would like to acknowledge their intellectual generosity in joining us for the sessions.

These sessions were sponsored by the Royal Geographical Society's Economic Geography, Developing Areas and Post-Socialist Geographies Research Groups, and we are very grateful for their intellectual and administrative support.

Some of the original ideas for these conference sessions and this collection arose during collaborative research conducted by Alison Stenning and Adrian Smith through an Economic and Social Research Council funded research project on 'Social exclusion, spaces of economic practice and post-socialism' (RES-00023–0695). We are very grateful to the ESRC for funding this research.

Ed Oliver in the Department of Geography, Queen Mary, University of London provided his usual cartographic excellence and proved to be the fount of patience in responding to seemingly never-ending requests for amendments to the range of maps and figures included in this book.

A version of Chapter 8 was previously published in *Antipode* 40(2), 2008. We are very grateful to Blackwell for allowing us to include a revised version of this publication in the collection.

Finally, we would like to thank Tamsine O'Riordan at Zed Books for her editorial guidance and patience in seeing this project through to the end, and to Susannah Trefgarne, formerly of Zed, who responded so positively to our initial enquiries about this publishing project.

INTRODUCTION

Social justice and neoliberalism

Katie Willis, Adrian Smith and Alison Stenning

Neoliberalism, understood as a set of ideas and practices centred on
an increased role for the free market, flexibility in labour markets
and a reconfiguration of state welfare activities, has become increasingly predominant across the world, particularly since the mid-1980s.
The supposed 'rolling-out' of neoliberalism as a response to the
perceived limitations of Keynesian or state socialist projects has
led to the neoliberalization of ever-increasing aspects of life in the
global North, global South and former 'communist' East (Watts
1994; Pickles and Smith 1998; Tickell and Peck 2003; Harvey 2005;
Saad-Filho and Johnston 2005; England and Ward 2007). As Giroux
(2004: xiii) has argued, 'Wedded to the belief that the market should
be the organizing principle for all political, social, and economic
decisions, neoliberalism wages an incessant attack on democracy,
public goods, and noncommodified values.' The ascendency of neoliberalization has brought with it important implications for social
justice, as the 'privatization of everything' (Watts 1994) constructs
a landscape of winners and losers and gives rise to a range of
social justice movements contesting and coping with the neoliberal
'revolution'. The contributors to this book consider these processes
through in-depth studies in particular communities across the world,

from South America, to southern Africa, to Europe. *Social Justice and Neoliberalism* seeks to ground neoliberalism in local struggles over everyday existence and the social reproduction of the lives of peoples and communities embroiled in the ever-widening reach of marketization. Such a grounded approach thus speaks to the call to recognize the embeddedness of 'actually existing neoliberalism' (Brenner and Theodore 2002) and the articulation of political-economic processes with everyday lives (Stenning 2005; Smith 2007).

The book focuses on neoliberal processes and outcomes 'from the margins', both geographically (global South, former state socialist East and peripheral communities in the global North) and socially. By drawing on perspectives from peoples and places that are often not considered in the construction, implementation or analysis of neoliberal-informed policies, the contributors aim to provide insights which might challenge existing perspectives on neoliberalism.

Using examples from both East and West Europe (see chapters by Hörschelmann; May et al.; Pattison; Smith et al.), Latin America (see chapters by North and Olson), sub-Saharan Africa (see chapters by Marx and May et al.) and Turkey (see Ergün's chapter), the contributors to this volume consider how neoliberalism has been experienced and contested in particular spaces; as well as how neoliberalization creates new possibilities for social justice campaigns and for alternative economic forms outside of, but articulated with, capitalism, which is positioned at the heart of neoliberal projects (Gibson-Graham 2006; Smith and Stenning 2006).

Aihwa Ong (2007: 3) has contrasted 'big N Neoliberalism' as 'a fixed set of attributes with predetermined outcomes' with the ways in which 'small n neoliberalism' operates in practice, 'as a logic of governing that migrates and is selectively taken up in diverse political contexts'. Many of the contributors to this volume draw both explicitly and implicitly on Ong's ideas of neoliberalism, not as a coherent set of ideas which are imposed in the same way throughout the world, but rather as a 'migrating set of practices.' In this way, they dispute Barnett's (2005) arguments regarding the 'non-existence' of neoliberalism, recognizing that there is something which ties such practices together such that grouping them as 'neoliberal' is a useful strategy for both theoretical and political purposes. Such a recognition, however, does not deny that 'The restless landscape of actually existing neoliberalism ... is characterized by deeply ingrained institutional geographies, as it is marked by a series of "local", *but interconnected*, neoliberalisms' (Peck 2008: 33, emphasis in the original). In pluralizing neoliberalisms, *Social Justice and Neoliberalism* seeks to explore both the commonalities and the diversity of neoliberalization and its experiences in contrasting social and geographical contexts (see also Larner 2003), and with variant implications for social justice.

The book deals with four main themes, which will be considered in turn in this introductory chapter and which we return to in our concluding chapter. First, we consider the ways in which neoliberalization has been resisted, either intentionally in large-scale social movements, or through smaller-scale practices. Second, the entanglement of neoliberalization with the forging of new identities, particularly around entrepreneurship and individualization, are considered. These are linked to new forms of governance, often mobilized around discourses of 'empowerment' and 'autonomy'. Third, we consider how the implementation of neoliberalism affects opportunities for social justice and how the material effects of neoliberalism may undermine campaigns for greater social equity. Finally, we draw on literatures around 'diverse economies' to decentre capitalism and examine alternative economic practices which may arise from, or exist alongside, forms of neoliberalized capitalism.

Neoliberalism and resistance

It is important to recognize that while it is not a coherent or homogenous ideology which unleashes a predictable 'economic tsunami' (Ong 2007), neoliberalism and neoliberalization practices have very real and often violent material outcomes (Giroux 2004; Hudson 2006; Springer 2008). These impacts are not, however, accepted passively by individuals, communities or households; rather, forms of resistance may be adopted or developed. By using this concept of 'resistance' we are not in any way reifying neoliberalism (Leitner et al. 2007), but rather we are recognizing that people and organizations challenge and contest the ways in which neoliberal policies threaten livelihoods, social cohesion and environmental conditions. Actions taken in the context of neoliberalization may be classified as resistance in political terms, but may also be seen as economic and social strategies for 'getting by'. While some such strategies reflect desperation, as we shall show later in this chapter in our consideration of debates over diverse economies, some can be interpreted as more explicit challenges to neoliberalization. A recognition of the contested nature of neoliberalism is vital if struggles for alternative futures are to be achieved. Neoliberalism itself is a product of contestation during the Fordist era (Leitner et al. 2007) and developed in a highly conflictual way (Peck 2008).

High-profile Latin American cases have become symbolic of resistance to neoliberalism and material examples of how 'another world is possible' (Fisher and Ponniah 2003). Such examples include Hugo Chavez's 'Bolivarian revolution' in Venezuela, social budgeting in Porto Alegre and the 'water wars' in Cochabamba, Bolivia, where local protests against water privatization were hailed as a success (Laurie et al. 2002; Laurie 2005). The barter, or *trueque*, networks set up in Argentina following the currency crisis and economic crash of 2001 are another symbolic case and represent a particular form of resistance to neoliberalization where local communities developed alternative currency forms and new economic spaces for non-capitalist forms of exchange (see North in this volume).

The role of IMF-led structural adjustment programmes (SAPs) in exacerbating existing marginal conditions for many communities in the global South and the former state socialist East has resulted in protests and other forms of resistance. Such resistance may, however, reflect actions which could be described as 'weapons of the weak' (Scott 1985). For millions of people, formal organized protests and resistance are very difficult to achieve given the precarious nature of their working existence and the hidden nature of their employment. In such cases, as described by Ergün in her chapter on Turkish garment workers, subtle strategies of resistance have to be adopted, using kinship networks or other forms of informal cooperation.

Previous research in many parts of the world has identified the importance of 'jumping scale' to achieve positive results in resisting neoliberal policies (see, for example, Kelly 1999 on the Philippines). Such scale-jumping is needed if 'local' campaigns are to have sustainable effects. New forms of trade-union organizing have adopted such strategies in the face of global capital, moving beyond national-level campaigns to transnational activities (Waterman and Wills 2001). 'Local' level campaigns may also achieve greater publicity and hence are more likely to achieve their goals, if they operate at a 'higher' geographical scale. This, for example, is the case with the Living Wage campaigns, outlined by Pattison for Manchester and May et al. for London, in their chapters. Living Wage campaigns started in Baltimore in the USA, but have been transferred and reconfigured for particular cities in the UK. Such campaigns work to resist the economic marginalization that is increasingly felt by large sectors of the population in waged work, resulting in the 'working poor' (see also Toynbee 2003, and Smith et al. this volume for a contrasting experience from East-Central Europe). Neoliberal policies, such as outsourcing and deregulation, have created conditions in which workers are unable to earn a 'living wage', which would enable their household's social reproduction. Many such workers are in sectors with limited trade union activity, resulting in less formal forms of resistance and in the emergence of new political movements around low pay in expensive global city locations (Wills 2004).

Identities, subjectivities and new forms of governance

Neoliberalization is often represented as being associated with the promotion of new forms of identity and subject formation, with a shift from collective forms of identity to more individualized subjectivities (Rose 1996). Such individualized subjectivities rest on notions of autonomy and choice, which have spread to all spheres of life, from employment to welfare provision, and generated new forms of governmentality. The underlying premiss is that when individuals are given choice within a free market, they are empowered; explanations for inequalities are then transferred from embedded unequal societal structures to individual recklessness or application (Beck and Beck-Gernsheim 2002). As Leitner et al. (2007: 4) argue, 'Under neoliberalism, individual freedom is redefined as the capacity for self-realization and freedom from bureaucracy rather than freedom from want, with human behaviour reconceptualized along economic lines.'

Such interpretations of individualization do, however, need to recognize the context-specific nature of these processes, both in spatial and in social terms. Ong (2007) argues that in the Indian and Chinese cases, the move towards neoliberal subjectivities is taking place within particular political formations and that, as a result, only a very small percentage of the population in both countries, for example the highly skilled IT workers in Bangalore, are encouraged or permitted to develop such identity formations. This is very different to the more ubiquitous process of individualization as highlighted in the global North. In some cases, individuals can benefit from such processes, being able to participate in new forms of consumption activities and enjoy the freedoms that come with economic success. Hörschelmann, in her chapter on young people in the former East Germany, highlights how, for some, new opportunities are viewed positively. The entrepreneurial aspects of the barter networks in Argentina (discussed by North in his chapter) can also be seen as having the potential for individuals to claim new subjectivities. However, this is not an automatic outcome of growing 'freedoms', as structural limitations on the ability to act in this new landscape of possibilities is greatly restricted. Smith et al. and Pattison, in particular, highlight how labour market restructuring and employment flexibilization are creating a discourse of individual opportunity alongside a reality of labour market marginalization and the emergence of in-work poverty.

Structural adjustment policies have been criticized for having implicit gendered identity assumptions which construct women as being previously 'unproductive'. Diane Elson (1995) argues forcefully that SAPs have been gender-blind in that they have assumed that women are available to enter the paid labour force at times of economic crisis and that they have a seemingly limitless supply of time and energy to contribute both paid work and increasing unpaid domestic reproductive work to household survival as welfare is increasingly privatized. Paid labour, especially in the expanding factories of multinationals and the companies they outsource to, also has a strong gender component with young, educated women often being the preferred labour force (Chant and McIlwaine 1995). These preferences are based on perceived essentialist characteristics of hard work, reliability and nimble fingers, which make such workers ideal in the new international division of labour. The fact that female workers usually command lower wages than their male counterparts is also of significant importance. In this respect, Ergün's chapter on Turkish clothing workers brings out the limited forms of worker autonomy, particularly for female workers, within the small-scale workshops found in Istanbul's periphery.

Hard work and application within the labour force are also found to have limited benefits for the Polish and Ghanaian immigrants discussed in the chapter by May et al., as well as the low-income populations of Manchester discussed by Pattison in his chapter, and of Bratislava and Kraków discussed by Smith et al. in their chapter. In each case, growing flexibility within the labour market, through subcontracting in the National Health Service, through payment per room in the hotel cleaning trade, and through the emergence of contingent service-sector work in East-Central European cities, has benefited businesses keen to cut costs in a competitive environment and to develop new strategies for capital accumulation. However, in this context, and as we suggest above, workers are increasingly unable to earn sufficient income to ensure a reasonable standard of living. Thus, rather than being able to take advantage of the new consumer choices which are available to them, these workers are excluded (see also Toynbee 2003). This has significant implications for social justice and the struggle for greater equity in societies throughout the world.

Social justice and neoliberalism

While the various critiques of neoliberalization have been extensive, not least in assessing the economic, social and gendered effects of rapid marketization and state withdrawal and reconfiguration, few have engaged explicitly with debates over social justice. As Pattison (this volume) notes, 'social justice [is] about fairness and equality of opportunity ... [Yet] Kitson et al. ... have noted that "neoliberal economic policies, by lifting the constraints on the exercise of unequal power, increase injustice and trigger a downward economic and social spiral".' Problematizing the links between social (in)justice and neoliberalization is thus at the core of this book's endeavours.

There is, of course, a long lineage of writing on social justice within the discipline of geography and beyond. David Smith (1994), among others, pioneered the development of a welfare geography in which analyses of social and spatial justice were key to understanding the unequal distributional consequences of social change. Others, such as David Harvey, found debates over space and social justice a useful, but not fully complete, basis for a more radical geography. For Harvey (1973), social justice became a route to Marxism. Yet Harvey was to return to an explicit engagement with social justice issues in his later reaction (1996) to the postmodern turn.

Conceptualizations of social justice have also played a key role in debates over the relative merits of civil society and the state in the face of market violence and neoliberalization. For example, Iris Marion Young (2000) has stressed the limits of civil society organizations to promote social justice agendas, through a critique of libertarian, communitarian and post-Marxist claims. In her focus on self-development in the promotion of justice, inclusion and democracy, Young argues that 'self-development cannot rely on the communicative and organizational activities of civil society alone, but requires positive state intervention to regulate and direct economic activity' (Young 2000: 184). As Young argues in *Justice and the Politics of Difference* (1990: 26), 'Evaluating social justice according to whether persons have opportunities, therefore, must involve evaluating not a distributive outcome but the social structures that enable or constrain the individuals in relevant situations.' Indeed, Young (2000: 185) recognizes that if 'promoting social justice means that societies should ... aim to make conditions for self-development available for everyone, then these endemic consequences of profit- and market-oriented economic processes ought to be corrected.' In this sense, Young provides a critique of neoliberalizing tendencies through social and state action (see also Fainstein 2007).

The discussion of resistance to neoliberal policies and practices earlier in this chapter highlighted the ways in which neoliberalism has been associated with perceived threats to social justice and growing inequalities. However, in common with debates around individualization, autonomy and empowerment, policymakers adopting a broad neoliberal line have not excluded consideration of social justice. For example, as part of 'roll-out neoliberalism', policies to combat social exclusion were often included (Brenner and Theodore 2002). This may be because of an ethical commitment to equity or greater fairness, as in the concept of 'Adjustment with a Human Face' (Cornia et al. 1987) or it could be that the inclusion of policies promoting justice and ethics are included within neoliberalism to maintain legitimacy (Leitner et al. 2007).

However, the particular kind of anti-social exclusion policies that are encouraged fit very well into broader conceptualizations of the neoliberal subject. Non-governmental, non-profit or community organizations (particularly what have been termed 'faith-based organizations') have been identified by governments and international institutions, such as the World Bank, as playing a key role in supporting marginalized groups. While this may be seen as a way of combining attempts to achieve social justice with neoliberal economic reforms, in many cases, these NGOs are constrained in how they can work with potential beneficiaries. As Mayer (2007: 100) states, 'Much of what used to constitute urban activism in this context now has demobilizing effects, where community-based organizations have become too busy training, feeding, and inserting their clients into job programs instead of representing them, lobbying for them'. Fyfe (2005) makes similar points regarding broader policies towards the so-called 'third sector' in the UK. In her chapter on religious organizations in Highland Peru, Olson discusses the changing nature of social justice campaigning from a period of widespread violence to a neoliberalizing economy.

NGOs and other such organizations, rather than being separate from the state and challenging government policies around neo-liberalization, are being increasingly drawn into forms of service provision. Funding opportunities often depend on particular governance structures (Mayer 2007), with groups becoming beholden to funders (including different parts of the state) rather than to their members or possible beneficiaries (Townsend et al. 2002). At the same time, as with other workers, NGO employees are encouraged to adopt more 'professional' identities and approaches to work, reinforcing the new forms of subjectivity associated with neoliberal policies (Bondi and Laurie 2005).

While such an analysis can present a rather pessimistic view, it is important to recognize the continued existence of spaces within which individuals and groups can campaign for greater social justice. These spaces may be newly created as part of neoliberalism, as with the new migrant spaces opened up by migration to London discussed in the chapter by May et al. These may revolve around religious institutions, or broader activities for social justice, as in the Living Wage campaign.

Diverse economies and neoliberalization

The concept of 'diverse economies' has received an increasing amount of attention in recent years (see, for example, Gibson-Graham 2006; Leyshon 2005; Smith and Stenning 2006). This book builds on this work, in its attempts to decentre the focus of economic activities on capitalism within neoliberal projects. Gibson-Graham (2006), for example, who has been at the forefront of the diverse economies agenda, uses the locally identified range of transactions, labour practices and enterprises within the municipality of Jagna, Bohol province, in the Philippines, to stress the contributions of non-capitalist activities to local livelihoods. She highlights that 'One effect of this representation of a diverse economy is that capitalist activity... is knocked off its perch so to speak, and with it goes the ordered certainties associated with development dynamics' (Gibson-Graham 2005: 13).

Diverse economies encompass a wide range of activities involved in the production and distribution of economic surpluses (Gibson-Graham 2006), and have the potential to present alternatives to capitalist development which are possibly less exploitative than capitalist labour practices. However, as Samers (2005) argues, it is vital that an identification of the components of diverse economies, particularly those which could be classified as 'informal economy' activities, are not romanticized (see also Smith and Stenning 2006). Samers points out how such activities are not always progressive and, rather than reflecting perceived positive dimensions such as trust, reciprocity and community cohesion, may be based on inward-looking practices based

on distrust. The links between capitalist and non-capitalist activities
are also difficult to identify, as has been argued in the long-standing
literature on the informal sector, particularly in the global South (see,
for example, Santos 1979).

Colin Marx in his chapter on informal activities in Durban, South
Africa, contributes to these debates around informality and diverse
economies, by highlighting particular spaces where certain economic
and social processes converge to make informal-sector activities viable
within a city which has experienced major neoliberalization. The
line between presenting such activities purely as 'coping strategies'
or 'survival strategies' in the face of extreme economic pressures
and more positive alternative economic forms is also clear in Smith
et al.'s chapter on Kraków, Poland, and Bratislava, Slovakia. Here,
household-based activities have become increasingly important in
the post-socialist transition period where employment shifts and the
restructuring of welfare provision has left many households exposed.
In both cases, the authors argue that these diverse economic activities
widen our conceptualizations of economic practices and, at least in
the Durban context, have the potential to provide alternatives to
capitalist development, drawing as they do on long-standing social
and moral practices.

Other forms of economic practice may represent much more
obvious alternatives within an increasingly neoliberal world. In particular, the growth of Local Exchange Trading Schemes (LETS) and
alternative currencies have received significant attention (Lee et al.
2004; North 2007). These community-based attempts to break out
of the mainstream capitalist economy and draw on the skills and
relationships in particular spaces may be high-profile alternatives,
but, as the Argentine barter networks demonstrate (see North in this
volume), their capacity to move beyond short-term survival activities
and the scale limitations on their scope mean that overly positive
interpretations need to be tempered.

Conclusion

Social Justice and Neoliberalism provides a set of global perspectives on
the diversity of forms, processes and experiences of neoliberalization

while also seeking to be attendant to the social justice implications
of the extension of market relations into more and more spheres of
social and economic life. The contributions to the volume each, in
different ways, seek to explore the ways in which ideas, practices
and materialities of neoliberalization travel; how neoliberal policies
and practices have global reach but are always constituted through
contingent social relations which create an uneven and differentiated
landscape of neoliberalization (see also Larner 2003; Leitner et al.
2007; England and Ward 2007). Through this contingent reading of
neoliberalization, the contributions seek to show how 'big projects'
are always constituted through place-based practices with their own
trajectories, histories and geographies. In these ways, this reading
asks us to consider the ways in which understanding 'big' political
economic projects such as neoliberalism always has to consider
their 'domestication' – how such phenomena are not 'simply "out
there" and all-powerful' but 'are always already particular domestic
and local phenomena – always mediated through everyday practice,
always made tolerable as best one can, through the lives of ordinary
people' (Smith and Rochovská 2007: 1165; see also Creed 1998). The
contributions to *Social Justice and Neoliberalism* also ask us to consider
how neoliberalization creates mobile subjects which translate processes of marketization across space – how neoliberalization and its
consequences have lives and bodies that connect places and peoples
at different scales and work to constitute and rework neoliberal subjectivities. It is through this translation, mobility and domestication,
therefore, that the contributions to *Social Justice and Neoliberalism* seek
to open up our conceptualization of how neoliberalization processes
literally 'take place' and how they are contested in varying contexts.

References

Barnett, C. (2005) 'The consolation of "neoliberalism"', *Geoforum* 36(1): 7–12.
Beck, U., and E. Beck-Gernsheim (2002) *Individualization: Institutionalized Individu-
alism and its Social and Political Consequences*, London: Sage.
Bondi, L., and N. Laurie (2005) Introduction to special issue on 'Working the
spaces of neoliberalism: Activism, incorporation and professionalisation',
Antipode 37(3): 394–401.
Brenner, N., and N. Theodore (2002) 'Cities and the geographies of "actually
existing neoliberalism"', *Antipode* 34(3): 349–79.

Chant, S., and C. McIlwaine (1995) *Women of a Lesser Cost: Female Labour, Foreign Exchange and Philippine Development*, London: Pluto Press.

Cornia, A., R. Jolly and F. Stewart (1987) *Adjustment with a Human Face: Protecting the Vulnerable and Promoting Growth*, Oxford: Clarendon Press.

Creed, G. (1998) *Domesticating Revolution: From Socialist Reform to Ambivalent Transition in a Bulgarian Village*, College Station PA: Penn State University Press.

Elson, D. (1995) 'Male bias in the development process', in D. Elson (ed.), *Male Bias in the Development Process*, 2nd edn, Manchester: Manchester University Press.

England, K., and K. Ward (eds) (2007) *Neoliberalization: States, Networks, Peoples*, Oxford: Blackwell.

Fainstein, S. (2007) 'Iris Marion Young (1949–2006): A tribute', *Antipode* 39(2): 382–7.

Fisher, W., and T. Ponniah (eds) (2003) *Another World in Possible: Popular Alternatives to Globalization at the World Social Forum*, London: Zed Books.

Fyfe, N. (2005) 'Making space for "neocommunitarianism"? The third sector, state and civil society in the UK', *Antipode* 37(3): 536–57.

Gibson-Graham, J.K. (2005) 'Surplus possibilities: Postdevelopment and community economies', *Singapore Journal of Tropical Geography* 26: 4–26.

Gibson-Graham, J.K. (2006) *A Post-Capitalist Politics*, Minneapolis: University of Minnesota Press.

Giroux, H. (2004) *The Terror of Neoliberalism: Authoritarianism and the Eclipse of Democracy*, Boulder CO: Paradigm.

Harvey, D. (1973) *Social Justice and the City*, London: Arnold.

Harvey, D. (1996) *Justice, Nature and the Geography of Difference*, Oxford: Blackwell.

Harvey, D. (2005) *A Brief History of Neoliberalism*, Oxford: Oxford University Press.

Hudson, R. (2006) 'On what's right and keeping left: or Why geography still needs Marxian political economy', *Antipode* 38(2): 374–95.

Kelly, P. (1999) *Landscapes of Globalization: Human Geographies of Economic Change in the Philippines*, London: Routledge.

Kitson, M., R. Martin and F. Wilkinson (2000) 'Labour markets, social justice and economic efficiency', *Cambridge Journal of Economics* 24: 631–41.

Larner, W. (2003) 'Neoliberalism?', *Environment and Planning D: Society and Space* 21: 509–512.

Laurie, N. (2005) 'Establishing development orthodoxy: Negotiating masculinities in the water sector', *Development and Change*, 36: 527–49.

Laurie, N., S. Radcliffe and R. Andolina (2002) 'The new excluded "indigenous"? The implications of multi-ethnic politics for water reform in Bolivia', in R. Seider (ed.), *Multiculturalism in Latin America: Indigenous Rights, Diversity and Democracy*, London: Palgrave Macmillan, pp. 252–76.

Lee, R., A. Leyshon, T. Aldridge, J. Tooke, C. Williams and N. Thrift (2004) 'Making geographies and histories? Constructing circuits of value', *Environment and Planning D: Society and Space* 22: 595–617.

Leitner, H., E.S. Sheppard, K. Sziarto and A. Maringanti (2007) 'Contesting urban futures: Decentering neoliberalism', in H. Leitner, J. Peck and E.

Sheppard (eds), *Contesting Neoliberalism: The Urban Frontier*, New York: Guilford Press, pp. 1–25.

Leyshon, A. (2005) 'Introduction: Diverse economies', *Antipode* 37(5): 856–62.

Mayer, M. (2007) 'Contesting the neoliberalization of urban governance', in H. Leitner, J. Peck and E. Sheppard (eds), *Contesting Neoliberalism: The Urban Frontier*, New York: Guilford, pp. 90–125.

North, P. (2007) *Money and Liberation: The Micropolitics of Alternative Currency Movements*, Minneapolis: University of Minnesota Press.

Ong, A. (2007) 'Neoliberalism as mobile technology', *Transactions of the Institute of British Geographers* 32: 3–8.

Peck, J. (2008) 'Remaking laissez-faire', *Progress in Human Geography* 32: 3–43.

Pickles, J., and A. Smith (eds) (1998) *Theorising Transition: The Political Economy of Post-Communist Transformations*, London: Routledge.

Rose, N. (1996) 'Governing "advanced" liberal democracies', in A. Barry, T. Osborne and N. Rose (eds), *Foucault and Political Reason: Liberalism, Neo-Liberalism and Rationalities of Government*, London: UCL Press, pp. 37–64.

Saad-Filho, A., and D. Johnston (eds) (2005) *Neoliberalism: A Critical Reader*, London: Pluto Press.

Samers, M. (2005) 'The myopia of "diverse economies" or a critique of the "informal economy"', *Antipode* 37(5): 875–86.

Santos, M. (1979) *The Shared Space: The Circuits of the Urban Economy in Underdeveloped Countries*, London: Methuen.

Scott, J.C. (1985) *Weapons of the Weak: Everyday Forms of Peasant Resistance*, New Haven: Yale University Press.

Smith, A. (2007) 'Articulating neo-liberalism: diverse economies and urban restructuring in post-socialism', in H. Leitner, J. Peck and E. Sheppard (eds), *Contesting Neoliberalism: The Urban Frontier*, New York: Guilford, pp. 204–22.

Smith, A., and A. Rochovská (2007) 'Domesticating neo-liberalism: Everyday lives and the geographies of post-socialist transformations', *Geoforum* 38(6): 1163–78.

Smith, A., and A. Stenning (2006) 'Beyond household economies: Articulations and spaces of economic practice in post-socialism', *Progress in Human Geography* 30: 190–213.

Smith, D. (1994) *Geography and Social Justice*, Oxford: Blackwell.

Springer, S. (2008) 'The nonillusory effects of neoliberalisation: Linking geographies of poverty, inequality and violence', *Geoforum* 39(4): 1520–25.

Stenning, A. (2005) 'Post-socialism and the changing geographies of the everyday in Poland', *Transactions of the Institute of British Geographers* 30: 113–27.

Tickell, A., and J. Peck (2003) 'Making global rules: Globalization or neo-liberalization?', in J. Peck and H. Wai-chung Yeung (eds), *Remaking the Global Economy: Economic and Geographical Perspectives*, London: Sage, pp. 163–81.

Townsend, J., G. Porter and E. Mawdsley (2002) 'The role of the transnational community of non-governmental organisations: Governance or poverty reduction?', *Journal of International Development* 14: 829–39.

Toynbee, P. (2003) *Hard Work: Life in Low-pay Britain*, London: Bloomsbury.

Waterman, P and J. Wills (eds) (2001) *Place, Space and the New Labour Internationalisms*, Oxford: Blackwell.

Watts, M. (1994) 'Development II: The privatization of everything', *Progress in Human Geography* 18: 371–84.

Wills, J. (2004) 'Organising the low paid: East London's living wage campaign as a vehicle for change', in W. Brown, E.G. Healy, E. Heery and P. Taylor (eds), *The Future of Worker Representation*, Oxford: Oxford University Press.

Young, I.M. (1990) *Justice and the Politics of Difference*, Princeton: Princeton University Press.

Young, I.M. (2000) *Inclusion and Democracy*, Oxford: Oxford University Press.

I

Voices from the trueque:

barter networks and resistance to

neoliberalism in Argentina

Pete North

In 1914, John Foster Fraser, a British visitor to what he called 'the amazing Argentine: land of enterprise', wrote:

> one cannot go through the country and see its fecundity, go into the killing houses … watch the ocean liners, with the Union Jack dangling over the stern, being loaded with many sides of beef, visit the grain elevators … pouring streams of wheat destined for European consumption into the holds of liners, without the imagination being stimulated when standing on the threshold of this new land's possibilities. (Fraser 1914: 70)

Fraser has not been the only commentator to point to Argentina as a place from which wider lessons could be drawn. Eighty-four years later, IMF secretary general Michel Camdessus invited Argentine president Carlos Menem to address the organization's plenary, the only head of state, apart from Bill Clinton, to be afforded the honour. Camdessus lauded Argentina thus:

> In many respects, the experience of Argentina in recent years has been exemplary … clearly, Argentina has a story to tell the world: a story which is about the importance of fiscal discipline, of structural change, of monetary policy rigorously maintained. (quoted in Blustein 2005: 58)

While Argentina's charismatic leader Juan Péron had, in the 1940s and 1950s, thrown the Union Jack if not off the liners, then off Argentina's railways,[1] and ensured that strong trade unions meant that the workers were well paid for their labour, latter-day Peronist Menem was lauded as an exemplar of good development practice by reinserting Argentina into the global economy and pegging the peso to the dollar, thereby bringing 'stability' to a formerly chaotic economy at the cost of reducing workers' wage levels, job security and working conditions. According to the IMF, following its 'sound policies' set Argentina apart from those other Southern countries that were not prepared to take the 'tough' decisions. Argentina, again, showed the way.

However, just as the cosy world of 1914 described by Fraser would soon be plunged into a world war that led to the great Depression, fascism and communism, so neoliberal success proved short-lived. While the peso-to-dollar peg did provide stability and gave Argentine elites access to a high-value currency that enabled them to live a First World lifestyle, the privatizations, bankruptcies and cuts in public-sector payrolls meant destitution for many. Some of the losers – the picket or *picquetero* movement – who were unable to strike (they were unemployed) or to affect the circulation of (increasingly virtual) capital, fought back by attacking neoliberalization in its concrete form by blocking roads to hit at the circulation of goods (Dinerstein 2001; Petras 2002). Others, mainly the new poor who had recently lost their jobs, responded to the crisis of liquidity caused by the peg by creating their own forms of money, traded through a network of markets. *Menemismo* was not, therefore, uncontested.

The protests grew, and things fell apart in a classic currency crisis in December 2001. The state had tried to meet a pending payment to the IMF by raiding pension funds, thus breaking confidence in its trustworthiness and financial competence. Convinced that the peg was no longer sustainable and that devaluation was inevitable, those who were able started moving their money out of the country. The state responded to the run on the currency by limiting the amount of cash people could take out of their accounts to an amount that barely allowed for subsistence. Enraged customers mobbed the now closed banks, banging pots and pans. When the state attempted to declare a state of emergency, Buenos Aires erupted into three days of street violence that saw thirty-six dead and the resignation of four presidents in a week. The fifth person to put on the presidential sash, the Peronist Duhalde, bowed to the inevitable and broke the peg.

As the peso fell to one-quarter of its previous value, the middle class found that their savings had been decimated and their retirements perhaps ruined. Previously, they had thought nothing of a shopping spree to Paris or Miami. The economy collapsed. GDP sank by 16.3 per cent in the first three months of 2002, whilst manufacturing output fell by 20 per cent. Some 52 per cent of the population, 19 million people, lived in poverty; 20 per cent of Argentines were reported as living in 'severe' poverty, which meant they could not meet basic daily nutritional needs. As many as 20 per cent were unemployed, while 23 per cent were underemployed (Rock 2002). As the crisis dragged on through 2002, Argentina moved from the status of IMF poster child to that of problem child.

If in 1914 and 1998 Argentina offered a vision of enterprise, by 2001 the crisis gave hope to many on the anti-capitalist left (Dinerstein 2002; Harman 2002; Klein 2003; López Levy 2004). Argentina seemed to be showing that 'it is possible in the 21st century for human development to be undone. "Progress" is not a given. It has to be fought for and defended' (López Levy 2004: 5). Neoliberal prescriptions were not only failing, but were being seen to fail spectacularly, while new forms of resistant practices spread like wildfire across Argentina. The pickets not only blocked roads, but some also created their own communal kitchens, organic gardens, schools and small enterprises in an effort to create more liberated forms of economic life (Chatterton 2005). In the cities, neighbourhood assemblies brought people together to talk about their problems and work out collective solutions to them (Dinerstein 2003). Sacked workers occupied closed enterprises, reopened them, and ran them on collective lines (North and Huber 2004; Dinerstein 2007). The new forms of economic organization generated by the resistance to the crisis seemed at last to answer the question, 'If you don't like neoliberalism, what would you do in its place?' The answer before seemed to be 'replace capitalism with something really nice', which is not a very convincing alternative. Argentina seemed to have provided a better answer.

Denied access to money, the luckiest were those who could join the barter networks, which through 2002 attracted literally millions of participants trading goods and services with money they produced themselves. These lucky few could meet basic needs and avoid destitution. Millions, it seemed, were developing a living example of an alternative to financial disciplining. If the IMF disciplined the Argentine government, and the government disciplined Argentine banks, which then restricted currency issuance, so disciplining individuals, then individuals, on the face of it, negated this disciplining by issuing their own currency. This chapter, based on fieldwork undertaken in 2002/3,[2] discusses the barter networks in the context of the Argentine crisis to examine the extent to which they were a form of resistance to neoliberalization and, perhaps, a vision of a more liberated economy – or just a coping mechanism, helping those decimated by the crisis to get by.

Alternative currencies and neoliberalism

While nation-states or banks are generally thought of as the originators of money, over the last twenty years subaltern groups of many kinds have responded to poverty, to globalization and to neoliberalization by creating and exchanging their own forms of money, known variously in different parts of the world as LETS, Hours, Talents or Time Money (North 2007b). Argentina's alternative currency networks were founded in 1995, during the Menem years. A Buenos Aires-based environmental NGO, Programa de Autosuficiencia Regional (PAR or Regional Self-sufficiency Programme) heard about Hours, the local currency circulating in Ithaca, upstate New York (Glover 1995). PAR, which at the time was mainly a conservation organization, wanted to use its knowledge of ecology and of the international Green movement to design new solutions to the poverty and unemployment that was seen all around (Primavera et al. 1998). While the original project started with twenty neighbours, as unemployment and poverty spread across Argentina through the second half of the 1990s, so did the Red Global de Trueque (Global Barter Network).

Participants joined the network by going along to a market, or *nodo* (node), where they were issued with a supply of money, called *creditos*,

FIGURE 1.1   Map of Argentina's barter networks discussed

created by the organizers of the market. In some well-organized *nodos* this money looked very like state-issued banknotes, but was less polished in bootstrap *nodos*. Participants might buy their first *creditos* for pesos, or be required to bring something to sell or that they had made in order to earn them. *Nodos* were typically in church halls, disused factories, car parks or baseball courts, and were held at a set

FIGURE I.2   Barter network meeting in Gualeguachu, Argentina

time each week. People could find out where and when *nodos* took place by word of mouth, or through the network's newsletters. By 2002 PAR claimed there were 4,500 markets across Argentina used by half a million people spending 600 million credits (Norman 2002). The real figure is unknowable. *Nodos* organized autonomously. Some used PAR's notes, some accepted currencies from nodes elsewhere, while others would not. As barter spread across Argentina, PAR's Red Global de Trueque (RGT) began to face criticism from nodes that organized themselves as the Red Global de Trueque Solidario (RTS), which argued for more explicitly solidaristic forms of organization.

Thus Argentina became the poster child not only for global capitalism, the IMF, and then the anticapitalist movement, but also for proponents of alternative currencies (De Meulinaire 1999).

The Argentine experience of alternative currencies is also of interest to a wider audience. Alternative currencies are in some ways a challenge to neoliberalism, while in others they resonate with it. The challenge comes first from claims that people's needs should be put *before* the need for financial discipline and that conventional money does not reward people fairly or equally for their contribution. All should be included and valued. Second, free trade at a global level is held to be

FIGURE I.3   Barter network vegetable market in Mendoza,
Argentina

ecologically unsustainable in that it leads to the creation of vulnerable
economic monocultures that can be devastated by currency crises, and
is built on unsustainable levels of fossil fuel use moving goods around
the globe that could be produced more locally (Helleiner 2000). Rather
than locating development in an international division of labour in
which all do what they do best and trade with each other, local currency
proponents argue for the localization of economies (Hines 2000) and
for the production of an economy that works at a slower pace, reusing
and recycling more. It is a radically Green vision of a localized, humane,
decentralized and participatory economy (Trainer 1995).

Yet, as discussed in more detail below, advocates of alternative
currencies also value forms of economic organization advocated by
neoliberals and generally rejected by the left. These include an attach-
ment to allocation through markets (as opposed to through planning);
to self-sufficiency and personal responsibility (as opposed to state
welfare); and to forms of economic organization centred on small
and micro-businesses. Alternative currency networks are essentially
markets through which small traders operating in perfect competition
exchange goods and services. As such, they constitute clear Smithian
utopias critiqued as such by normally supportive, Marxist-influenced,
Green commentators like Wall (2005: 62) and Kovel (2007). Hayek

(1990), for example, called for money to be denationalized and for there to be a choice of currencies. If it is not necessarily the responsibility of the state to run enterprises and provide welfare, Hayek asked, is it necessarily the state's role to provide money?

So alternative currencies, generally promoted by Greens for their ecological outcomes (Douthwaite 1996) and by leftists for their egalitarian outcomes (Bowring 1998), also have neoliberal resonances. Dividing lines therefore become blurred. Has neoliberalism lost its definition as an object of antagonism for the left? Has it become so hegemonic that left and Green supporters have been seduced by elements of it, or lost confidence in their critique of the market and in their defence of collectivism and planning? Or does it mean that, as Larner argues, 'the new political configurations of what we call neoliberal are more multi-vocal than might previously have been understood' (Larner 2005:11)?

This ambivalence suggests that in considering neoliberalism we need to pay more attention to economic diversity. In particular, we need to move on from thinking that market-based economic activity is inevitably neoliberal (Gibson-Graham 2006). Markets and entrepreneurs existed long before neoliberalization, and they existed in formally state-controlled economies like the former Soviet Union (Ledeneva 1998). If neoliberals advocate markets, is this always something to be opposed? Might some kinds of market-based economic activities provide more enjoyable, resilient and prosperous livelihoods, at a slower, less stressful and more ecologically sustainable rhythm, than exploitative, dehumanizing paid work for an employer? Might community-controlled, participatory forms of welfare provide more dignified solutions than doled-out state welfare? Are we guilty of erasing the exploitative nature of Fordist-era work and welfare, focusing too much on what we have lost and indulging in rose-tinted nostalgia for that which has gone (Larner 2005: 10–11)?

Rethinking neoliberalism in this way follows Larner's (2003, 2005) concern to recognize that more is going on than the inscription throughout the world of plans that were originally developed in Chicago and rolled out from the global centres of Thatcher's Britain and Reagan's America though processes of neoliberalization coded as the imposition of Northern agendas on a powerless global South. We need to

identify the ways that neoliberalization was co-constructed by and
resisted by Southern actors, and that this process was more diverse
than previously considered. Some elements of neoliberalism *do* indeed
look like they are part of a wider class process to revitalize capitalism by
reimposing capitalist discipline and making the ideology of capitalism
a new 'common sense', thus securing the extraction of profits for the
next generation (Harvey 2005). The similarities in neoliberal projects
throughout the globe can make them look like they were rolled out
(Peck and Tickell 2002) according to a script written by World Bank
bureaucrats who do not even leave their hotel rooms when they para-
chute into the latest crisis (of their own making) (Stiglitz 2002). We
need not go as far as arguing that because we cannot reduce all social
and economic change to neoliberalism, then 'there is no such thing
as neoliberalism!' (Barnett 2005:9). But it is to say, following Larner,
that we need to be attuned to the complex and cross-cutting nature
of these changes. Elsewhere, I discuss the extent that Argentine and
IMF elites co-produced the neoliberalization of that country (North
2007a). In this chapter, I examine the extent to which the barter
networks co-constituted and resisted neoliberalization in Argentina,
but in subaltern ways.

Resisting or recoding neoliberalization?

The ecological activists who founded the barter networks claimed that
their aim was to do more than just alleviate hardship. The networks,
for them, were a civil-society-based response to neoliberalism that
provided the opportunity to establish a better, saner, more humane,
ecological form of money with the potential to humanize markets so as
to include those formerly outside them. They did not oppose markets
tout court and argue for a return to the state-planned Argentina of the
past, but felt that a new form of money would enable markets to work
to what they called 'different rhythms' (Primavera et al. 1998). They
argued that Argentina, traditionally one of the richest countries in
Latin America, had been decimated by the 1976–84 military dictatorship and the hyperinflation and chaos of the lost decade of the 1980s.
The 1990s saw the burial of both the welfare state and much of Argentina's cherished educational and cultural infrastructure. The impact

was both economic – the rise of a new poor – and psychological – a loss of hope and a rise in people seeking psychological help. The retrenchment of the state meant that it could no longer be expected to provide solutions, which would have to be generated through civil society. Barter was seen as a laboratory through which responses to the crisis could be developed based on solidarity, entrepreneurship, political responsibility and ecology – that is, through which neoliberalization, seen as marketization and state withdrawal, could be reimagined and reconstituted in more liberated ways.

This can be seen very clearly in the networks' value base:

- Our fulfilment as human beings need not be conditioned by money;
- We believe in the possibility of replacing competition, profit and speculation with reciprocity among people;
- We assume that our actions, products and services may respond to ethical and ecological standards rather than the will of the market, consumerism and short-term profit;
- Participants should produce and consume: be 'prosumers';
- Every member is responsible for their actions and for what they exchange;
- The network is a free association. Membership does not imply a relationship of dependence. (Primavera et al. 1998: 5–6)

In these values we see a claim that the barter networks are a market that operates to ethical, rather than purely economic, rhythms. We see an interesting mix of the language of challenge and resistance (solidarity, ecology, valuing people not money) and, perhaps, the influence of neoliberalism (trading, entrepreneurialism, markets, personal responsibility). Taking personal responsibility meant having regard to the wider health of the network by ensuring that an individual's trading relations were based on reciprocity. Reciprocity was opposed to the action of egotistical individualists taking advantage of their fellow prosumers[3] by, for example, buying up all of the produce of people who were new to the game and were charging too little, at times right in front of them. The culture of personal responsibility to ensure reciprocity was supported by an induction process to ensure that prosumers understood how they should contribute to the reproduction of the value based on their trading decisions, and by coordinators and/or stewards walking round the markets to ensure that no one was creating a disturbance by selling obviously shoddy goods, charging too much or too little, or being rude or disrespectful to others. Values were also communicated through posters and leaflets around markets. In all communications, the reciprocal, communal and solidaristic nature of trading, 'prosumer' values, and the changed 'rhythm' were stressed. The slow pace of trading, with purchases interspersed with promenades around the stalls, conversations, watching a samba band or play by local kids, a quick stop for an *empañada*[4] or a longer one to share some *mate*[5] indicated the changed, non-neoliberal rhythm. This was a market, but an ethical, reciprocal market, not one where profit, competition and efficiency governed values. We do not see a call for a return to the past, but for the present to be reconstituted in more liberated ways.

The second reason why local money is often seen as an explicit form of resistance to neoliberalization is its local nature (Pacione 1997; North 2006). Most alternative currencies circulate in a defined and often quite small geographical area, in an attempt to create an ecological diversity of currencies. Here, again, Argentines reimagined globalized utopias in subaltern ways rather than resisting them. The currency note produced by PAR, the *arbolito*, circulated among nodes who would accept it without restriction, right across Argentina. PAR did not support the opposition of the local to the global, believing that the local can be small-minded and xenophobic, while globalization can imply connection, solidarity, communication and support. They mentioned the support agencies like Amnesty International had given to Argentines during the military dictatorship, and the value of the Internet to a country as far away from what they regarded as the centres of global culture in Europe and North America (North 2005). They argued for global solutions, that given the scale of the wider economic crisis enough currency should be printed to meet demand, and that waiting for groups to form and print their own money locally, in an endogenous manner, would be too slow. Months could be taken up on arguments on the name of the currency, how to value it, what 'local' meant, what 'local' did not include, how far away was 'too far', and so on. It was recognized that this process could be speeded up. PAR therefore developed a franchising network through which they sold 'start-up kits' (for pesos) to a number of regional representatives, who would sell them on to local coordinators. The kits enabled a local coordinator to establish a network in a top-down manner, from which individuals could establish new micro-enterprises through barter before, in time, entering the formal market. This is one of the reasons why barter spread so quickly across Argentina during 2001 and 2002.

However, the wide geographical spread nature of PAR's franchises also led to problems. Some of PAR's franchise holders turned out to be rather unsavoury – Peronist clientelists, crooks, con artists, and snake-oil salesmen. As inflation began to hit the networks, critics argued that PAR was over-emitting the currency, and as there was no democratic control over policy for emitting the currency there was nothing that could be done about this. Critics challenged the legitimacy of selling *arbolitos* for pesos, arguing that prospective members should be required to produce. They argued that PAR was getting wealthy from selling the kits, and that this was illegitimate. PAR countered that they were not over-emitting, but that unknown people had been seen handing out fifty *credito arbolitos* from the backs of vans, and that the police had found criminal gangs with *arbolito* printing presses. PAR suspected that Peronist thugs were behind it, and denied any personal benefit from the networks.

Either way, during 2001 the networks split and a rival network, the Red Global de Trueque Solidario (Solidarity Barter Network – RTS) emerged. RTS argued that the Red Global de Trueque was beginning to mimic the pathologies of capitalism – boom and bust, inflation, and making a minority wealthy at the expense of the majority. They argued that the best way to maintain the integrity of the currency and to ensure that barter *did* act as a laboratory for a new form of market was to ensure that the markets and processes for money issuance were democratically controlled locally, from below. They discouraged use of the *arbolito*, and issued local money that did not circulate out of those networks that actively agreed to accept them. They argued that *creditos* should be collectively owned and managed, not imposed from outside.

RTS nodes from across the country met monthly to coordinate their work and to agree collectively to print and accept their notes.

They insisted on an active decision by all groups on whether or not to accept a new node into the network and on how much currency to print. They argued that strong community-building mechanisms should be used at nodes to ensure that the prosumer values of the network were understood, maintained and reproduced. What mattered was the effective management of local nodes to ensure trust, transparency, order, and to manage prices and distribution.

RTS's critique, that PAR had lost sight of the anti-neoliberal values that had first inspired them, was taken further by the coordinator of the Mar-y-Sierras RTS in the coastal city of Mar del Plata. He argued that if the new form of money did not lead to a participatory economy, then it had no value. What mattered was the forms of economy generated, not the form of money itself. Consequently, Mar-y-Sierras *nodos* were strictly coordinated with three coordinators and three administrators in each *nodo*, and all decisions were made at a mass meeting at the beginning of each trading session. This was a highly regulated and collectively run market. PAR responded by arguing that RTS were imposing their political views on an economy that should be open to all, and that *trueque* was a market, not a 'chamber of deputies'. They saw barter as a market in which all could participate, not just those opposed to neoliberalization.

The final way in which barter was seen as a form or resistance to neoliberalism was its acephalous nature. The movement had no head, being at best a federation of like-minded, locally organized nodes (RTS), or independent, self-organized nodes facilitated through PAR's start-up kits (RGT). No one was 'in charge'. There was no way to restrict money issuance if individuals independently agreed to accept money from each other that they had created themselves. The Argentine Central Bank may have tried to enforce economic discipline and capitalist rationality through the peg and a tight monetary policy; the IMF might have tried to control the Argentine Central Bank; and George Bush might have tried to control the IMF (Helleiner 2005). But if individuals, in their thousands if not millions, decide not to submit to this disciplining and create their own form of money, then the disciplining will be limited. This is a conception of denationalized, private money not expected by Hayek.

We see here an interesting process whereby some elements of neo-liberalization were recoded in more liberated ways from below. This is more than the imposition of neoliberalization from without and from above on hapless Southern communities; it is a more interesting process whereby subaltern groups recoded and reimagined neoliberal tropes into more interesting forms. But we cannot make too much of this without recognizing the power imbalances here. While for some organizers barter was (hopefully) a bridge to a new form of economy and a manifestation of resistance to the destruction of the Argentine welfare state, for others it was more of a coping mechanism. The discussion now turns to barter not as revolutionizing the economy, but as a vehicle for social solidarity in an intense capitalist crisis that enabled those caught up in it to come out the other side, but through which, in the absence of calls for the reinstatement of state welfare, neoliberal tropes were less reimagined than internalized by former opponents.

Internalizing neoliberalism? Barter networks as welfare

At the height of the networks' extent, in 2001–02, barter was operating in an environment where the Argentine economy had collapsed. The rich looked after themselves (it was widely thought), having whisked their money out of the country on the eve of devaluation, while the working classes were protected by Peronism and/or the pickets. Poor Peronists, it was thought, were looked after through clientelist networks, while the pickets looked after their own either through community-based projects or by acting as a vehicle for agitating for and then distributing state welfare payments. The class that had really suffered, that did not have anyone looking after its interests or helping it to survive the crisis, barter members often argued, was the 'new poor'. The 'new poor' constituted a self-described class 'in the middle', between rich and poor, who saw their savings, pensions and the possibility of a well-paid job disappear.[6] While Mar-y-Sierras did try to build links with the other protest groups, most organizers saw barter specifically as a way of helping the middle classes survive the crisis with the wider objective, in time, of providing a better form of market economy than capitalism.

When barter was at its height in 2001–02, it did this generally quite well. Interviews with prosumer after prosumer indicated that an active node visitor who set up a stall and who was able to produce something that others wanted or had something to sell could feed and clothe themselves and their family, get their hair cut and their nails done, hire a car, and buy some luxuries and presents. Some of the middle class lived off their fat by selling some non-essential possessions, meaning that poorer people could buy things that previously would have been beyond their reach. Others set up new small businesses, making honey, pizzas, *empañadas*, bread, biscuits, preserves, chutney and the like. These were not forms of resistance, nor were they political – they were ways of coping with an economic collapse. When a 'proper job' became available, it would be taken up in a flash. For example, one prosumer, Susanna, was a psychiatrist and her husband a painter. She was frustrated with the *nodos*. For a long time both of them were producing what was required – food – but they got fed up with what they saw as a subsistence lifestyle. They wanted to practise the work they loved and had trained for. Susanna then offered English lessons, psychiatry sessions and tango lessons, but hardly anybody ever wanted those – they needed the bare necessities. Asked if she could not offer her services in many more *nodos*, to have a greater chance of getting clients, she responded that she did not have the time. She needed to earn money. Another prosumer commented: '*trueque* is all an illusion, a necessity, not for salvation. It's for the day; I sell and I eat.'

While *trueque* helped the middle classes to live off each other's fat and recycle unwanted goods, the poorest were excluded: they had little ability to produce, and thus to participate. As a social justice mechanism, it was therefore wanting. Worse, when the crisis became really acute in 2002–03 and the poorest bought *creditos* in large numbers at knock-down prices and flooded into the *nodos*, often buying up as much as they could as quickly as possible, selling it on, or offered what were thought of as substandard goods, they were castigated as *vivos*, or wideboys. The overwhelmed nodes could no longer manage their affairs according to their vision of reciprocity and a more humane vision, feeling that something briefly beautiful had been destroyed.

As the crisis hit, the Peronists took advantage of PAR's franchising system to set up their own barter networks. Some violently attacked rival non-clientelist nodes. By late 2002, problems such as inflation and forgery of *arbolitos* had become widespread, the result, PAR claimed, of Peronist infiltration and attempts to discredit barter, or of criminal action commissioned by Peronists. Then, in November 2002, a television programme claimed to expose what it called the 'great barter rip-off': food was poor quality, stolen goods were being sold, the schemes were a scam and many of the notes were forgeries. The television channel was controlled by supporters of former President Menem, standing at the time in the 2002 presidential election as one of three Peronists, claiming to be the only one able to return Argentina to its former dignity. Menem argued during the 2003 election campaign that the pickets should be 'eliminated' – a form of language too close for some to that of the murderous 1976–84 military government. Similarly, the image of millions of Argentines getting by through a 'primitive' form of economics like barter did national dignity no good, and barter needed also to be 'eliminated' for the good of the nation.[7]

If RTS found PAR's businesslike approach problematic, other barter organizers were happy to accept that PAR were the innovators who had come up with the idea that had spread like wildfire across Argentina. The standardization of the currency, the *arbolito*, the franchising process and the start-up kit were PAR's innovations from which they were entitled to benefit. They parted company, however, because RTS felt that PAR had made some naive and imprudent decisions in their choice of franchisees, had grown too quickly, had become dazzled by runaway success, and could not cope organizationally with the millions-strong economy they had created seemingly overnight. What had worked well, in a haphazard and grassroots manner, was no longer enough. There was a lack of transparency and no audit trail. This approach is best characterized by the Zona Oeste barter network in suburban[8] Buenos Aires, run by the charismatic *caudillo*-like Fernando Sampayo. Sampayo ran his networks from the top down in a businesslike but hierarchical – and honest – manner. He developed links with farms outside Buenos Aires and trucked in wheat and vegetables. The aim was not to reinvent capitalism: it was to organize professionally run and audited nodes that met people's needs and helped them develop new small businesses. Organized from above, Zona Oeste did more to meet basic needs than some of the nodes in central Buenos Aires patronized by the 'exploded' middle class. Sampayo specifically saw himself as a retired successful businessman who was now 'giving back' to a community within which he had built many businesses and drawn a good life. He rejected any connections to the wider Argentine protest movement. Barter was a new support structure that would encourage self-help and facilitate the generation of new small businesses. His values were aligned more with the subaltern capitalism of Hernando do Soto, seeing in informal businesses the wealth creators of the future (de Soto 1989).

Others in the RTS saw barter as a way of helping the 'exploded' middle class first to survive the crisis, and then become independent by creating their own forms of livelihood which, they hoped, would provide better alternatives to paid work. They did not mourn the lost jobs, seeing them as often exploitative. They wanted to turn the crisis into an opportunity to do something better. Charli, one of the organizers of RTS in the centre of Buenos Aires, argued that while there were no obvious opportunities for paid employment, there were still things that had to be done, needs to be met, things to be made and sold. The state could no longer be expected to look after people, nor in many ways should it, as it did so in clientelistic ways. State welfare was seen as at worst corrupt, at best patronizing relations of dependency rather than of dignity and equality. Charli saw barter's role as that of helping those traumatized by the severity of the economic crisis to feel better about themselves, and to feel they could do something about it by changing their mindset from that of a prospective employee to that of a prosumer who would eventually join the formal market by creating their own opportunities:

> It's a matter of changing people's way of thinking ... from that of an employee to that of a businessperson who runs a micro enterprise, a producer. All this means changing people's ways of thinking. ... They say: 'There are no jobs.' I respond: 'There is no employment, but there is work.' ... And there is work, because there are needs to be met; and some of these we can cover with work, no? (Charli, RTS, Capital Federal, Buenos Aires)

Charli's 'capacity building' strategy was a form of disaster relief. It aimed at lifting people's spirits, helping them work cooperatively to build new forms of livelihood for themselves through the creation of an economy based on reciprocal exchange using new, socially controlled, money. It was based on the understanding that alternative forms of liberated livelihood needed to be built in the here and now, but with a different rhythm. It accepted the need to be entrepreneurial, to take responsibility for oneself, but also the need to be honest, not to exploit others, to think of what fellow prosumers need, and perhaps to work to a different, more ecological and slower rhythm. And crucially it recognized that there *is* such a thing as society. While some elements of neoliberal tropes were absorbed, such as the critique of 'dependency', the valorization of personal responsibility and of enterprise, and an absence of demands on the state, this is a vision of an ethical, Smithian market rather than a neoliberal capitalist market where the objective is profit maximization alone.

This was a strategy, interestingly, shared by all the barter networks. Difference in emphasis lay in the extent to which the capacity-building strategy was seen as realistic or not, and the extent to which collective or individual forms of capacity-building were the focus. PAR and Zona Oeste were both based in quite marginal parts of greater Buenos Aires, places that had been devastated by neoliberalization over many years. They felt that Charli's strategy of encouraging individuals to take control of their economic lives through small, participatory barter nodes was too slow, that the extent to which people in such a poor area could be expected to self-actualize was limited, and that people needed more help than that which they could reasonably be expected to generate themselves. The solution was to organize the basics from the top down, and give people a base from which to rebuild. From the left, only Mar-y-Sierras saw barter not as a generator of new small businesses, but as a new community-run economy in which people would rebuild their economies collectively. But none of them wanted or expected the state to step in and provide the security they needed – it was down to individuals and communities to build their own futures. To this extent, neoliberal tropes had been internalized. But does this mean that 'neoliberal' tropes like entrepreneurialism (if done collectively) and personal responsibility (if focused on needs of subaltern collectivities) are something that the left should remain antagonistic to? Perhaps the Argentine experience suggests that this needs to be rethought.

Conclusion

To some extent, Argentina's barter networks rose to the level they did because of uniquely Argentine conditions. Argentina was a country that had thought of itself as part of the First World until it went through an economic collapse of unprecedented severity. The welfare system was decimated, and for months people could not get access to their own money. This economic crisis explains the push towards developing barter networks. Having experienced many changes of currency over the past fifty years, and having experienced hyperinflation, Argentines were used to informal and unorthodox economic solutions to problems. Barter was not seen as strange or suspect. It was the latest scheme to get by. These contexts help to explain the pull which led to mass usage of barter networks. But the experience of barter was also of more generalizable interest. The politics on which this edifice was built was a mix of traditional ecological and leftist concerns, combined with a Smithian utopia of small traders using Hayekian denationalized money. Those involved valued globalization, entrepreneurialism and personal responsibility, and wanted to remake markets and trading so they worked to different rhythms. This suggests that markets can be rewritten into more progressive forms, and are more than a facet of a process of neoliberalization that is imposed top-down from above.

However, to finish our analysis we must recognize that barter, like so many alternative economic experiments, was attacked by forces of economic conservatism and global economic processes, and ended in disbandment, defeat and disgrace (Gibson-Graham 2002: 25). For the middle class with something to sell, or those with skills to exchange, barter did bounce them through the crisis. But it did not last. In time, barter began to mimic the pathologies of the capitalist system, and succumbed to political attack through inflation and forgery. The November 2002 television broadcast led to an overnight crisis of confidence, and a two-thirds drop in participation in barter. By the middle of 2003, the networks were between a tenth and a quarter of their previous size, and, as the economy revived into 2004/5 on the back of the newly competitive peso and an export boom in soya to China, the networks died.

The barter networks had large numbers of participants, but this was the result of a financial crisis that overwhelmed them. By 2003, many of the nodes were no longer fashionable as people in desperate need fought over a dwindling number of resources. The solidarity economy that some hoped would enable a market that worked at different rhythms to capitalism did not emerge. The networks provided an opportunity for petty, kitchen or household-level production of food, clothes and the like, for people to exchange the skills they needed, and for the middle class to recycle unwanted goods to get by. Bankrupt stock could be sold. But there was no significant *production* of new goods and services beyond some small micro-businesses that, once the economy began to revive, moved into the mainstream economy. No connections were built to the recovered factories, and levels of capital generated by subaltern groups, even if these subalterns described themselves as 'middle class', were not large enough to develop the range of production a modern complex economy needs. Furthermore, the very poor were excluded. Grassroots initiatives resisted neoliberalization, helped those at the hard end of the crisis to survive it, but did not provide – yet – an alternative. Does this mean that their experience is a failure? In this analysis, barter can be seen as a glimpse of a more liberated form of market that was dragged down by a financial crisis and political attack that was not the making of the organizers. A vision of an alternative was produced, and that vision was not dulled.

Notes

1. Péron nationalized the British-owned railways.
2. Thanks to Uli Huber for her help with fieldwork and with developing some of the ideas on which this chapter is based, and to the University of Liverpool for providing funding. Fieldwork was undertaken in April 2002, and March–June 2003, in Buenos Aires (Capital Federal and Mar del Plata) and Mendoza. Methods included interviews with organizers and prosumers, and participant observation at barter nodes.

3. A contraction of producer and consumer, used to imply that participants can not only consume but must also produce goods and services.
4. A small pasty – an Argentine staple.
5. A hot herbal drink sucked through a straw from an ornate beaker. Argentines would never be without their *mate* kit – a flask of hot water, some *mate* and the beaker and straw. A tranquil couple of hours sipping *mate* in convivial company and putting the world to rights is an important part of the day.
6. A contemporary cartoon had a taxi driver talking to a *cartonero*, a scavenger who survives by collecting waste paper for recycling. The *cartonero* says that before the crisis he used to drive a taxi. The taxi driver responds that he used to be an architect.
7. Menem won the first round of the 2003 presidential election, but dropped out of the run-off before the second round of voting when it became clear that he would lose heavily to his Peronist rival, Néstor Kirchner.
8. 'Suburban' does not imply suburbia. The area was part of Buenos Aires' vast hinterland, characterized by housing that did not fit the label of *villas miserias* (shanty towns or informal settlements), but neither was it bourgeois suburbia. Rather, it was a sprawling, at times formal, at times semi-informal, area of working-class and 'new poor' housing.

References

Barnett, C. (2005) 'The consolations of "neoliberalism"', *Geoforum* 36(1): 7–12.
Blustein, P. (2005) *And the Money Kept Rolling In (and Out): Wall Street, the IMF and the Bankrupting of Argentina*, New York: Public Affairs.
Bowring, F. (1998) 'LETS: An eco-socialist initiative?', *New Left Review* 232: 91–111.
Chatterton, P. (2005) 'Making autonomous geographies: Argentina's popular uprising and the Movimiento de Trabajadores Desocpados (Unemployed Workers Movement)', *Geoforum* 36(5): 545–61.
De Meulinaire, S. (1999) 'Reinventing the market: Alternative currencies and community development in Argentina', *International Journal of Community Currency Research* 4, www.geog.le.ac.uk/ijccr/volume4/4no3.htm.
de Soto, H. (1989) *The Other Path: The Invisible Revolution in the Third World*, New York: Harper & Row.
Dinerstein, A. (2001) 'Roadblocks in Argentina: Against the violence of stability', *Capital and Class* 74: 1–7.
Dinerstein, A. (2002) 'The battle of Buenos Aires: Crisis, insurrection and the reinvention of politics in Argentina', *Historical Materialism* 10(4): 5–38.
Dinerstein, A. (2003) 'Que se vayan todos! Popular insurrection and the *asambleas barriales* in Argentina', *Bulletin of Latin American Research* 22(2): 187–200.
Dinerstein, A.C. (2007) 'Workers' factory takeovers and new state policies in Argentina: Towards an 'institutionalisation' of non-governmental public action?', *Policy and Politics* 35: 529–50.

Douthwaite, R. (1996) *Short Circuit: Strengthening Local Economies for Security in an Uncertain World*, Totnes: Green Books.

Fraser, J.F. (1914) *The Amazing Argentine: Land of Enterprise*, London: Funk & Wignalls.

Gibson-Graham, J. (2002) 'Beyond global vs local: Economic politics beyond the binary frame', in A. Herod and M.W. Wright (eds), *Geographies of Power: Placing Scale*, Oxford: Blackwell, pp. 25–60.

Gibson-Graham, J. (2006) *A Post Capitalist Politics*, Minneapolis: University of Minnesota Press.

Glover, P. (1995) 'Ithaca hours', in S. Meeker Lowry (ed.), *Investing in the Common Good*, New York: New Society Publishers, pp. 72–80.

Harman, C. (2002) 'Argentina: Rebellion at the sharp end of the world crisis', *International Socialism* 94: 3–48.

Harvey, D. (2005) *A Brief History of Neoliberalism*, Oxford: Oxford University Press.

Hayek, F. (1990) *Denationalisation of Money: The Argument Refined*, London: Institute of Economic Affairs.

Helleiner, E. (2000) 'Think globally, transact locally: Green political economy and the local currency movement', *Global Society* 14(1): 35–51.

Helleiner, E. (2005) 'The strange story of Bush and the Argentine debt crisis', *Third World Quarterly* 26(6): 951–69.

Hines, C. (2000) *Localisation: A Global Manifesto*, London: Earthscan.

Klein, N. (2003) 'Argentina: A new kind of revolution', *Guardian*, 25 January: Weekend, 14–22.

Kovel, J. (2007) *The Enemy of Nature*, London: Zed Books.

Larner, W. (2003) 'Neoliberalism?', *Environment and Planning D: Society and Space* 21: 509–12.

Larner, W. (2005) 'Neoliberalism in (regional) theory and practice: The Stronger Communities Action Fund in New Zealand', *Geographical Research* 43(1): 9–18.

Ledeneva, A. (1998) *Russia's Economy of Favours: Blat, Networking and Informal Exchange*, Cambridge: Cambridge University Press.

López Levy, M. (2004) *We Are Millions: Neo-liberalism and New Forms of Political Action in Argentina*, London: Latin America Bureau.

Norman, K. (2002) 'Barter Nation', *Buenos Aires Herald Magazine*, 6 April: 14–19.

North, P. (2005) 'Scaling alternative economic practices? Some lessons from alternative currencies', *Transactions of the Institute of British Geographers* 30(2): 221–33.

North, P. (2006) *Alternative Currencies as a Challenge to Globalisation? A Case Study of Manchester's Local Money Networks*, Aldershot: Ashgate.

North, P. (2007a) 'Neoliberalizing Argentina?', in K. England and K. Ward (eds), *Neoliberalization: States, Networks, Peoples*, Oxford: Blackwell, pp. 127–62.

North, P (2007b) *Money and Liberation: The Micropolitics of Alternative Currency Movements*, Minneapolis: University of Minnesota Press.

North, P., and U. Huber (2004) 'Alternative Spaces of the "Argentinazo"', *Antipode* 36(5): 963–84.

Pacione, M. (1997) 'Local exchange trading systems as a response to the globalisation of capitalism', *Urban Studies* 34(8): 1179–99.

Peck, J., and A. Tickell (2002) 'Neoliberalizing space', *Antipode* 34(3): 380–404.

Petras, J. (2002) 'The unemployed workers movement in Argentina', *Monthly Review* 53(8): 32–45.

Primavera, H., C. De Sanzo and H. Covas (1998) 'Reshuffling for a new social order: The experience of the global barter network in Argentina', paper presented at conference, Enhancing People's Space in a Globalising Economy, Espoo, Finland.

Rock, D. (2002) 'Racking Argentina', *New Left Review* 2/17: 55–86.

Stiglitz, J. (2002) *Globalisation and Its Discontents*, London: Allen Lane.

Trainer, T. (1995) *The Conserver Society*, London: Zed Books.

Wall, D. (2005) *Babylon and Beyond: The Economics of the Anti-Capitalist, Anti-Globalist and Radical Green Movements*, London, Pluto Press.

2

Confounding neoliberalism: priests, privatization and social justice in the Peruvian Andes

Elizabeth Olson

> The human economy, then, is embedded and enmeshed in institutions, economic and noneconomic. The inclusion of the non-economic is vital. For religion or government may be as important for the structure and functioning of the economy as monetary institutions or the availability of tools and machines themselves that lighten the toil of labor. (Polanyi 1992: 34)

The aim of this chapter is to understand the relationship between 'the non-economic' and neoliberalism through the historical and contemporary work of religious social justice activists working in the Southern Andes of Peru. More specifically, my discussion explores the relationship between neoliberal ideology and normative evaluations of economic policy in the context of a liberation-theology-inspired Catholic Church functioning within an environment of internal conflict and dramatic shifts in state economic regimes. The analysis contributes to existing work on economy and society by considering how faith organizations become a part of the 'rolling out' of neoliberalism (Peck and Tickell 2002) under the premiss of economic development. Faith-based development organizations and movements often position themselves as advocates of 'human development' (Marshall and Keough 2004), a phrase intended to signal a more holistic understanding of needs than what is possible through economic solutions. Religious actors therefore are faced with evaluating the processes and anticipated outcomes of economic policies against a faith-based normative standpoint. In regions like the Southern Peruvian Andes, where historical movements in support of land redistribution presented clear links to liberation theology, some policies undertaken as part of neoliberalization have been greeted with relative ambivalence, signalling in part the struggle that religious leaders, laity and activists face when evaluating the potential social impacts of economic change.

I begin my analysis by briefly considering academic debates about the intersection between economic and non-economic social processes – including religion – through the ideological and normative spaces of neoliberalism. I then turn to the case of the liberation-theology-inspired Iglesia Surandina, the Southern Andean Church, and compare the ardent activism of leaders and laity in the 1980s with the perspectives and activities at the turn of the century. From the late 1970s and through the beginning of the twenty-first century, the Surandina was among the most influential economic and social justice networks in the region, yet the role that economic policy and reform have played in conceptions of social justice has changed considerably from a focus on livelihood rights to one of democratic participation. The case study provides some insight into the role of non-economic ideology in the construction of responses to neoliberalization.

Neoliberalism, ideology and the non-economic

The challenge to give neoliberalism an 'identity crisis' and pay more careful attention to its ideologies has generated a wealth of rich empirical research on the diversity of both economic policies and technologies of governance associated with neoliberalism (Larner 2003). Neoliberalism becomes enacted and materialized in and through other non-economic social processes and partnerships (Larner and Craing 2005), and functions as a 'mobile technology' moving through and across networks to become embedded in places in different ways (Ong 2007). But giving neoliberalism an identity crisis has also come with some growing pains. Castree (2006: 2) has critiqued this work for its imprecision, leaving us with the option either to accept 'distinct kinds of neoliberalism' or to embrace neoliberalism as an abstract, ideological category that then cannot be 'held responsible for anything'. Though Castree's critical realist approach is welcomed, I suggest that understanding neoliberalism – and being able to blame it for things – also requires a more empirical approach to understanding converging and contested ideologies. In this context, religion and its institutions are generally considered either instruments of neoliberal progress or a final space for ideological resistance.

The centrality of ideology in the constitution of the economy draws upon the classic debates of scholars such as Max Weber and Émile Durkheim, who insisted on understanding the co-constitution of economy and society. For Weber, economic practice had to be rationalized by its participants, and the emergence of ascetic religion played a critical role in the functioning of capitalism (Weber 1930; Collins 1992). Polanyi (1992) argued that differences in economic organization reflected differences in social norms, such that the motives for exchange in a pre-industrial society might be dominated by reciprocity rather than profit. Yet there is also a concern that these perspectives have given undue power to 'the economic', and Mitchell (2008: 5) has subsequently argued that the economic should instead be understood 'as a series of competing projects' brought into being by the deliberately narrow production of economic 'findings'. The economy is thus self-constitutive, emerging out of the generation of knowledge produced from particular ideological standpoints.

This view of economic projects as self-actualizing is also reflected in much of the research on contemporary neoliberalism (Peck and Tickell 2002: 382; see also Chopra 2003), but with a focus on the characteristics and practices that are particular to a neoliberal 'logic'. Neoliberalism is understood to penetrate or subsume all scales of social being and social relations, ranging from the body to the globe, and acts as a disciplinary regime which generates new neoliberal subjects who become managed, counted, and professionalized in order to operate under the (idealized) conditions of a freed market and a disinvested state (Katz 2005; Mitchell 2006). A central operative myth underpinning neoliberal logic is that of the freed individual who is unhindered by the economic constraints of a state-led economy. Thus, under neoliberalism, 'logics of individualism and entrepreneurialism' (Leitner et al. 2007: 2) are based on self-interest and 'freedom from bureaucracy rather than freedom from want' (Leitner et al. 2007: 4). From Bourdieu's (1998) perspective, the neoliberal world-view achieves 'nothing other than the oldest dream of capitalism, the establishment of a framework for the accumulation and distribution for profit according to Darwinian principles' (Chopra 2003: 424). Neoliberalism, then, is 'an economic project but it is also a moral one – a project of individualising ethics' (Smith and Rochovská 2007: 1166) which is hostile to less exploitive social ideologies and ethics, such that

> the hegemony of neoliberalism, alongside the naturalization of capitalist values, influences the ability to make choices on one's own behalf in the daily lives of economically marginalized as well as economically privileged communities around the globe. (Mohanty 2002: 508)

Research into the everyday places of neoliberalism presents a more challenging space for examining and theorizing how neoliberal ideologies intersect with other ideologies. Smith and Stenning (2006), in referring to Gibson-Graham's work on diverse economies, emphasize that exploitation is not exclusive to capitalism or neoliberalism and can just as easily occur in other 'social' spaces. As a result, it is not possible to '*a priori*' position diverse economies as liberatory. Rather, what is required is careful attention to the always already present forms of power bound up within different economic practices' (Smith and Stenning 2006: 207). Smith and Rochovská's (2007: 1167) investigation of the 'domestication of neo-liberalism' in the post-socialist Slovak Republic emphasizes the everyday activities of Slovak citizens who are trying to make neoliberal transformations more tolerable. Rather than thinking of 'non-economic' spaces such as the household as antagonistic to neoliberalism, the authors demonstrate how neoliberalism's 'success', in the case of contemporary Slovakia, is largely contingent on non-market, informal labour such as trans-generation childcare or alternative systems of food production which draws upon systems of reciprocity and kinship in these 'constitutive outsides' (Smith and Rochovská 2007: 1172). The case study begins with a discussion of the ethics of neoliberalism, but the analysis understands the 'everyday' as a practice-based, material space with less attention to its constitutive ethics or alternative ideologies.

A complementary approach to existing analyses of neoliberalism in the everyday might place normative evaluation and ideology in the centre of empirical research alongside material practices. Lee (2006: 415), in his reflections on the construction of value, emphasizes that values (such as individualism, egalitarianism, and so on) 'can never be merely suppressed, ignored or reduced to trivial relations of economically marginal significance. Indeed, they shape the conduct and consequences of economic geographies in a myriad of ways.' Values, or the things people hold 'inalienable', act as a system of knowledge that is critical in the evaluation of social activity (Lee 2006). Lee offers a brief vignette of novice winemakers and explains that the decision to go into business and the ability to remain in business despite economic failures depended upon valuations by neighbours and banks which, though not socially progressive, are not reflective of neoliberal individualism.[1] Transformative politics, in this very complex view of economic life, is therefore more likely to be found in 'the weaker performative incorporation of a diversity of values into all forms of economic activity' (Lee 2006: 429).

Religious ideology appears to be a particularly powerful means for incorporating diverse values into economic practice, but arguably also an effective route for embedding neoliberal ideology in non-economic spaces. Modern interpretations of Weber's focus on Calvinism, such as Zelizer's (1979) research on the establishment of life insurance in the nineteenth-century United States, suggest that the expansion of capitalism into 'sacred' areas depends upon the justifications furnished by religious leadership. Contemporary research from the UK and New Zealand on the work of religious voluntary and social welfare organizations recounts a range of ways that religious ethics, as embodied through volunteers or religious organizations, absorb or adjust to contexts of neoliberalization (see Cloke et al. 2005, 2007; Conradson 2008), often filling the spaces of the absent state with a justificatory discourse of faithful work. In her consideration of the future of the left, Wills (2006) suggests that the high levels of activism by faith-based groups in the London Living Wage campaign should not be conceptualized as a re-emergence of the left, but as a

FIGURE 2.1   Map of Peru

different kind of movement comprising groups who may have different normative aims, with participants 'deliberately not talking about
their own particular doctrines and differences' (Wills 2006: 219). In
places where secularism is less taken for granted, religious and neoliberal ideologies can be either incompatible or mutually sustaining.
Gokariksel and Mitchell (2005) demonstrate how the shift toward
the free market in the 1980s in France and Turkey was discursively
and practically wrapped up with the emergence of democracy and
liberalized religion, such that 'traditional' Islam, often embodied
in the female Muslim, became conceived as the roadblock to state
progress. However, Halvorson's (2005) research with girls in Pakistan

provides a different perspective on the links between Islamic ethics and neoliberalization. As new economic structures shift the spaces in which women work, assumptions about women's belonging in public spaces also shifted. The result was not an increased status for girls in society, but the broadening of their mobility as a necessary adaptation to the changes wrought through neoliberalization.

The remainder of this chapter explores more deeply the ways that religious ideology and economic ideology meet through a more historical perspective of social justice activism by religious leaders in the Iglesia Surandina (Surandina). It draws upon ethnographic research conducted in the Southern Andes for twelve months in 2001 and 2002 (Figure 2.1), following the changing work of several religious leaders and laity who have been present in the region since the early phases of activism.

State-led development and activism in the Southern Andes

Neoliberalization in Latin America has distinctive characteristics reflecting both the contexts of Latin American politics and society and historical shifts in foreign and transnational influences (see also North, in this volume). In Peru, domestic economic policy was heavily influenced by foreign banks, corporations and governments several decades prior to John Williamson's reflections on the 'Washington consensus' in 1990 (Pastor and Wise 1999). Until 1990 there was an uneven embrace of state-led development characterized by early dependence on external financing and public firms, overlaid with a tense relationship with domestic private investors and an inability to coordinate social policy effectively, regardless of the development model selected (Wise 1994). State-led import-substitution industrialization in the first half of the 1960s was followed by a period of redistribution policy and nationalization under the left-leaning military dictatorship of General Juan Velasco (1968–75). Velasco also initiated agrarian reform with the intent of radical land redistribution, but was followed by a centrist, Francisco Morales Bermúdez, who implemented IMF stabilization policies in 1978, and Fernand Belaunde, whose failed attempts to privatize state industry were hampered by a lack of available investors and the presence of government 'gatekeepers' who were interested in keeping control of their respective sectors (Pastor and Wise 1992: 88). By the early 1980s, rapidly rising inflation was coupled with a decrease in social spending, and pressures to try and 'fix' the uneven and ineffective distribution of land that took place during agrarian reform increased steadily.

Alan García thus began his first presidency in 1985 with a plan for economic heterodoxy. After instituting price controls, privatizing banks, and angering the international finance community by publicizing his reduction in debt repayment, the modest economic growth which accompanied his first two years in office was drastically reversed. These decades of economic and social chaos supported the growth of the Maoist-inspired revolutionary movement Sendero Luminoso, the Shining Path. By the mid-1980s, Sendero had spread its activities beyond its organizational home in the central Andes of the district of Ayacucho. In addition to attacks on critical resources in Lima, Sendero's most notable accomplishment during this period was its access to, and influence in, the countryside in the Southern Andes. García proved inept at defeating Sendero, and counterinsurgency efforts under his administration became as feared in many rural parts of Peru as Sendero itself. By the time he left office in July 1990, annual inflation had reached a shocking 3,000 per cent (Gonzales de Olarte 1993) and Sendero appeared largely unshaken.

The politics and economics of the 1980s thus presented a range of challenges for social activists working on behalf of the nation's poor, and an even greater challenge for the rural poor in the Southern Andes. Peasants still found themselves without access to land following agrarian reform, while terrorism and government counterinsurgency added another threat to their well-being. These hardships galvanized the Church of the Southern Andes, the Surandina, an alliance of the five Prelates of Cusco, Sicuani, Ayaviri, Puno and Juli, who worked to redefine the meanings and demands of *la justicia* (justice) alongside the plight of the rural peasants.

The Surandina and economic activism in the 1980s

The 'years of terrorism' dramatically changed many aspects of social activism and economic development throughout the Peruvian Andes, with many state and private organizations abandoning activities in rural locations. The Surandina had a very different response to this period of crisis, with five bishops of the region showing a strong stance of solidarity with the *campesinos*, the rural peasants, who tended to be of Quechua and Aymara descent. The leaders and lay workers of the Surandina had developed a vibrant practice of liberation theology beginning in the 1960s with a distinctive imprint of 'Andean' ontology and spirituality (Marzal 1969). The liberation theology of the Surandina not only recognized the obligation that the Church had to the poor, but also attempted to reconcile its own violent perpetration of inhumanity towards indigenous ideology, community and organization. Its radical activism often drew the ire of the more conservative Peruvian Church, and attracted the critical eye of the Vatican throughout the 1970s and 1980s (Klaiber 1992).

Male and female Church leaders publicly demanded state responses to resolve the plight of the Peruvian rural peasant, with access to land and livelihood providing a central theme in the letters and liturgy. For many Church leaders, justice became defined by the ability of men and women to reap the benefits of their own labour and to be treated with respect, with a wealth of biblical metaphors to support their position. In his pastoral letter to 'those who govern', Luis Vallejos Santoni, then Archbishop of Cusco, outlined his concerns over the agony of the peasants in the countryside and the disappointments following agrarian reform:

> To be just signifies giving each one that which he [*sic*] is owed. This refers to the material blessings of nature. Here, the best example would have to be compensation for work and the named right to the fruit of one's own work and one's own land. But man [*sic*] is also owed his reputation, respect and consideration ... how many tears have drenched our *tierra cusquena* [Cusco land] because of injustice! (IPA, n.d.: 44–5, author's translation)

This explicit link between justice, land and respect helped to shape the Surandina's own labour in the 1980s. This was especially true in the Ayaviri Prelate, a region that had been given the dubious distinction as being the 'second Ayacucho' for its level of Sendero presence and activity, and the High Provinces of Cusco which bordered on this region of conflict. Securing the basic civil rights of citizens was a defining element of the Surandina's work at this time, but this period also marked an impressive range of activism targeted at agricultural productivity and livelihoods. In addition to a more formalized agricultural centre in Ayaviri and several humanitarian interventions during severe climate events, leaders also supported and directly engaged in broader peasant movements addressing land access and markets. Two very different examples of activism help to reveal the scope and scale of this activism: a small-scale intervention to help peasants improve the local market prices of their goods in the High Provinces, and a dramatic land occupation in Ayaviri.

The first illustration of economic activism took place in a rural pueblo of the High Provinces of Canas, Cusco. Former parish priest Victor Ramos arrived in the rural parish in 1974 to work with two nuns from the Company of Mary. Agricultural reform had already transformed the dynamics of the countryside, with government-created agrarian leagues coming into contest with community federations which existed well before the 1969 agrarian reform (see Alfaro Moreno 1994). Ramos and the sisters focused their social work on educating the population about the agrarian reform. 'Considering that it was a law that had to do with the life of the peasants,' Ramos explains, 'they had been absent from the law. They weren't familiar with it.' Educating the parish population about the law also provided a basis for envisioning the Church as a space for resolving other problems related to production. In the course of their regular meetings, the catechists voiced their frustration over low market prices for their products:

> They started a discussion about the theme of commercialization. This theme led to the issue of prices. You know that here in Peru the *campesino* sells cheap and buys expensive. They noticed this. And so we worked on this theme, and they arrived at a plan among themselves, the catechists did this, the men and the women [themselves] – they decided that they would fix a pricing scheme ... they would set a minimum price for which they would sell each of their products. (interview with Victor Ramos, November 2002)

The *campesinos* recognized that fixing prices would require a different kind of market space, as the existing market was spread around the pueblo's plaza where it was easy for sellers to push prices down. Their solution was to leave the commercial sellers – those who brought in fruits imported from the jungle, household goods, and other items not produced locally – in the plaza, but to move their own products within the walls of the church grounds. The discussion encouraged a broader conversation with the presidents of the community, initially led by the catechists but eventually taken over by community leaders.

The second example, the *marcha por la tierra* (march for the land), was a more radical attempt to address the failures to distribute land in a more equitable manner. In Ayacucho, like other parts of the rural Andes, the majority of land post-reform was held by about fifty cooperatives with very little reserved for either *campesino* communities or individual holders (Rénique 1987). Cooperatives were often inefficient and corrupt, and in the region of the Surandina pressure to sell to former landowners was great. Reform adjustments stalled under President Belaunde, and by November 1985 the *campesino* federations of Ayaviri were insisting on a reorganization of the cooperatives in order to comply with the original intent of land redistribution. When Alan García's government failed to respond, the peasants began a series of land invasions. Sendero also instigated its own marches for the land, but in Ayaviri the most visible representatives were the leaders of the Catholic Church who walked with the peasants and even led the marches.

The Bishop of Ayaviri between 1982 and 1992 was Monsignor Francisco d'Alteroche, a French Dominican who had spent most of his service in Argentina and Peru. For the Monsignor and others, the fight for the land resonated with Surandina liberation ideals of justice and dignity through having control of one's land and one's labour. In reflecting on the power of the marches, the Monsignor explained that 'The fight for the land is a political problem, but it's interesting how we related the fight for the land with the fight for life … in this area, without land there is not life – material, spiritual, communitarian, cultural or religious life.' By affiliating itself with the *campesino* federation and the Izquierda Unida (United Left), the Church was also overtly aligning itself with organizations that were considered legitimate representatives of peasant interests (Smith 1991).

Though quite different in character and scope, both examples point to the importance of a normative alignment with the aims of economic justice in motivating and inspiring the activism of the Surandina. The right to land and the fruits of a person's labour became central to how Church leadership defined social justice and envisioned their social practice. They were not purely 'economic' concerns, but became associated with the very survival of the Andean peasant and failed to be addressed adequately by either the economically liberal approaches of Belaunde or the heterodox programmes of García. In the two decades which followed, however, the centrality of land and production became gradually replaced with concerns over democratic governance as Peru turned towards neoliberal economic policies to upright its economy.

Privatization and democratic politics

Alberto Fujimori was elected in 1990 with a promise to stabilize the economy without forcing the country into recession. His moderate economic reform was replaced by an aggressive shift towards stringent financial and economic reform after his election – dubbed 'fujishock' – justified by the economic shambles left by García's first presidency (Wise 2004). When Alejandro Toledo was elected to the presidency in April 2001, his campaign included a promise not to continue the privatizations which had been planned but not executed during the Fujimori government. Once in office, however, Toledo found it difficult to improve the economy and create jobs without responding to pressure from international banks and investors to privatize state-held sectors. Pressure also came from within the Toledo government, for in his eagerness to ensure a climate that would be favourable to international investors Toledo appointed two fiscal conservatives to the key positions of finance minister and prime minister (Arce 2005).

In 2002, the Toledo government attempted to sell two electricity distributors, the Empresa de Generación Eléctrica de Arequipa (Egasa) and the Empresa de Generación Eléctrica del Sur (Egsur). In June that year the sales collapsed under widespread protest throughout the south and in other regions which participated in strikes in a show of solidarity. In July, Toledo was forced to declare a month-long state of emergency in Southern Peru. The crisis came to a close when a committee headed by the Archbishop of Arequipa brokered a peace agreement and the government put the sales on hold for an indefinite period of time. The decision not to carry on with the privatization was interpreted by some as a warning to foreign investors of Peru's 'problem' with globalization (León 2002: 90). The costs of the protests were high, with several deaths and untold injuries, and extensive damage to infrastructure in the city of Arequipa. The response reflected frustration with Toledo's unreliability and a general distrust of privatization. Though utility privatization in Peru does appear to have increased access to services to the urban poor, consumption fell across all economic groups due to higher prices (Tórero and Pascó-Font 2001; see also Birdsall and Nellis 2003). In contrast to the Church mobilization around the economic concerns of the 1980s, the public outrage over privatization did not encourage notable support among the religious leaders of the Surandina.

From economic activism to democratic governance

The Iglesia Surandina also experienced change during this time. An increasingly conservative Peruvian Church meant that new appointments were not always entirely sympathetic to liberation and indigenous theologies. Despite these changes, many of the lay workers, priests and nuns who had been present in the Surandina in the 1980s remained in the region or returned to it in subsequent years. Community catechist associations also persisted during this time in many parishes, and the swelling of the Catholic Church's social work through a range of social organizations ensured increasingly diverse spaces for direct participation by members (Olson 2006; Riedel 1999). The economic projects of the Church also became increasingly institutionalized through the 1990s. These new activities had the effect of interlacing Church social action about poverty to international and bilateral aid agencies, particularly the Catholic agency Caritas and USAID. Concerns over livelihood and labour which inspired the march for the land were reoriented around microcredit projects, youth development projects, and 'capacity-building' among small-scale producers.

This was the context in the High Provinces of Cusco when Monsignor d'Alteroche, who had left his service in Ayaviri after ten years,

FIGURE 2.2   Market held outside the Catholic Church during Easter celebrations in the Andes, Peru

agreed to take on the responsibility as parish priest of a rural parish in 1996. Two sisters who had also worked in Ayaviri during the 1980s accepted an invitation to serve in one of the parish's pueblos. The Monsignor and the sisters participated in the organization of development activities with greater attention to education and politics than economic distribution, with the alleviation of poverty a focal point primarily of the formalized 'social teams' organized under the Prelate, which enacted the projects funded by Caritas and USAID. But the role that anti-neoliberalization policies might play in these conversations was less clear, a point which became most apparent during the anti-privatization protests. During the many public conversations in the plaza about the kind of support that the pueblo should give to the protesters in the south, and whether they should block the road leading through the high provinces to Ayaviri, the Monsignor expressed his concerns about the suitability of participation. In one such conversation, he replied abruptly that it would be *una tonteria* (stupidity) to block the roads. His reasoning was that such an action would prevent the teachers, virtually all of whom commuted in daily on the bus from the town of Sicuani, from attending school. And

FIGURE 2.3   Encouraging voting among Sunday churchgoers in the Andes, Peru

given the number of protests that had already taken place this year, it already appeared that classes would have to be held straight through the summer in order to compensate for missed days.

When I later asked the Monsignor about his position, he explained that he did not see privatization as a pressing issue for the particular communities of this region. In addition to them not being in the region of the privatization plan, the main pueblos of the parish did have electricity that had been brought in through a government-sponsored electrification programme, but the majority of the households in slightly more distant communities did not. Nor did households with electricity use it with any great regularity. The Catholic chapels in communities closer to the pueblos had been wired and were used for both religious and community-oriented events, with the communities themselves paying the electric bills with funds gathered from all households within the community boundary. If supporting a strike meant that teachers could not be bussed in from Sicuani and that the children would miss another day of school, the Monsignor argued that he could not support it. In the end, the community did not participate in the road blockage, and though it is difficult to say what influence the Monsignor's vocal opposition had upon the final decision, his unique presence as a well-educated foreigner and a charismatic religious leader did mean that his arguments would later be repeated and discussed. But he also confided his frustration with the current conditions of injustice. 'It used to be clear what the fight was for', he explained to me one evening. 'There were the peasants without land, the landowners, the Church fighting alongside the peasants. Today there is a system. How do you fight a system?'

His own response was to improve democratic capacity, and he channelled his activism into improving the quality of local democracy and government. In addition to supporting a range of democratic educational seminars sponsored by the local Vicaría de Solidaridad (Vicary of Solidarity), the Monsignor brokered an agreement which was signed by the ten mayoral candidates, indicating their willingness to abide by certain rules intended to improve both the civility and the outcome of the 2002 local and regional elections. The Monsignor had been upset to hear that other candidates were calling one of two women running an 'uneducated peasant', and began speaking with candidates and community leaders to try and improve the conduct of the campaign. In a meeting held in the parish, candidates and public officials agreed to a contract of good behaviour – no insulting of candidates, only their policies; refusal to engage in corrupt politics; and an agreement to support and work with whomever was elected in the end, among other points. When the Monsignor spoke of the agreement, he emphasized the importance of improving the democratic process at the local level, and of improving concepts of responsibility and community.

The shift in Surandina activism from radical action for redistributive economics to an emphasis on democratic politics – and established development networks to promote alleviation from poverty – seems to suggest that this is yet another example of the 'contradictory character of the neoliberal project' in Peru and the ways that it becomes enacted through non-economic social processes (Laurie and Bonnett 2002: 32). Like the march for the land decades before, working for fair elections and a quality democracy seemed an appropriate outgrowth of Surandina liberation theology ideals of solidarity and justice for the poor. Resisting privatization, on the other hand, was not equivalent to standing up to 'the system' which perpetuates inequality and injustice.

Conclusion: confounding neoliberalism?

How does the case of the Surandina, and a focus on ideology more generally, inform our understanding of neoliberalism as a mobile technology? The changing emphasis of the actors in the Surandina reflects both a shifting political–economic context and an altered Church. Those working in the 1980s envisioned their influence being felt through direct intervention in economic policies aimed at highlighting the importance of redistributing wealth. With the arrival of Toledo's government, and after twelve years of relatively consistent – if corrupt – neoliberalization, intervention on economic matters has been largely institutionalized and professionalized within the Church, with the potential for radical change envisioned as happening through democratic process. In the contemporary context, institutionalization of development activities streamlined economic justice aims into projects. It could be argued that the promise of democracy, the search for good governance, and the professionalization of economic activism are an integral part of the depoliticizing force of neoliberalization. From this perspective, the work of the Southern Andean Church could very well be seen as encouraging compliance with the rolling out of neoliberalism.

There are, however, two alternative explanations for these shifts. First, from the perspective of the Surandina, the contemporary plight of the indigenous and the poor is understood from a longer historical timeline reaching from colonialism through to the afterlife. Neoliberalism is not understood as the cause of injustice, but as the most recent expression of ongoing inhumanity, suffering and redemption. Against a backdrop of servitude and indentured labour, neoliberalism can appear quite docile. Given that contemporary conditions of suffering and inequality are already deplorable, policies such as privatization of utilities may be interpreted as not nearly as important to economic justice as a reliable education system or a fair and incorruptible government. Weyland (2004) reminds us that in Latin America much of the success of neoliberal economic policy has been predicated on the recognition that there are very few good alternatives (see also North, in this volume). In a place that has seen very few good alternatives for a very long time, there is a sense among activists that a benevolent political rule could provide the foundations for a benevolent economic system.

The second explanation underpinning the Surandina's modest response to neoliberalization is the difficulty activists encounter in accurately interpreting the potential material or normative outcomes of neoliberal economic policies. There is a clear frustration about what can be known and what needs to be known about development activities ranging from microcredit to privatization. Whereas these activists had little difficulty judging the normative resonance of uneven land distribution or fair local market prices with Surandina liberation theology, neoliberal economic policy outcomes for an already marginalized population are difficult to anticipate. Privatization in places where utilities are already poorly supplied and too expensive for most residents is not understood as the triumph of harsh individualism over communal compassion. When set against the problems of a dire educational system, crop infestations and familial violence, privatization appears to be a comparatively elite concern of the upper poor or middle class in urban areas. And for those communities where there is presently no electricity in communal buildings or educational centres, gaining immediate access for communal use can be more important than holding out for an alternative system under some future electrification plan.

This second point suggests that the adaptability of neoliberalism cannot be thought of only in terms of policies and technologies that can be manipulated to fit the needs of a given state or place, but may also reflect the potential to reshape and modify its central values. In contrast to other historical models of exchange, neoliberalism as an ideology can appear – rightly or wrongly – to be more undecided in its prejudice and more amenable to revisions. Indeed, the formal development activities of the Surandina are riddled with changes made by leaders and laity in order to make school lunches or microcredit better reflect a liberal Catholic ethic (see Olson 2008). Though there is little evidence from this case that the alternative normative aims of Surandina liberation theology have substantially changed the state model of economic development, it did clearly help legitimize processes in which a market economy or a system of private land ownership might be expected to reflect the values of equity and human dignity. Whether these alternative values can be inserted into Peru's future development through more formalized and state-based democratic models is decidedly less certain.

The case of the Surandina thus leaves us with a critical question: to what extent can the normative aims of neoliberal ideology be altered through its intersections with non-economic factors? Can economic policies generally associated with neoliberalization be adjusted and manipulated to reflect very different aims through democratic reform? Scholars on the left have been rather unoptimistic about this possibility, given that democratization, participation and even community caring have been important technologies for the rolling out of neoliberalism (see Staeheli 2008). It is in this vein that Leitner et al. (2007) encourage us to consider where neoliberalism has been changed so much that it no longer truly resembles neoliberalism. The experiences of activists might encourage us to continue to seek out the more subtle ways that the 'non-economic' is seen as a means for confounding the exploitive ideological underpinnings of neoliberalism.

Notes

Special thanks are extended to the religious and non-religious organizations that supported and participated in the research for this study in the region of the Iglesia Surandina, and to Charmalee and Edward Dias for assistance in fieldwork. An earlier draft of this chapter was presented at an ESRC Neoliberalism seminar series in Glasgow, and it has been improved considerably with the helpful guidance of the editors of this volume. All errors remain my own.

1. The story implies that the neighbours were anxious for their property not to be purchased by 'outsiders'.

References

Alfaro Moreno, J. (1994) *Los Greminos Rurales*, Lima: Fundación Friedrich Ebert.
Arce, M. (2005) *Market Reform in Society: Post-Crisis Politics and Economic Change in Authoritarian Peru*, University Park: Pennsylvania State University Press.
Birdsall, N., and J. Nellis (2003) 'Winners and losers: Assessing the distributional

Impact of Privatization', *World Development* 31(10): 1617–33.

Bourdieu, P. (1998) *Acts of Resistance: Against the Tyranny of the Market*, New York: New Press.

Castree, N. (2006) 'Commentary: From neoliberalism to neoliberalisation: Consolations, confusions, and necessary illusions', *Environment and Planning A* 38: 1–6.

Chopra, R. (2003) 'Neoliberalism as Doxa: Bourdieu's theory of the state and the contemporary Indian discourse on globalization and liberalization', *Cultural Studies* 17(3–4): 419–44.

Cloke, P., S. Johnsen and J. May (2005) 'Exploring ethos? Discourses of "charity" in the provision of emergency services for homeless people', *Environment and Planning A* 37: 385–402.

Cloke, P., S. Johnsen and J. May (2007) 'Ethical citizenship? Volunteers and the ethics of providing services for homeless people', *Geoforum* 38(6): 1089–101.

Collins, R. (1992) 'Weber's last theory of capitalism: A systematization', in M. Granovetter and R. Swedberg (eds), *The Sociology of Economic Life*, Boulder CO: Westview Press, pp. 85–110.

Conradson, D. (2008) 'Expressions of charity and action towards justice: Faith-based welfare in urban New Zealand', *Urban Studies* 45(10): 2117–41.

Gökariksel, B., and K. Mitchell (2005) 'Veiling, secularism, and the neoliberal subject: National narratives and supranational desires in Turkey and France', *Global Networks* 5(2): 147–65.

Gonzales de Olarte, E. (1993) 'Economic stabilization and structural adjustment under Fujimori', *Journal of Interamerican Studies and World Affairs* 35(2): 51–80.

Halvorson, S. (2005) 'Growing up in Gilgit: An exploration of girls' lifeworlds in northern Pakistan', in G. Falah and C. Nagel (eds), *Geographies of Muslim Women: Gender, Religion, and Space*, New York: Guilford Press, pp. 19–44.

IPA (Instituto Pastoral Andino) (n.d.) 'Carta pastoral de Luis Vallejos Santoni, Arzbispo del cusco, con motivo de sus Bodas de Plata Sacerdotales', *Memoria de dos Pastores, Testigos de Nuestra Fe*, Instituto Pastoral Andina, Jr. Jose Carlos Mariategui B-11, Urb, Sta. Monica, Wanchaq, Cusco, Peru.

Katz, C. (2005) 'Partners in crime? Neoliberalism and the production of new political subjectivities', *Antipode* 37(3): 623–31.

Klaiber, J.L., SJ (1992) *The Catholic Church in Peru 1821–1985: A Social History*, Washington DC: Catholic University of America Press.

Larner, W., and D. Craing (2005) 'After neoliberalism? Community activism and local partnerships in Aotearoa New Zealand', *Antipode* 37(3): 402–24.

Larner, W. (2003) 'Guest editorial: Neoliberalism?', *Environment and Planning D: Society and Space* 21: 509–12.

Laurie, N., and A. Bonnett (2002) 'Adjusting to equity: The contradictions of neoliberalism and the search for racial equality in Peru', *Antipode* 34(1): 28–53.

Lee, R. (2006) 'The ordinary economy: Tangled up in values and geography', *Transactions of the Institute of British Geographers* 31: 413–32.

Leitner, H.E., S. Sheppard, K. Sziarto and A. Maringanti (2007) 'Contesting urban futures: Decentering neoliberalism', in H. Leitner, J. Peck and E.S. Sheppard (eds), *Contesting Neoliberalism: Urban Futures*, New York: Guilford Press, pp. 1–25.

León, R. (2002) 'Peru's globalization problem', *Foreign Policy* 133: 90–91.

Marshall, K., and L. Keough (2004) *Mind, Heart and Soul in the Fight against Poverty*, Washington DC: World Bank.

Marzal, M. (1969) 'La Christianización del Indígena Peruano', *Allpanchis Phuturinqa* 1: 89–122.

Mitchell, K. (2006) 'Neoliberal governmentality in the European Union: Education, training and technologies of citizenship', *Environment and Planning D: Society and Space* 24(3): 389–407.

Mitchell, T. (2008) 'Rethinking economy', *Geoforum* 39(3): 1116–21.

Mohanty, C.T. (2002) 'Under Western Eyes' revisited: Feminist solidarity through anticapitalist struggles', *Signs: Journal of Women in Culture and Society* 28(2): 499–535.

Olson, E. (2006) 'Development, transnational religion, and the power of ideas in the High Provinces of Cusco, Peru', *Environment and Planning A* 38: 885–902.

Olson, E. (2008) 'Common belief, contested meanings: Organizational culture in faith-based development', *Tijschrift voor Econonische en Sociale Geografie* 99(4): 393–405.

Ong, A. (2007) 'Boundary crossings: Neoliberalism as a mobile technology', *Transactions of the Institute of British Geographers* 32: 3–8.

Pastor, M., and C. Wise (1992) 'Peruvian economic policy in the 1980s: From orthodoxy to heterodoxy and back', *Latin American Research Review* 27(2): 83–117.

Pastor, M., and C. Wise (1999) 'The politics of second-generation reform', *Journal of Democracy* 10(3): 34–48.

Peck, J., and A. Tickell (2002) 'Neoliberalizing space', *Antipode* 34(3): 380–404.

Polanyi, K. (1992) 'The Economy as Instituted Process', in M. Granovetter and R. Swedberg (eds), *The Sociology of Economic Life*, Boulder CO: Westview Press, pp. 29–51.

Rénique, J.L. (1987) 'Estado, partidos políticos y lucha por la tierra en Puno', *Debate Agrario: análisis y alternativas* 1: 55–76.

Riedel, F. (ed.) (1999) *Una Iglesia en marcha con el Pueblo*, Prelatura de Sicuani and Centro de Estudios y Publicaciones (CEP), Cusco: Sicuani.

Smith, A., and A. Rochovská (2007) 'Domesticating neo-liberalism: Everyday lives and the geographies of post-socialist transformations', *Geoforum* 38(6): 1163–78.

Smith, A., and A. Stenning (2006) 'Beyond household economies: Articulations and spaces of economic practice in postsocialism', *Progress in Human Geography* 30(2): 190–213.

Smith, M.L. (1991) *Rural Development in the Crossfire: The Role of Grassroots Support Organizations in Situations of Political Violence in Peru*, International Development Research Centre, Report 3–A-88–4267, Ottawa.

Staeheli, L. (2008) 'Citizenship and the problem of community', *Political Geography* 27(1): 5–21.

Tórero, M., and A. Pascó-Font (2001) *The Social Impact of Privatization and the Regulation of Utilities in Peru*, World Institute for Development Economics Research, Discussion Paper no. 2001/17, United Nations University, New York.

Weber, M. (1930) *The Protestant Ethic and the Spirit of Capitalism*, New York: Scribener's.

Weyland, K. (2004) 'Neoliberalism and democracy in Latin America: A mixed record', *Latin American Politics and Society* 46(1): 135–57.

Williamson, J. (ed.) (1990) *Latin American Adjustment: How Much Has Happened?* Washington DC: Institute for International Economics.

Wills, J. (2006) 'The left, its crisis and rehabilitation', *Antipode* 38(5): 907–15.

Wise, C. (2004) 'The Politics of Peruvian Economic reform: Overcoming the legacies of state-led development', *Journal of Interamerican Studies and World Affairs* 36(1): 75–125.

Zelizer, V. (1979) *Morals and Markets: The Development of Life Insurance in the United States*, New York: Columbia University Press.

3

Travelling neoliberalism: Polish and Ghanaian migrant workers in London

Jon May, Kavita Datta, Yara Evans, Joanna Herbert, Cathy McIlwaine and Jane Wills

Neoliberalism can no longer be understood as a homogeneous set of principles and practices. Just as it displays a variety of origins, so too it takes a variety of locally specific, or 'path dependent', forms (Harvey 2005; Larner 2000). It also, and obviously, travels. A small body of scholars have begun to trace the movements of neoliberal ideas (Beckman 1992; Bockman and Eyal 2002), and of the elite band of politicians, policymakers and analysts responsible for promulgating those ideas (Peck 2006). A second, more extensive body of work considers the multitude of others whose movements are shaped by rather than shape 'travelling neoliberalism' (Castles and Miller 2003). In this chapter we attempt to bring these two bodies of work together: following both the movement of neoliberal principles and practices from their heartland in North America and Western Europe into sub-Saharan Africa and East Central Europe (ECE), and the movement of people – as migrant workers – to Britain following their displacement from these regions in the aftermath of neoliberal restructuring. Here, the notion of 'travelling neoliberalism' thus invokes a double movement; of both ideas and people, of neoliberal principles and practices and of those whose lives have been radically reshaped by those principles and practices.

As Castles and Miller (2003) have argued, we live in the age of migration. Millions of people are on the move: with the predominant flows of international economic migration moving south to north, and east to west. Such movements can, in part at least, be understood as a result of the movement of neoliberalism into the Global South and East Central Europe. As countries in the global South continue to work through the aftershocks of IMF and World Bank imposed structural adjustment programmes (SAPs) and poverty reduction strategies (PRSs), and the countries of ECE move through 'transition', hundreds of thousands of workers have relocated, heading north and west. At the same time, the neoliberalization of Western economies – characterized by the rapid restructuring of those economies and labour markets – has itself fuelled demand for these workers (Sassen 1991, 1998).

Despite the obvious symmetry of such movements, surprisingly few attempts have been made to chart the exact contours of these flows – connecting up this flow of neoliberal ideas with the subsequent flows of people from north to south and south to north, west to east and east to west (though see Misra et al. 2004; Mitchell 2004). In this chapter we try to do exactly this: tracing, first, the movement of neoliberal ideas from Washington, Brussels and London to Ghana and Poland; and second, the subsequent movements of Ghanaian and Polish workers from those countries to London. In the final parts of the chapter we explore the impact of neoliberal restructuring on the London economy itself, tracing the creation of a demand for these workers and of a new 'migrant division of labour' in London, and contrast the very different experiences of Polish and Ghanaian migrants working in London's low-wage economy.

Within this apparently simple logic, migration emerges less as a simple response *to* neoliberal restructuring, than as a complex set of practices sitting *alongside* that restructuring and interacting *with it* in complex ways. Not least, whilst migration offers workers an opportunity to escape the consequences of restructuring in their home countries, they must in turn negotiate the effects of restructuring at their point of destination. These effects, and these experiences, are also complex. The arrival of more and more overseas workers has increased competition in London's low-wage economy, leading to conflict between different groups – and between workers from sub-Saharan Africa and ECE especially (Herbert et al. 2008). For many migrant workers, life in London is incredibly – and increasingly – hard. But people also find ways of coping with these hardships, whilst migration itself continues to offer migrants their best hope of securing a better future for themselves and for their families – whether in London, Warsaw or Accra (Datta et al. 2007).

In telling this story, the chapter draws upon material from a wider project examining the experiences of low-paid migrant workers in London (Datta et al. 2007; Evans et al. 2007; May et al. 2007). As part of that project, the authors interviewed over one hundred low-paid migrant workers in different sectors of London's economy, and over two dozen policymakers, community organizations and employers. Reflecting the current make-up of London's low-paid migrant workforce, the single largest group of workers interviewed came from sub-Saharan West Africa, notably Ghana and Nigeria – both countries subject to sustained restructuring over recent decades. Among those who had made their way to Britain from ECE, Polish workers predominated. Though these had also come to London in an effort to carve out a better life for themselves after the shock of transition, their experiences of life in London were very different from the experiences recounted by those from sub-Saharan Africa. Contrasting the experiences of Polish and Ghanaian workers in London's low-wage economy thus offers important insight into the complexities of labour migration, and of the relationships between international labour migration and neoliberalism.

Structural adjustment, transition economies and migration

Structural adjustment is perhaps one of the most significant and far-reaching forms of 'travelling neoliberalism': a model of social and economic 'reform' born in the corridors of Washington and visited upon struggling nation-states far beyond the engine rooms of neoliberal thought (Bayart 1993; Beckman 1992). Although the precise nature of structural adjustment may have changed over the years, with the recent shift towards poverty reduction strategies, for example, the basic prescription remains the same: fiscal austerity, the liberalization of trade agreements, a reduction of import tariffs, and wide-ranging cuts to public expenditure (Simon 2001). Initially with loans, and later debt reduction, dependent upon take-up of a SAP or implementation of a PRS, recipient countries have little choice but to accept the medicine doled out by the IMF and the World Bank (Coombe and Stoller 1994; for a rather different reading of PRS, emphasizing the differences between SAPs and PRS, and the consultative nature of the latter, see Craig and Porter 2003).

If we are to understand structural adjustment as a form of 'travelling neoliberalism', however, we need first a rather more sophisticated understanding of the ways in which neoliberalism – and theory more generally – travels. Whilst ideas may move, they also tend to mutate as they come into contact with other ideas, and are enacted under locally specific conditions (Clifford 1989). And, whilst it is tempting to read structural adjustment as a simple illustration of US hegemony – a prime example of the 'one size fits all' development mantra – we need also to understand the ways in which such programmes are received in and put into practice by recipient nations (Mohan 2007).

In the case of Ghana, for example, key tenets of the structural adjustment programme introduced in 1983 already had a long domestic history by the time Jerry Rawlings turned to Washington, with the Busia government of 1969–72 liberalizing controls on foreign direct investment, and the Acheampong administration of 1972–78 moving to impose the country's first austerity programme. Even if they were 'imposed' from outside, then, the prescriptions of the IMF and the World Bank introduced in the early 1980s certainly fell on fertile ground in Ghana, and have been enthusiastically followed since – as the country has emerged as one of the continent's keenest advocates of neoliberal economic reform (Manuh 2001).

Though the close accord between Washington's and the Ghanaian government's own view of the most effective route to economic prosperity may appear unusual, a very similar story can in fact be told in relation to Poland and to the 'imposition' there of neoliberal principles of economic restructuring. In the mid- to late 1990s Poland was held up as one of the most successful of East Central Europe's transition economies – a 'soaring eagle' in the words of the International Monetary Fund – and proof positive, it seemed, of the ability of bodies like the IMF and the European Round Table of Industrialists to impose order upon ailing post-communist economies (De Broeck and Koen 2000). And yet, as Shields (2006a) makes clear, capitalism did not simply 'drop from the sky' into Poland in 1989. Rather, the 'transnationalization of production … [of] finance, and the ideological component[s] of neoliberal hegemony can be traced in the Polish political economy since [at least] the 1970s' (Shields 2006a: 20). As with Ghana, the roots of transition are much deeper in Poland than is sometimes assumed. The 'transmission' of neoliberal ideas and practices west to east has also been complex. In the case of Poland, neoliberalism has been neither simply 'imported' from the West, nor entirely 'home grown'. Rather, a particular and locally specific form of neoliberal restructuring has emerged in Poland: the result of a complex blend of ideas and practices bought over from Washington and Brussels but reworked by the Polish state and carried through by a newly emergent, indigenous (though fully transnational) capitalist class (Shields 2006b).

The movements of neoliberal principles and practices are in fact therefore remarkably complex. The effects of those principles and practices are far clearer. After more than a decade of stringent neo-liberal 'reform', for example, by the mid-1990s even the World Bank was doubtful of Ghana's prospects for long-term recovery (Armstrong 1993). Most obviously, whilst the 1980s and early 1990s saw a sharp rise in Ghana's GDP, both under- and unemployment also rose through this period, partly at least as a result of the privatization of some two-thirds of the country's parastatal enterprises and significant reductions in its civil service. Though the country's service sector has expanded, manufacturing activity has shrunk. Despite attempts to enforce fiscal control, inflation has risen and with it the cost of both housing and basic commodities. Whilst Ghana's transport and telecommunications networks have both grown, significant cuts have been imposed in the country's education and health-care systems. As a result, structural adjustment has proved very hard indeed for Ghana's poor. But the middle classes have also suffered – with declining job opportunities (and wages) in the public sector especially forcing many to look beyond traditional forms of managerial and professional employment, and beyond Ghana, in an effort to support their families (Manuh 2001). A remarkably similar dynamic can be traced in Poland. After an initial period of growth in the early years of transition (when GDP growth hovered around 5 per cent p.a.), by 2002 annual growth rates in Poland had fallen to just 1.2 per cent, leaving the country with a gross national income per capita of less than $5,000 (World Bank 2004a, 2004b). With attention focused on developing the country's service sector, agriculture and manufacturing – key sectors in the state-socialist era – have gone into meltdown. Following the rolling out of a programme of privatization, unemployment has soared – even as social welfare programmes have been cut (Misra et al. 2004; OECD 2003). For those able to find work, job security is a thing of the past and real wages have declined significantly (see also Smith et al. in this volume), whilst working conditions in the new private enterprises are often more reminiscent of the nineteenth rather than the early twenty-first century (Kowalik 2001). Transition has been particularly painful for those in southern and eastern Poland and in rural districts, for older workers previously employed in manufacturing or farming, and for younger, low-skilled workers in general.

Given such conditions it is hardly surprising that people have sought an escape. In Ghana, levels of emigration rose progressively through the 1980s as restructuring began to bite, with people leaving to take up opportunities in North America, the Middle East and Western Europe – including Britain (Mohan et al. 2000). Indeed, so significant was this exodus that it has been estimated that by the mid-1990s somewhere between 10 and 20 per cent of Ghanaians lived abroad: rich and poor (though rarely the poorest), men and women, its urban middle class as well as those from the countryside (Peil 1995). In Poland, mass emigration began almost as soon as the Berlin Wall came down – such that, for the first time in decades, in 1990 Poland became a country of net emigration. Though the economy grew in the 1990s, the results of economic growth were markedly uneven, and levels of emigration continued to rise through the late 1990s and into the early years of the twenty-first century (Iglicka 2005).

From a world-systems perspective, international migration is mainly structured by exactly these 'disruptions and dislocations ...

in the process of [uneven] capitalist development' (Massey et al. 1994: 445). Such movements are then given more specific shape by a number of key institutional actors. Certainly, just as they have played a role in the restructuring driving these movements, both the Ghanaian and Polish states have sought to shape the resultant migration flows in a number of ways. Most obviously, though never explicitly formulated as policy, until very recently (when concerns over labour shortages have seen the Polish government seeking ways of bringing workers home again) mass emigration was viewed as an attractive option by the Polish state: one way in which to tackle the otherwise seemingly intractable problems of mass unemployment that came with transition. Thus, through the 1990s the Polish government entered into a series of bilateral agreements with several Western European countries to secure the rights of Polish workers to move abroad on a temporary basis (Kicinger 2005), whilst since 1 May 2004 a new European Community treaty agreement with the UK has granted freedom of movement to and de facto residence in Britain (for details, see Currie 2006). In Ghana, 2001 saw the first Home Coming Summit organized by the government-sponsored Ghana Investment Promotion Centre in an effort to find ways of making the remitting of money from Ghana's diasporic community easier. In 2002, the Ghanaian state moved to 'capture' the diasporic community itself more effectively, introducing dual citizenship and, in 2006, the right to vote in Ghanaian national elections for Ghanaian nationals living abroad (Mohan 2007).

Neoliberalism and migration reconsidered

At one level, then, international migration can be understood as an attempt by both individual households and the state to manage the fallout of neoliberal restructuring. For individual households, migration offers an escape from the hardships of restructuring and a chance to realize opportunities no longer available at home. For the state, it offers a way out of the legitimation crises that restructuring can engender: providing an outlet for the un- or under-employed, and a vital source of foreign earnings through the flow of overseas remittances (Datta et al. 2007). Indeed, within such a reading, migration can emerge not only as a *response to* neoliberal restructuring, but as *enabled by* it. In the case of Poland, for example, even as the period leading up to EU accession saw a deepening penetration of neoliberal principals of marketization and flexible labour practices (Shields 2006b), the act of accession itself – seen by advocates as a key moment in European 'free market' integration – has provided thousands of Polish workers with a means of escaping the hardships ushered in by those very processes.

Yet, though clearly structured by these broader processes, migration must be understood as also and always deeply 'embedded in [a range of] ... complex economic, social, and ethnic networks' (Sassen 1998: 62, quoted in Misra et al. 2004: 5). Indeed, in Ghana, as elsewhere in West Africa, there is a long history of temporary migration – with movement between regions and across national borders one way in which households have long sought to safeguard their survival (Peil 1995). More recently, large-scale migration from Ghana to Britain began not in the late 1980s/early 1990s – as the previous, rather oversimplified, narrative might suggest – but in the 1960s and 1970s, as people fleeing the increasing hardships experienced under the Nkrumah government looked to older (colonial) ties between Ghana and Britain (Koser 2003). In Poland too, although between 1945 and the collapse of Communism in 1989 Poland's migration policy was based on isolationism (such that the country never provided the fertile ground for the recruitment of labour into Western European economies that it might otherwise have been expected to), people still left. In the post-war period much of this emigration was politically driven, though many thousands of people also left in search of work: moving mainly to Germany – both legally, on a temporary basis, and illegally (Iglicka 2005).

Rather than wholly new, or a process brought in to being by the roll-out of neoliberal principles and practices across the global South and ECE, then, the mass migrations of recent decades may be better understood as reflecting the *re-emergence* on a new scale of tried and tested household survival strategies. In Ghana, especially, migration is deeply embedded in the household economy, in kinship networks and the wider community. The costs involved in moving between continents, the difficulties in obtaining the necessary papers (whether legally or illegally) and the uncertainties associated with finding a place to live and work when one reaches one's destination, all mean that migrants must depend upon their families and wider social networks for support throughout the migration process. Likewise, if 'successful' on reaching their destination, people are likely to remit monies not only to kin but to the wider community (via Hometown Associations, for example) in an attempt to improve their status at 'home'. For these reasons, Mohan (2006) prefers to see migration not as the simple working through of an overly economistic logic, but as moving around a set of social relations and obligations (to the household, kin and community) that exist as much within a *moral* universe as an economic one, as involving issues of status and belonging as much as finance and survival (Mohan 2006: 870–71).

In Poland, the recent and rapid rise in emigration seems more obviously related to the survival strategies of individual households, a result of the equally rapid internalization of a new and aggressively neoliberal individualism even (Garapich 2007), than it does to the kind of dynamics evident in Ghana. But if so, the wider social networks built up over the years through friends and family, neighbours and colleagues in Poland (Stenning 2003), continue to be important in facilitating the migration process by, for example, providing people with an initial point of contact on reaching their chosen destination (Eade et al. 2007).

Tracing the 'prehistory' of these flows is important because it changes the ways in which we understand both migration and neoliberalism, and the relationships between the two. As research in Poland and other East Central European countries has shown, though everyday life in ECE has certainly been transformed with the transition from state socialism to 'free' market capitalism, people have found ways to manage that transition. Far from being entirely displaced, the modes of sociality and means of making a living that developed under state socialism have been adapted – but continue. In short, households have found ways to survive (if rarely to prosper) in the transition economy (Stenning 2003, 2005). For Smith (2007) such practices need understanding not as a simple response to the hardships ushered in by neoliberal restructuring (that is, as existing outside of and always in a subordinate relationship to a formal 'economy' run on neoliberal lines) than as part and parcel of a 'wider frame of culture-economy and non-essentialist economic practices' that *together with* a neoliberalizing market economy make up the 'diverse economies' of East Central Europe (Smith 2007: 216).

So too with migration. Though given renewed impetus, and certainly transformed in scale in recent years, the movement of households from Ghana and Poland to the USA, Britain and other Western European countries pre-dates the restructuring of their national economies along neoliberal lines. Rather than as a simple response *to* neoliberal restructuring, migration thus emerges as a long-standing set of practices sitting *alongside* that restructuring and interacting with it in complex ways. Such practices are diverse, and give rise to quite different patterns of movement by very different groups. As we show below, such differences are often of crucial importance in shaping the experience of migrants when they reach their chosen destination.

Neoliberal restructuring, the London economy and the return of the repressed

Many of the key tenets of neoliberal thinking that were to be developed in Washington and Brussels, and that were to wreak such havoc in Ghana and Poland, first emerged in London: from government and quasi-governmental organizations, think-tanks and analysts in the 1970s and 1980s (Massey 2004). Far from being only the place to which so many of those displaced by neoliberal restructuring in sub-Saharan Africa and ECE have made their way, London can thus be thought of as a key site in the *production* of the ideas that helped shape those movements in the first place (Massey 2007). Those same ideas have also helped engender a radical restructuring of the London economy itself along neoliberal lines over the past three decades, thus fuelling the demand for migrant labour.

As in Ghana and Poland, the state has played a crucial role in this restructuring process. Most obviously, labour market deregulation, welfare 'reform' and the introduction of new immigration policies have helped shape the emergence of a distinctive 'migrant division of labour' in London over the past decade or so, in which those coming to London from countries like Ghana and Poland must now find a place (May et al. 2007).

For example, by the mid-1990s it was apparent that the UK, and London in particular, faced a peculiar problem. Alongside high levels of growth and rising demand from employers for both highly skilled and low skilled workers, there remained high levels of unemployment (among British minority ethnic communities in particular) and economic inactivity (GLA 2002). With shortages of highly skilled workers, and with welfare 'reform' apparently unable to shift sufficient numbers of the lower skilled off benefits and into (low-wage) work, employers began to lobby government to ease the restrictions on the use of foreign labour (Flynn 2005).

The result was the introduction, in 2002, of a new system of 'managed migration': designed to reduce levels of asylum and illegal immigration and manage legal migration in the interests of the UK economy (Morris 2002). Following the introduction of 'managed migration', the number of people legally entering Britain to work rose very considerably, from around 40,000 a year in the mid-1990s to over 200,000 a year in 2004 (Flynn 2005). Crucially, managed migration also introduced a strict hierarchy of classes of entry and associated privileges: ranging from the right to settle for the highly skilled, to only temporary admission with no rights to benefits for the low skilled (RSA 2005). Importantly, too, these channels of entry and associated privileges mapped on to quite particular immigration flows. Broadly speaking, those coming to Britain from high-income (northern hemisphere) countries were more likely than native Londoners to find managerial and professional work, whilst those coming from the global South were more likely either to find no work at all, or – even if arriving with tertiary-level qualifications – only low-paid employment (Spence 2005). Ineligible for benefits, such workers provided employers with a ready pool of cheap, and highly flexible, labour.

Cross-cutting the more general inequality in London's labour market, and clearly racialized patterns of employment and unemployment, then, by the turn of the new millennium a distinctive 'migrant division of labour' also existed in London. Indeed, by 2002/3 46 per cent of the city's elementary positions (domestics, cleaners, caretakers, refuge collectors and labourers) were filled by workers born abroad – the single largest group having come to London from the global

South (Spence 2005). Levels of pay for those in elementary occupations are extremely low, and working conditions extremely poor. In a recent survey of London's low-paid workers, for example, May et al. (2007) found as many as 92 per cent earning less that the Greater London Authority's London Living Wage (of £6.70 an hour in 2005) and over half working unsociable hours (the early, late or night shift).

Yet, the introduction of managed migration was in fact to be only the first step in a more radical overhaul of Britain's immigration system. On 1 May 2004 the British government found itself confronted by a seemingly inexhaustible supply of (cheap) labour. Having originally estimated an annual in-flow of between 5,000 and 13,000 new arrivals from the EU accession states (Dustmann et al. 2003), between May 2004 and March 2006 more than 350,000 people registered with the government's Worker Registration Scheme, almost 200,000 of them Poles (Home Office et al. 2006). Though by no means all those registering were newly arrived in the UK, and only a proportion came to London, such a large supply of new workers has provided London with a major boost to its labour 'reserve'. To ensure such labour can be used to best effect, those entering Britain from the EU accession countries also do so under very specific conditions. Though with a de facto right to reside in Britain (Currie 2006), people can only (legally) work if they subsequently register on the Worker Registration Scheme, and cannot claim benefits until continuously registered for twelve months. Under such conditions, continued labour market flexibility is assured.

Partly because it seems employers are now increasingly favouring white workers from ECE over either black and minority ethnic (BME) candidates or applicants from the global South (Herbert et al. 2008), workers from the EU accession states have been remarkably successful in finding work. For the British government, the continuing supply of (white) workers from the EU accession states has enabled further restrictions to be placed on the number of work permits issued to 'low-skilled' workers from beyond the EU (Home Office 2006; Home Office and Foreign and Commonwealth Office 2007), thus easing fears over the kind of public backlash that characterized earlier periods of mass immigration when migration streams were dominated by people from the New Commonwealth countries (Smith

1989). For workers themselves, however, with three-quarters of those recently arrived from Poland also employed in routine or semi-routine occupations (Eade et al. 2007), competition at the low-paid end of London's labour market has increased significantly. It is within this shifting context that the respondents from Ghana and Poland, whose voices we give space to below, must carve out a living.

'So the hotel looks wonderful, but what is happening behind the scenes?'

Even as neoliberalism strives to create a world without borders for capital, it continues to rely on border controls and restrictive immigration regimes to curtail the movement of some workers and increase control over others (Chacón 2007). Nonetheless, for people like Julia the decision to look for work in London was relatively straightforward. Growing up in Tychy, in southern Poland, Julia had to leave high school before she could graduate when it became clear that her father's wages from the mining company where he worked were no longer sufficient to support the family. Julia's subsequent employment history in Poland is not unusual, with frequent moves between various low-paying jobs in catering, retail and small-scale manufacturing (see Smith et al., in this volume). Having worked first in one of Tychy's growing number of fast-food restaurants, for example, she moved to a florist, which went bankrupt, and from there to a small clothing company. She took the decision to leave Poland in the spring of 2005 for the 'same reason that 80 per cent of Polish coming here [do] – for work ... because of the wages'.[1] Though the thought of leaving Poland was a little daunting, she was not the first person in her family to do so. Throughout the 1980s, her father had regularly worked on building sites in Germany and still made occasional trips west to supplement his wages from the mine.

The move itself was relatively easy to organize. A friend of Julia's sister's friend was also moving to London and had made contact with a Polish landlady there who had contacts with the agencies that supply London's hotels with back-of-house staff. Nonetheless, arriving in London was a shock. The house they moved into was spread over three floors, with the landlady occupying the ground floor. Five bedrooms, one kitchen and one bathroom were shared by no fewer

FIGURE 3.1   A Polish woman cleans the foyer of one of London's numerous corporate headquarters

than twenty-five tenants. After having her own room at home, the house was 'something unimaginable ... [with] mattresses scattered all over the floor ... [When I] saw the conditions there, I almost had a nervous breakdown'.

As Jan Mokrzycki, president of the Federation of Poles in Great Britain confirms, the kind of loose networks of 'chain migration' drawn upon by Julia, as too the often appalling accommodation in which those moving to London (initially at least) tend to find themselves, are common features in the stories of Polish émigrés (Mokrzycki 2006). Like Julia, more and more Polish women especially are taking on work in London's hotels (Evans et al. 2007). In 2002, the British hotel industry employed over 280,000 workers, with close to 10 per cent of the nation's hotel rooms located in London (Evans et al. 2007: 88). Though the industry has always tended to draw upon agency staff to provide numerical flexibility, over the past decade or so it has undergone significant restructuring: engaging in what Evans et al. (2007) refer to as 'subcontracting by stealth'. Thus, British hotels have tended to increase their reliance on agency rather than in-house staff, for example, taking advantage of a new oversupply of agency workers – mostly migrants – to lower both pay and conditions of work. Hence, although London hotels still tend to pay in-house staff an hourly rate, agency cleaning staff are more often paid by the room – a piece rate whose hourly equivalent is often set below the national minimum wage (Evans et al. 2007). The move towards piece work has led to both a downward pressure on wages and a marked intensification of workloads, as subcontractors seek to retain their profit margin through increased productivity. Indeed, average wages in the sector are the lowest in Britain (with full-time mean earnings standing at just £210.80 a week in 2005), whilst hotels have one of the highest rates of labour turnover and the lowest levels of union density of any sector of the British economy (ASHE 2005; Smith and Carroll 2003; Wills 2005).

Like Julia, Zofia (aged 20 from Łódź in central Poland) was put in contact with an employment agency servicing the hotel sector by the brother of a Polish friend, with whom she shared a flat. Working mostly with other Poles and Lithuanians, she got on well with her colleagues, but the pay remained extremely poor – with Zofia earning just £2.00 for each room she cleaned. As Zofia and Julia make clear, such work is often backbreaking. Yet, with such low levels of pay, people also sometimes find it necessary to take on second jobs:

> Once a week ... the main manager from the agency came to check our work. She would complain about everything. Girls on their knees were cleaning skirting in the corridors, I had to clean the lamps in the corridor, doors, frames, everything. So the hotel looks wonderful, but what is happening behind the scenes – to get this effect – is very hard work. (Zofia)

> My friend said to me, 'listen Julia, in this bakery the owner needs someone ... I know that you are ... not afraid of working hard'. So I went to the bakery but I didn't resign from the hotel. I was working at night at the bakery and at the hotel during the day. I was sleeping like two hours a day and survived that way for one and a half weeks, but after that ... I just couldn't do it any more. (Julia)

Though Zofia got on well with the other chambermaids, her relationships with her supervisors were more difficult. Partly these problems related to the intensity of the work, with supervisors pushing their teams to take on more and more rooms. But racial tensions were also evident, with Zofia complaining about a black African supervisor in particular who seemed to want to make her life at the hotel as difficult as possible:

My manageress was from the Ukraine, the other one was – I don't know, she was black, somewhere from Africa … Whatever I did wasn't good enough … she always gave me the girls without experience, so I had to help them a lot. They also worked slower … [the girls] would say that it is very hard work and that they feel humiliated. They are humiliated, it is true.

More generally, working as a chambermaid was extremely lonely – as Zofia found herself working 'on my own all the time in those rooms'. Indeed, loneliness is a recurring theme in the accounts of many of the Polish workers with whom we talked. Nor was this loneliness eased by her connections with the wider Polish community in London. Rather, in common with other respondents, Zofia tended to view her co-nationals as a threat – as competing for the same jobs and housing, and as more generally not to be trusted, as Julia explains (see also McIlwaine 2005):

> In Poland I had more time for friends and would spend more time with them. Here I have friends, but not many. I have also learnt that the Polish are a very jealous people – the worst I have come across … Even black people keep together, but the Polish – they never help each other, they stab you in the back. I have seen it here – we are so afraid that someone will do better than us.

Yet, whilst life outside of work too was often difficult, people sought to put their difficulties in perspective. Most obviously, however hard to bear at the time, life in London was seen by most as providing them with opportunities unavailable at home and bearable because it was *temporary*, as Julia concluded:

> You know, if we take into account earnings this is what keeps me here in London. That I can provide for myself. Pay for a flat, for food, buy tickets, cosmetics, clothes and still put some money aside. In Poland it would be impossible, because if I wanted to live on my own, unfortunately I would not even have enough to rent a small studio flat.

Of course, the tendency to view migration in these terms is largely a product of the freedom that those from the EU accession states have to come and go from Britain as they please. As Grażyna, pointed out, Poland is 'not so far – only one and a half hours from Stansted'. Viewed in these terms, life in London was tolerable because it was recognized for what it was: a welcome means of gaining some independence, of easing the burden on their families in Poland, and (even if difficult) of saving enough money to enable a better life on their *return home*.

This ability to return is not only a question of geographical distance, time or money. For those seeking work in Britain, it is primarily a question of legal status. For those without the appropriate entry visa, there is no right to stay and to build a new home, *or* to return to the one left behind. For those lacking such rights, life in London can be very different.

'When you present your documents… that's mostly what they look out for'

In contrast to the ease with which the Polish respondents made their way to Britain, people from Ghana had travelled to London by a variety of, often circuitous, routes. A few had come to London many years earlier to join relatives under the British government's Family Reunification scheme. Others had travelled as a dependant on their partner's visa. A few had moved first to another European Union country, gained an EU passport and only then made their way to Britain. Though not surprisingly people were often wary of discussing their immigration status in any great detail, it is clear that some were in Britain illegally. Most often people had overstayed on an initial visitor's or student visa, earning them the ambiguous label of an 'irregular' migrant. Though no one knows the true size of the irregular population in Britain, studies suggest that these experiences are by no means unusual – with estimates of that population ranging from 310,000 to 570,000 people in 2001 (Woodbridge 2005).

Since EU accession, the British government has again announced plans to clamp down on irregular migration seeking to stem the flow of illegal migrants coming to Britain from beyond the EU. As part of that process, the British state has sought to further secure its extraterritorial borders: tightening up on the procedures relating to the issuing of visas in Britain's overseas consulates, for example, as Kwasi, from Ghana, explains: 'When you present your documents for the visa, that's mostly what they look out for: are you going back to your country when you finish what you are doing?'

For those with irregular status, life is precarious. Not least, there is the constant fear of arrest and deportation. As Abina, also from Ghana, says, 'If you come and you don't have papers then you will be in serious trouble.' Finding work is also becoming more difficult as employers, wary of the fines accruing to those employing people in contravention of their immigration status, are turning to the new supply of legal workers from ECE instead.

Yet, whilst the majority of Polish respondents were relatively young, the Ghanaian people we worked with tended to be older: typically in their thirties or forties. Many had dependent children, either having been joined in Britain by their families, having had children once already in Britain, or (both men and women) having left their children with family in Ghana whilst they sought work overseas. For these people, in particular, the main reason to come to Britain was to secure enough money to make regular remittances to their family back home, as Ama makes clear: 'I've been able to give, like, daily bread to my family; given them food by sending them money every month so they can buy food … If I were back home my salary would not even be enough for me.'

As such, the difficulties people had in finding work, and the very low levels of pay associated with the kind of jobs most did secure, had ramifications far beyond their own immediate well-being. Neither the scale and significance of such remittances, nor the difficulties people must go through in order to provide them, should be underestimated. Overseas remittances are now estimated to be Ghana's third largest source of foreign earnings (Anarfi et al. 2003) and for many households provide a vital source of income – used to fund both projects designed to secure a better future (frequently, a child's education) and day-to-day living. Over 80 per cent of the Ghanaian workers we spoke to regularly sent money home: with amounts varying according to circumstance but averaging around £100 a month – out of an average monthly income of just £850. Though making an invaluable contribution to the family at home, such amounts are a significant drain on the incomes of those providing them (Datta et al. 2007). Adding to this financial strain is the emotional pain suffered by those who must leave their children behind while they seek work overseas so that they can better provide for their children's future (Datta et

FIGURE 3.2 'So does that mean because of your colour, what you want to do you will not be able to do it?' A Ghanaian woman cleaning toilets at the London headquarters of a major international bank

al. 2006; see also Aranda 2003; Parreñas 2005). Indeed, one of the most invidious aspects of British immigration policy is, of course, that those living in Britain without permission cannot risk leaving the country – to visit family back home, for example – lest they are unable to get back in.

Such narratives are all the more striking when one considers that many of the people we talked with had previously held managerial or professional positions in their home country (over half arrived in Britain with tertiary-level qualifications) – positions that would once have provided considerable security and a decent living in Ghana. Yet, in Britain, these people too had been able to secure only low-wage jobs. For some, the problems they encountered in finding appropriate employment must be put down to their irregular status. Overseas qualifications are also not always recognized by British employers. But even those who had trained in Britain, and been granted indefinite leave to remain, often faced difficulties. For these people, problems in finding professional employment are most obviously explained with reference to continued racism in the London labour market (Herbert et al. 2008). Mary, who in Ghana had held a high-level position in a port inspection company but who had seen her wages fall and the opportunities for promotion curtailed as the Ghanaian economy stalled, was now studying for a certificate in housing management. She recounted her experiences as follows:

A friend of mine told me 'Mary this course you are doing at university, I promise you, you are not going to get work with it in this country, so why are you worrying yourself?' ... So does that mean because of your colour, what you want to do, you will not be able to do it? ... it's something that I'm battling with.

Whilst Mary continued with her course, Obi from Nigeria worked as a cleaner on the London Underground. Processes of subcontracting are particularly well developed on the London Underground system, with cleaning contracts now outsourced by Transport for London to a small number of international cleaning companies. As Obi makes clear, these companies have proved especially adept at drawing on London's supply of workers from the global South to keep their labour costs low and, more recently, of playing off these workers against new workers from ECE as a means of reducing their wages bill even further:

> Now they [the contractor are] introduc[ing] people from Romania, Bulgaria[2]... What they do is when they bring them in, they remove some of these Africans. They tell them these people are Europeans and they have better right to work than you ... we are getting what we are getting because some of us don't have the papers. So you can subdue us, you can do anything, make us lick the floor. We will do it because if you don't we are sacked, and when they say you are sacked, it gives you fear. How do you survive? You can't go elsewhere to work because if you go elsewhere they'll tell you 'where is your [papers]', you know? ... If you speak out against anything, then they'll threaten you ... 'We know you don't have the papers so we can sack you any moment' ... [And] ... these people when they come in, they don't care how much you pay them. Like the lady from Romania who was later made a supervisor ... when I was still getting six pounds, she was getting three or four pounds something. She didn't mind, she was so happy, she said, 'Look this money in Romania can buy, can buy a lot of things.'

In light of such competition, the reward for workers is increasingly poor. As a cleaner on the underground, Kwasi – who in Ghana had worked as an architect – earns just £220 a week. As he explains, such work is not only poorly paid, it is also extremely demanding; with workers constantly stooping and carrying to clear the trains and platforms of rubbish, all the while without daylight or fresh air:

[Picking – cleaning – trains is] very hard. Because we've got a lot of rubbish and because – you know carbon dioxide [*sic*]? Sometimes, if you use like cotton, white cotton… you see there is a black carbon deposit because of the electricity down here … put your hand on the wall, or use some glove to clean it, before you know it, it's black. It's no good for our health.

In light of such hardships, it is important to consider how people got by in London – in both financial and emotional senses – carving out not only a living but a life for themselves in Britain. Like the Polish respondents, Ghanaians too tended to draw upon networks of co-nationals to find work and secure accommodation – often sharing housing with other Ghanaians. Yet, partly because – unable to leave – many had been in London far longer than they had intended (longer certainly than the Polish respondents), and partly perhaps because their experiences of racism led many to turn inwards towards the Ghanaian community rather than seek friendships beyond that community, these networks tended to be more extensive and somewhat 'deeper' than those described by the Polish respondents. They also served a rather different function (Herbert et al. 2008; c.f. Eade et al. 2007).

Most obviously, as well as a source of material support, such networks provided a way for people to maintain a connection with the wider Ghanaian diaspora in London, and with Ghana itself. Few of those we talked with were members of Hometown Associations – a transnational space that seems, in London at least, to be dominated by middle-class elites (Mohan 2006). Rather, people used funerals and memorial services (important occasions for Ghanaians) and especially the Church as a way to keep in contact with family and friends in London and Ghana, to speak in their native tongue, and to catch up on news from home.

Such networks thus provided people with a means of sustaining a powerful and enduring sense of Ghanaian identity when far from home. More important even than this, perhaps, is the role that the Church played in fostering a sense of dignity and self-respect among these workers. For those doing the 'dirty work' of neoliberalism (Herod and Aguiar 2006), lack of respect is a key issue – one brought home to them every time they collect their wages, and every time the people whose offices and carriages they clean walk past them without acknowledgement as though they are invisible (see Wills 2006). For many of the Ghanaian respondents, this lack of respect was exacerbated by a sense of racial prejudice, by the knowledge that the qualifications and experience they bought with them from Ghana were of little value in Britain, and by the persistent and pervasive sense of themselves as – often unwelcome – outsiders. Yet, at Church, as Kobie explains, not only are neoliberalism's invisible workers made visible, they are made welcome – not as low-paid workers, not as migrants, but as members of a single community brought together through faith and self-respect: 'In my church, when you get there, you see that you are really in a community, you are embraced. Be you a Ghanaian, an American or whatever …they'll see you as a church member … you feel at home.'

Conclusions

Piecing together these narratives it is possible to draw at least two, radically opposing, conclusions regarding the relationships between neoliberalism and migration. On the one hand, it is possible to tell a story of unremitting woe. Pushed out of their countries by the hardships that have followed in the wake of neoliberal restructuring, people from Poland and Ghana have gone to London only to be confronted by yet more hardship, as they battle to secure a life and a living in an economy that has itself been radically altered by three decades of neoliberal 'reform'. On the other hand, one could suggest that the very restructuring that has led to such hardship has, in the case of Poland at least, also enabled thousands of Poles to escape a struggling economy in search of new opportunities in a 'single Europe'; whilst the restructuring of the London economy has created the demand for low-wage work that gives people from both Poland and Ghana the chance – however slim – of carving a better life for themselves and their families by earning the kind of money unimaginable at home.

Neither conclusion would be satisfactory. Rather than searching for the either/or, we need to understand the contradictions inherent within neoliberalism (Harvey 2005) and the complexities of the relationships between these contradictory processes and the equally complex practices of migration. Once these complexities are recognized, it should come as no surprise that the lived experiences of those whose movements most obviously embody 'travelling neoliberalism' are equally complex.

For example, it is clear that with EU accession competition in London's low-wage economy has increased. As a result, tensions are now emerging between different migrant groups, as well as between migrants and British nationals, in competition for the same low-wage jobs. Competition is especially evident between East Central Europeans and an earlier group of migrants from the global South, and sub-Saharan Africa in particular (Herbert et al. 2008). Such tensions arise not only in the labour market, as – for a variety of reasons – employers are more and more likely to favour workers from ECE over those from the global South, but on the shop floor: as supervisors, of whatever country, tend to favour their co-nationals in the allocation of tasks, recommendations for promotion and so on (Datta et al. 2007). These tensions, often presented by workers themselves within a racial frame, are evident here in the remarks of both Polish and Ghanaian workers about their counterparts.

There is also little doubt, in the short term at least, who the losers in this competition will be. As the British government tightens up on irregular migration and further restricts the flow of 'low-skilled' workers from beyond the European Union, it will become more and more difficult for people from countries like Ghana to access the London labour market, whilst those already in London will face greater insecurities and hardship. The opportunities open to different migrant workers are, in other words, powerfully racialized, as people have to negotiate an obviously racialized immigration system. Over the medium to long term too, even if they are able to stay in Britain, the evidence is that non-white migrant groups fare less well than their white counterparts in the London labour market: as they continue to confront problems of racial discrimination (Wheatley-Price 2001).

And yet many of the workers we spoke with – Poles and Ghanaians alike – also spoke at length about how much they valued the opportunity to live and work alongside people from all over the globe and their sense of ease among other Londoners (Herbert et al.

2008). Similarly, whilst British immigration policy currently works to compound the racial disadvantage already faced by migrants from countries like Ghana, some state labour market policies have been crucial in securing important gains for such workers. Most obviously, with the exception of the hotel and hospitality sector, our surveys of London's low-wage economy suggest that employers tend to abide by the national Minimum Wage, even if they rarely pay the higher London Living Wage (May et al. 2007). Whilst both sender and recipient states clearly play a crucial role in shaping migration flows, and in shaping the lives of those who migrate, then, the state too needs to be understood as a complex, and often contradictory, institution. State policy is also open to change. Through the spring and summer of 2007, for example, the British government found itself under increasing pressure to launch a regularization programme and grant amnesty to the hundreds of thousands of irregular migrants who play such a key role in Britain's and, especially, London's economy (www.strangersintocitizens.org.uk).

The campaign for regularization has been led by a broad-based affiliation of trade unions, pressure groups and – especially – faith-based organizations. Just as the Church plays a crucial role in the day-to-day lives of many of London's migrant workers, providing people not only with a space in which to sustain a sense of identity and belonging when overseas, but a rare space of respect in lives characterized by disrepect, it is faith groups rather than more traditional political organizations that may hold the best hope for improving the lives of many migrant workers, whether battling for a living wage, or regularization (Wills 2004). Such campaigns are vital, not only because they demonstrate that resistance to neoliberalism is possible, but to secure a better future for those who most obviously carry the burden of 'travelling neoliberalism'.

Notes

The research on which this chapter draws was funded by the Economic and Social Research Council (Award RES00230694: *Global Cities at Work*), the Greater London Authority, Oxfam, Queen Mary, University of London and Unison. It was conducted in collaboration with London Citizens. Photos were taken by Chris Clunn (www.chrisclunn.com) and were commissioned by the ESRC Identities and Social Action Programme (www.identities.org. uk). Copyright is held by Chris Clunn. The authors would like to thank all those, and especially the workers, who took the time to talk to us during the research and without whom there would have been no project.

1. Interviews with the Polish respondents were conducted in Polish, and later translated in to English. To maintain clarity of meaning, the material presented here has been corrected for grammatical errors introduced in the translation process. Interviews with Ghanaian respondents were conducted in English. The material from these interviews has been presented verbatim. To preserve anonymity, the names of all workers have been changed.

2. In fact, Bulgarians and Romanians may only work in Britain if granted a (temporary) work permit under the UK's Sector Based Scheme – a programme enabling employers in (low-skill) industries facing a shortage of labour to apply for a temporary work permit on behalf of applicants from Bulgaria and Romania. Since the scheme does not include cleaners (unless working in staff canteens or restaurants) it is unlikely the people Obi is referring to are Bulgarian or Romanian. More likely is that they are from one of the accession states, though his comments make clear a more general tendency found in comments by both workers and employers whom we interviewed to draw crude distinctions between 'Africans' and 'Eastern Europeans'.

References

Anarfi, J., and S. Kwankye (2003) *Migration from and to Ghana: A Backround Paper*, Development Research Centre on Migration, Globalisation and Poverty, University of Sussex.

Aranda, E.M. (2003) 'Global care work and gendered constraints: The case of Puerto Rican transmigrants', *Gender and Society* 17(4): 609–26.

Armstrong, R. (1993) *Ghana Country Assistance Review: A Study in Development Effectiveness*, Washington DC: World Bank.

ASHE (Annual Survey of Hours and Earnings) (2005) 'Table 4.1a: Weekly Pay – Gross – for all employee jobs in United Kingdom', www.statistics.gov/uk/downloads/theme_labour/ASHE.2005/2005_industry.pdf; accessed 25 March 2008.

Bayart J. (1993) *The State in Africa: the Politics of the Belly*, Harlow: Longman.

Beckman, B. (1992) 'Empowerment or repression? The World Bank and the politics of African adjustment', in P. Gibbon (ed.), *Authoritarianism, Democracy and Adjustment: The Politics of Economic Reform in Africa*, Uppsala: Nordiska Afrikainstitutet, pp. 83–105.

Bockman, J., and G. Eyal (2002) 'Eastern Europe as a laboratory for economic knowledge: The transnational roots of neoliberalism', *American Journal of Sociology* 108(2): 310–52.

Castles, S., and M.J. Miller (2003) *The Age of Migration*, London: Palgrave Macmillan.

Chacón, J.A. (2007) 'Migrant workers: Casualties of neoliberalism', *International Socialist Review* 54, July–August, www.isreview.org/issues/54/casualties.shtml.

Clifford, J. (1989) 'Notes on travel and theory', *Inscriptions* 5, http://humwww.ucsc.edu/CultStudies/PUBS/Inscriptions/vol_5/clifford.html.

Coombe, R., and P. Stoller (1994) 'X marks the spot: The ambiguities of African trading in the commerce of the black public sphere', *Public Culture* 15: 249–74.

Craig, D., and D. Porter (2003) 'Poverty reduction strategy papers: A new convergence', *World Development* 31(1): 53–70.

Currie, S. (2006) '"Free" movers? The post-accession experience of Accession 8 migrant workers in the United Kingdom', *European Law Review* 31(2): 207–29.

Datta, K., C. McIlwaine, Y. Evans, J. Herbert, J. May and J. Wills (2006) *Work, Care and Life amongst Low Paid Migrants in London: Towards a Migrant Ethic of Care*, Global Cities at Work Working Paper Number 5, Department of Geography, Queen Mary, University of London.

Datta, K., C. McIlwaine, J. Wills, Y. Evans, J. Herbert and J. May (2007) 'The new development finance or exploiting migrant labour? Remittance sending among low-paid migrant workers in London', *International Development Planning Review* 29(1): 43–67.

De Broeck, M., and V. Koen (2000) *The Soaring Eagle – Anatomy of the Polish Take-Off in the 1990s*, IMF Working Papers, Washington DC: International Monetary Fund.

Dustmann, C., M. Casanova, M. Fertig, I. Preston and C. Schmidt (2003) *The Impact of EU Enlargement on Migration Flows*. Home Office Online Report, London, www.homeoffice.gov.uk/rds/pdfs2/rdsolr2503.pdf.

Eade, J., S. Drinkwater and M. Garapich (2007) *Class and Ethnicity: Polish Migrant Workers in London*, Full Research Report – ESRC End of Award Report. RES-000–22–1294, Swindon: ESRC.

Evans, Y., J. Wills, K. Datta, J. Herbert, C. McIlwaine and J. May (2007) '"Sub-contracting by stealth" in London's hotels: Impacts and implementation for labour organising', *Just Labour: A Canadian Journal of Work and Society* 10: 85–98.

Favell, A., and R. Hansen (2002) 'Markets against politics: Migration, EU enlargement and the idea of Europe', *Journal of Ethnic and Migration Studies* 28(4): 581–601.

Flynn, D. (2005) 'New borders, new management: The dilemmas of modern immigration policies', *Ethnic and Racial Studies* 28(3): 463–90.

Garapich, M. (2007) 'The builder, the fighter, and the conman: Individualism and identity among transnational Polish migrants', paper presented to the Department of Geography, Queen Mary, University of London, October.

GLA (2002) *London Divided: Income, Inequality and Poverty in the Capital*, London: Greater London Authority.

Harvey, D. (2005) *A Brief History of Neoliberalism*, Oxford: Oxford University Press.

Herbert, J., K. Datta, Y. Evans, J. May, C. McIlwaine and J. Wills (2008) 'Multicultural living? Experiences of everyday racism amongst Ghanaian migrants in London', *European Urban and Regional Studies* 15(2): 103–17.

Herod, A., and L.L.M. Aguiar (2006) 'Introduction: Cleaners and the dirty work of neoliberalism', *Antipode* 38(3): 425–34.

Home Office (2006) *A Points Based System: Making Migration Work for Britain*, London: Home Office.

Home Office and Foreign and Commonwealth Office (2007) *Managing Global Migration: A Strategy to Build Stronger International Alliances to Manage Migration*, London: Home Office and Foreign and Commonwealth Office.

Home Office, Department of Works and Pensions, HM Revenue and Customs and Department of Communities and Local Government (2006) *Accession Monitoring Report, May 2004 to March 2006*, London: HMSO.

Iglicka, K. (2005) *EU Membership Highlights Poland's Migration Challenges*, Country Profiles, Migration Information Source, Centre for International Relations, Warsaw.

Kicinger, A. (2005) *Between Polish Interests and the EU Influence: Polish Migration Policy Development 1989–2004*, Central European Forum for Migration Research Working Paper 9, Warsaw.

Koser, K. (2003) 'New African diasporas: An introduction', in K. Koser (ed.), *New African Diasporas*, London: Routledge, pp. 1–16.

Kowalik, T. (2001) 'Ugly face of the Polish success', in G. Blazyca and R. Rapacki (eds), *Ugly Face of the Polish Success*, Cheltenham: Edward Elgar, pp. 33–53.

Larner, W. (2000) 'Neoliberalism: Policy, ideology, governmentality', *Studies in Political Economy* 63: 5–26.

Manuh, T. (2001) 'Ghanaian migrants in Toronto, Canada: Care of kin and gender relations', *Research Review* 17(2): 17–26.

Massey, D. (2004) 'Geographies of responsibility', *Geografiska Annaler* 86B(1): 5–18.

Massey, D. (2007) *World City*, Cambridge: Polity Press.

Massey, D.S., A.B. Gross and K. Shibuya (1994) 'Migration, segregation, and the geographic concentration of poverty', *American Sociological Review* 59(3): 424–45.

May. J., J. Wills, K. Datta, Y. Evans, J. Herbert and C. McIlwaine (2007) 'Keeping London working: Global cities, the British state and London's new migrant division of labour', *Transactions of the Institute of British Geographers* 32(1): 157–62.

McIlwaine, C. (2005) *Coping Practices amongst Colombian Migrants in London*, Department of Geography, Queen Mary, University of London.

Misra, J., J. Woodring and S.N. Merz (2004) 'The globalization of care work: Immigration, economic restructuring and the world-system', unpublished paper, Department of Sociology and Centre for Public Policy and Administration, University of Massachusetts–Amherst.

Mitchell, K. (2004) *Crossing the Neoliberal Line: Pacific Rim Migration and the Metropolis*, Philadelphia: Temple University Press.

Mohan, G. (2006) 'Embedded cosmopolitanism and the politics of obligation: the Ghanaian diaspora and development', *Environment and Planning A* 38: 867–83.

Mohan, G. (2007) 'Making neo-liberal states of development: The Ghanaian diaspora and the politics of development', unpublished manuscript.

Mohan, G., E. Brown, B. Milward and A. Zack-Williams (2000) *Structural Adjustment: Theory, Practice and Impacts*, London: Routledge.

Mokryzcki, J. (2006) President of the Federation of Poles in Great Britain, personal interview.

Morris, L. (2002) *Managing Migration: Civic Stratification and Migrants' Rights*, London: Routledge.

OECD (Organisation for Economic Co-operation and Development) (2003) *Trends in International Migration*, Paris: OECD.

Parreñas, R. (2005) 'Long distance intimacy: Class, gender and intergenerational relations between mothers and children in Filipino transnational families', *Global Networks* 5(4): 317–36.

Peck, J. (2006) 'Liberating the city: between New York and New Orleans', *Urban Geography* 27(8): 681–713.

Peil, M. (1995) 'Ghanaians abroad', *African Affairs* 94(376): 345–67.

Rees, P., and P. Boden (2006) *Estimating London's New Migrant Population*, London: Greater London Authority.

RSA (2005) *Migration: A Welcome Opportunity? A New Way Forward by the RSA Migration Commission*, London: RSA.

Sassen, S. (1991) *The Global City: New York, London, Tokyo*, Princeton: Princeton University Press.

Sassen, S. (1998) 'The de facto transnationalizing of immigration policy', in C. Joppke (ed.), *Challenge to the Nation State*, Oxford: Oxford University Press, pp. 49–86.

Shields, S. (2006a) *Transnational Capital, Class Configuration and the Social Implications of Poland's On-going Transition to a Market Economy*, Centre for International Politics, University of Manchester.

Shields, S. (2006b) *Historicizing Transition: The Polish Political Economy in a Period of Global Structural Change*, University of Manchester Centre for International Politics Working Paper Series, No. 17, University of Manchester.

Simon, D. (2001) 'Neo-liberalism, structural adjustment and poverty reduction strategies', in V. Desai and R. Potter (eds), *The Companion to Development Studies*, London: Arnold, pp. 86–92.

Smith, A. (2007) 'Articulating neo-liberalism: Diverse economies and urban restructuring in post-socialism', in E. Sheppard, H. Leitner and J. Peck (eds), *Contesting Neoliberalism: The Urban Frontier*, London: Guilford, pp. 204–22.

Smith, M., and M. Carroll (2003) 'Branch report for hotel and restaurants in the UK', unpublished report for European Foundation for the Improvement of Living and Working Conditions, Dublin.

Smith, S.J. (1989) *The Politics of 'Race' and Residence*, Cambridge: Polity Press.

Spence, L. (2005) *Country of Birth and Labour Market Outcomes in London: An Analysis of Labour Force Survey and Census Data*, London: Greater London Authority.

Stenning, A. (2003) 'Shaping the economic landscapes of post-socialism? Labour, workplace and community in Nowa Huta, Poland', *Antipode* 35(4): 761–80.

Stenning, A. (2005) 'Post-socialism and the changing geographies of the everyday in Poland', *Transactions of the Institute of British Geographers* 30(1): 113–27.

Strangers into Citizens (2007) *Call for a Pathway to Legal Status for Long Term Migrants*, www.strangersintocitizens.org.uk; accessed 26 July 2007.

Wheatley-Price, S. (2001) 'The unemployment experience of male immigrants in the English labour market', *Applied Economics* 33(2): 201–15.

Wills, J. (2004) 'Campaigning for low paid workers: The East London Communities Organisation (TELCO) Living Wage Campaign', in W. Brown, G. Healy, E. Heery and P. Taylor (eds), *The Future of Worker Representation*, Oxford: Oxford University Press, pp. 262–82.

Wills, J. (2005) 'The geography of union organising in low-paid service industries in the UK: Lessons from the T&G's campaign to unionise the Dorchester Hotel, London', *Antipode* 37(1): 139–59.

Wills, J. (2006) 'Low wage urban labour markets and the fight for respect', Department of Geography, Queen Mary, University of London, unpublished paper available from the author.

Woodbridge, J. (2005) *Sizing the Unauthorised (Illegal) Migrant Population in the United Kingdom in 2001*, London: Home Office.

World Bank (2003) *African Adjustment Study: The Case of Ghana*, Washington DC: World Bank.

World Bank (2004a) *World Development Indicators*, Washington DC: World Bank.

World Bank (2004b) *Global Development Finance*, Washington DC: World Bank.

4

Neoliberalization and its discontents: the experience of working poverty in Manchester

Vincent Pattison

I grew up hearing over and over, to the point of tedium, that 'hard work' was the secret of success: 'Work hard and you'll get ahead' or 'it's hard work that got us where we are'. No one ever said that you could work hard – harder even than you ever thought possible – and still find yourself sinking ever deeper into poverty and debt.
(Ehrenreich 2002: 220)

Debbie[1] is a 25-year-old cleaner at a Manchester hospital. Her work is dirty, hard and important for the running of the hospital but this is not reflected in her pay. She earns £5.88 per hour, which is above the current national minimum wage rate of £5.73 per hour,[2] but is not enough for her to meet all her basic needs. After rent, bills and transport costs, Debbie has just enough to buy food for the week. She buys economy brands and relies on food that will fill her up rather than food that is healthy and nutritious. Her limited income means that she rarely socializes. Recently she had to give up her one and only social outlet – playing football – because she could not afford the travel and match fees. Debbie takes pride in her work and believes she deserves to be paid more. With more money she could afford better food, a social life, some new clothes or have a savings account. She could even think about moving out of her mum's home and getting her own place. However, these seemingly basic requirements in twenty-first-century Britain are currently out of her reach. Debbie is one of over 5 million low-paid workers (defined as earnings below £6.50 per hour) and 2.2 million 'working poor' in the UK (Cooke and Lawton 2008; for a parallel account of the working poor in Poland and Slovakia, see Smith et al. this volume). For Debbie and others like her, work is not working.

Debbie was one of over a hundred participants involved in research into living wages and working poverty in Manchester, some of the summary findings of which are presented in this chapter. The research proceeded in two distinct, yet related, phases. First, I aimed to calculate a living wage for different working households in Manchester. Second, I aimed to use these figures to assess the effects of the disparity between what workers needed to earn to meet their basic needs locally (the living wage) and their actual wages at or around the national minimum wage. The aim was to provide a critique of processes of neoliberalization in Manchester using the social justice concept of the living wage and 'the micro-contexts of everyday routines' (Barnett 2005: 9) of Manchester's working poor. The research aimed to add to an underdeveloped literature on *actually experienced* neoliberalism through an investigation of how these processes impacted the everyday productive and reproductive spheres of low-wage workers.

Much of the work on neoliberalism has been concerned with identifying, theorizing and critiquing the various processes of neo-liberalism and how these processes manifest themselves across space and time (see, for example, Peck and Tickell 2002; Brenner and Theodore 2002). However, the literature on how these processes are experienced on the ground by low-income workers and communities is less well developed (but see Radcliffe 2004; Smith and Rochovská 2007; Smith et al. in this volume; Ward et al. 2007). This research is important because, as Benhabib (1986: 102) has argued, 'the task of criticism is to show how trans-subjectivity can become inter-subjectivity'; that is, how the global trends of textbook neoliberalism manifest themselves in the lives of individuals within a specific spatial context. As such, to critique anything we need to evaluate how experiences have changed for various groups of people within specific places under neoliberalism and with what consequences. The chapter focuses on how changes in the labour market driven by neoliberalism affect the meaning and experience of working poverty in Manchester and what this means for issues of social justice. It begins with a brief overview of labour market change and the rise of the living wage concept as a means of contesting these labour market changes and their effects on workers. The two stages of the research are then introduced and the findings discussed before concluding with a brief assessment of the future of social justice – in the form of the living wage – in the UK.

Neoliberalism and urban labour markets: why work no longer works

Since the 1970s, neoliberalism has diffused 'from a gleam in Friedrich Hayek's eye to become everyday discourse and practice' (Leitner et al. 2007: 1) to varying degrees around the world. Originally emerging as an alternative to the then dominant political economic project of Fordist Keynesianism, neoliberalism has become popular academic shorthand to describe the economic supply-side reforms that have been used to varying degrees to revitalize the political economies of many industrialized nations in the so-called 'post-Fordist' period (Amin 1994; Jessop 2003). After the perceived successes of early neoliberal experiments in Chile and other Latin American countries (Harvey 2005; North in this volume; Olson in this volume), neo-liberalism became *the* 'strategic political response to the sustained global recession of the preceding decade' (Brenner and Theodore 2002: 2–3) in the late 1970s and early 1980s, particularly under Reagan and Thatcher.

Brenner et al. (2005: 1) have argued that the 'neoliberal ideology rests on the belief that open, competitive and unregulated markets, liberated from state interference and the actions of social collectivities represent the optimal mechanism for economic development.' This ideology was premised on the notion that the failures of Fordism in the 1970s 'occurred *in* the market, not *because* of the market' (Peck 1996: 2, emphasis in original). As such, those introducing neoliberal reforms favoured the creative destruction (see Brenner et al. 2005) or

TABLE 4.1 Worker security in Fordist and neoliberal labour markets

Security	Fordism	Neoliberalism
Labour market	Adequate employment opportunities, through state-guaranteed full employment.	Full employability ensures a large reserve army of workers, thus keeping wage inflationary pressures low. Increasing insecurity in labour markets.
Employment	Protection against arbitrary dismissal, regulations on hiring and firing, imposition of costs on employers, etc.	Vastly reduced protection against arbitrary dismissal, regulations on hiring and firing, imposition of real employment costs shared between employers and state (through in-work subsidies).
Job	A niche designated as an occupation or 'career', plus tolerance of demarcation practices, barriers to skill dilution, craft boundaries, job qualifications, restrictive practices, craft unions, etc.	Erosion of jobs-for-life mentality brought about by assault on notions of collectivity. Processes of flexibilization have resulted in a decline of internal labour markets.
Work	Protection against accidents and illness at work through health-and-safety regulations and limits on working time, unsociable hours.	Limited protection against accidents and illness at work through health-and-safety regulations. Reduction in provisions such as sick pay. Working time regulation in some industries but not others.
Skills reproduction	Widespread opportunities to gain and retain skills, through apprenticeships, employment training, etc.	Limited opportunities to gain and retain skills, through apprenticeships, employment training, etc.
Income	Protection of income through minimum wage machinery, wage indexation, comprehensive social security and progressive taxation.	Limited protection of income through minimum wage legislation. In-work benefits available to top up income. Regressive tax/benefits system leading to poverty trap.
Representation	Protection of collective voices in the labour market, through independent trade unions and employer associations incorporated economically and politically into the state, with the right to strike, etc.	Reduced protection of collective voices in the labour market, through independent trade unions and employers associations. Right to strike in many countries curtailed through legislation.

Source: Adapted from Standing 1997: 8–9.

rolling back (see Peck and Tickell 2002) of extant Fordist Keynesian regulatory institutions through a variety of neoliberal experiments which aimed to:

> minimise the size of government, make space for competitive forces, enlarge the scope and reach of the private sector, (re)distribute wealth on the basis of market principles [and] break down labour unions and other 'anti-market' or 'anti-competitive' institutions. (Tickell and Peck 2003: 13)

One area that has been profoundly affected by these processes is the labour market, which has been fundamentally re-regulated and flexibilized with the aim of re-establishing market rule through the partial re-commodification of labour (Esping-Anderson 1985). In the last twenty-five years, workers at the lower end of the labour market have experienced the effects of these processes first-hand through a reduction of labour market securities vis-à-vis those which existed under Fordism (see Table 4.1).

In the UK, since the rise of British neoliberalism under Thatcher in the late 1970s, capital-oriented labour market flexibilization and re-regulation strategies have led to a race to the bottom in worker security and the rise of non-standard contracts at the lower end of the labour market which are 'associated with rock-bottom wages, coercive management, intensified labour processes, unsocial hours and high rates of job turnover' (Felstead and Jewson 1999: 3). The increasing prominence of this type of employment has been fuelled by workplace flexibilization strategies – such as outsourcing in both the public and the private sectors – and the decline of collectivist institutions – such as trade unions – through the use of legislation. Taken together these changes constitute a profound shift for workers in terms of their relationship to their employer, to colleagues and to the labour market in both the public and private sectors (see Perrons 2000; Rubery et al. 2005; Peck and Tickell 2007). The main legacies of labour market restructuring under the Thatcher administrations were rising poverty, social exclusion and social inequalities (Powell 2000). When New Labour came to power in 1997 they inherited a labour market which was profoundly different from the one Labour last presided over in 1979.

The Third Way politics of New Labour represented both important continuities and discontinuities with Thatcherism in terms of industrial policy as it attempted to 'transcend both old-style social democracy and neoliberalism' (Giddens 1998: 26). Blair embraced many of the supply-side policies of Thatcherism, such as a commitment to outsourcing, labour market flexibilization and an intolerance of trade unions. However, unlike Thatcher, Blair was keen to balance market-oriented flexibility with a commitment to minimum standards of 'fairness at work'. As such, New Labour implemented a set of policies that aimed to *make work pay* through a combination of a statutory minimum wage floor and Working Tax Credits[3] as a means of incentivizing work (Davies and Freedland 2007). In 1998, the trade and industry secretary (1997–98) Margaret Beckett 'promised that the new national minimum would "end the scandal of poverty pay" and would begin to close the growing gap between rich and poor' (quoted in Abrams 2002: 169).

However, the rhetoric of New Labour and the reality for low-paid workers could not be more different. When the national minimum wage was implemented in 1999 the level for adult workers over 21 was set at £3.60 per hour. Rather than ending poverty pay, it appeared as though New Labour was effectively institutionalizing it, as these levels were set with the remit that they should not 'create onerous burdens on business' (Howell 2004: 5). This was so that they did not 'violate the core components of neoliberal economic policy, those of maintaining low inflation and fiscal austerity' (Craig and Cotterell 2007: 508). Minimum wage levels were also set with no reference to what people needed to earn to meet their basic costs of living (Veit-Wilson 2004). As such, the new legislation did not provide *living* wages for working households and is one reason why the numbers in working poverty continue to rise (Grover 2005; Palmer et al. 2007).

Of course, this situation is not unique to the UK. The perceived failure of federal and state minimum-wage legislation to provide an adequate wage floor for workers has been a source of community discontent in the USA. This led to the emergence of local grassroots movements for living wages in the early 1990s which demanded a fair day's pay for a fair day's work (Merrifield 2002). The living wage is about paying workers enough so that they can meet their basic needs and so avoid poverty and social exclusion. In the words of one Unison (2002) report, it is about 'justice not charity'. The living wage aims to really *make work pay* at the lower end of the labour market by putting upward pressure, through progressive local activism, on local working pay and conditions.

As a movement, the living wage has re-empowered some low-wage workers in some US and UK urban areas and has re-energized the local labour movement by filling the void vacated by the demise of old leftist institutions, such as trade unions (see Wills 2006). The broad-based coalitions that have coalesced around the living wage issue are typically made up of a range of local organizations encompassing religious groups, trade unions, community organizations, academic institutions and workers' associations, which are all united by an interest in issues around low pay, poverty, social exclusion and social justice. The living wage provides a means for workers and communities to contest some of the processes of neoliberalism that have 'zapped' labour within place and resulted in a downward pressure on their working pay and conditions (Peck 2002).

The contemporary living wage movement began in the US city of Baltimore in 1994 (see Niedt et al. 1999; Harvey 2000; Walsh 2000) and has since spread to over 130 urban areas across the USA (Luce 2004; Weldon and Targ 2004; Levin-Waldman 2005). The living wage concept has also been internationalized to other countries sharing similar political economic trajectories to the USA, such as the UK. The first Living Wage campaign in the UK began in East London in 2001 as one of several campaigns by The East London Communities Organisation (TELCO) (see Wills 2001a, 2004, 2007; Grimshaw 2004). The campaign coalesced around research by academics at Queen Mary, University of London into low pay in London (see Wills 2001a). This research used commissioned work from the Family Budget Unit at the University of York, which calculated a living wage level for Londoners. The research showed that workers needed £6.30 per hour to meet their basic needs in the capital, which was £2.20 per hour more than the prevailing national minimum wage of £4.10 (October 2001) (see Wills 2001a).

What is interesting about the living wage in the UK is the concerted effort to rigorously calculate local living wage levels. There has been a growing research agenda which aims to calculate the amount households need to earn per hour to meet their basic needs. The preferred method for the costing of needs in the UK has been to use budget standards, a basket of services and goods which, if consumed, would give a household a predetermined standard of living. There are variants of this methodology but the favoured method has been the Low Cost but Acceptable (LCA) budget standard, which costs a basic and low-cost but inclusive lifestyle. The money needed to acquire this basket of services and goods is the minimum income needed by a household to meet its basic needs locally. This method has been used to calculate living wage levels in several UK cities, such as York (Parker 1998); London (Wills 2001a; GLAE 2005, 2006, 2007); Swansea (Parker 2002); Brighton (Ambrose 2003); Birmingham (Pierson 2005); and Cardiff (Littman and Murphy 2006) (see Table 4.2). As such, it was the method used to calculate a living wage for Manchester.

TABLE 4.2   Living wage levels calculated in various UK urban areas using the LCA budget standards methodology

Urban area	Year	Living wage (£/hour)	Adult national minimum wage (£/hour)
York	1998	5.58	3.60
London	2001	6.30	4.10
Swansea	2002	5.56	4.20
Brighton	2003	6.38	4.50
Birmingham	2005	6.50	5.05
London	2005	6.70	5.05
Wrexham	2006	6.00	5.35
Cardiff	2006	6.50	5.35
London	2006	7.05	5.35
London	2007	7.20	5.52
London	2008	7.45	5.73[*]

Note: [*] Updated from £5.52 on 1 October 2008.
Source: Derived from Parker 1998, 2002; Wills 2001a; GLAE 2005, 2006, 2007, 2008; Ambrose 2003; Brighton 2003; Pierson 2005; Littman 2006; Low Pay Commission 2007.

A living wage for Manchester

Manchester was chosen as the study site because it provides a good example of the paradox of the neoliberal city. Juxtaposed against extreme affluence – which has been attracted by the city council's 'entrepreneurial turn' – is the extreme poverty of 'old' Manchester. This poverty is untouched by the new affluence of the city but bears the brunt of the negative elements of the neoliberal processes. Here 'problems of localised deprivation, of endemic low pay in many parts of the economy [and] of political and social alienation' (Peck and Ward 2002: 3) are rife.

Currently, Manchester is ranked the fourth most deprived local authority in England, behind Liverpool, and Hackney and Tower Hamlets in London. More than half of the city's population live in wards which are among the top 10 per cent most deprived areas in England (Manchester Partnership 2007). The level of inequality between the winners and losers of Manchester's neoliberal political economy is such that George Osbourne, shadow chancellor of the exchequer, has described the city as 'perhaps the most starkly evident example of a new divide between rich and poor' in the UK (Ottewell 2007), whilst a recent report by the Centre for Cities (2007) has ranked Manchester as *the* most unequal city in the UK. Such inequalities are having severe consequences for social justice in the city. As such, Manchester is similar in terms of both historical and contemporary political economic context to many of the living wage cities in the USA.

The method chosen to calculate a living wage for Manchester was the Family Budget Unit's Low Cost but Acceptable budget standards (LCA). Due to the size of the local authority and the difficulty in creating an illustrative living wage for such a large area, it was decided that the research should be conducted at ward level. The wards of Ardwick and Baguley (see Figures 4.1 and 4.2) were chosen as they were both areas characterized by high numbers of low-income households, high levels of multiple deprivation and high proportions of social housing – a key indicator of social inequality.

It was decided that living-wage levels would be calculated for three main hypothetical household types: (i) a couple with two children;

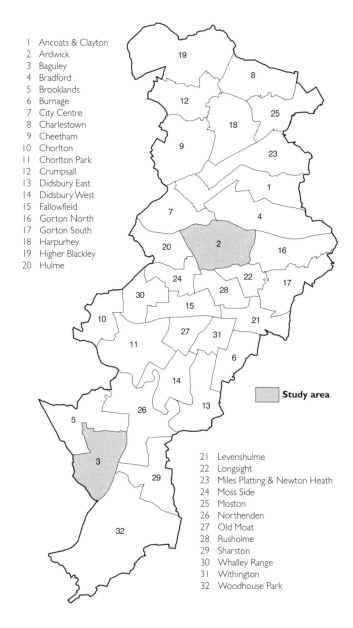

1 Ancoats & Clayton
2 Ardwick
3 Baguley
4 Bradford
5 Brooklands
6 Burnage
7 City Centre
8 Charlestown
9 Cheetham
10 Chorlton
11 Chorlton Park
12 Crumpsall
13 Didsbury East
14 Didsbury West
15 Fallowfield
16 Gorton North
17 Gorton South
18 Harpurhey
19 Higher Blackley
20 Hulme

Study area

21 Levenshulme
22 Longsight
23 Miles Platting & Newton Heath
24 Moss Side
25 Moston
26 Northenden
27 Old Moat
28 Rusholme
29 Sharston
30 Whalley Range
31 Withington
32 Woodhouse Park

FIGURE 4.1   Manchester and the study area wards:
Ardwick and Baguley

FIGURE 4.2   Manchester: a juxtaposed cityscape of poverty and affluence

(ii) a single parent with two children; and (iii) a single adult; living in each of the two Manchester wards in differing situations – for example, in social housing and private rented accommodation, with and without a car, claiming Working Tax Credit and not claiming, and working different hours. These were the predominant household types used in previous research and in Manchester.

One of the aims of the research was to update the LCA budgets for 2007 consumption patterns. The LCA budgets were constructed in 1997 and have not been updated since. As such, the research fully updated the constituent elements of the budget using behavioural and consumption data and low-income focus-group feedback to give them contemporary relevance (for a full account of this process, see Pattison 2008a). Another aim of the research was to attend to previous critiques of the LCA budget standard by attempting to vary housing tenure (social housing is the only housing type used in the original LCA budget) and by including savings and debt repayments as 'active' rather than merely listed items (see Pattison 2008a). The budgets were then finalized using the focus-group feedback and priced locally to produce the weekly cost of meeting the living standard locally, which could then be used to derive the living-wage levels.

In total sixty-four different living-wage levels were calculated for the different household types and lifestyle permutations (see Pattison 2008a). All but four of the wage levels came out well above the national minimum wage; those four fell below when Working Tax Credit was factored in because the majority of the income needed to meet the budget was derived from government subsidies. Whilst the living-wage figures differed markedly depending on the household's circumstances, the headline living-wage figure for Manchester was £6.50 per hour. This figure provides an hourly wage threshold below which households are in danger of experiencing poverty. However, the figure is problematic for several reasons, including that it does not allow all household types to meet their basic needs and it assumes a full uptake of available benefits and the availability of social housing (see Pattison 2008a). Despite this, for the purpose of this chapter, it is sufficient to note that the living wage for Manchester – that is, the hourly wage level needed for a household to meet all its basic needs locally – was higher than that currently earned by low-income households in the city. The second question investigated, therefore, was: 'what is the lived experience of working poverty given that the national minimum wage rate represented a *sub-living wage* level in Manchester?' The following section explores these experiences through a selection of quotations from interviews with contract workers at Wythenshawe Hospital.

The experience of working poverty in Manchester

> Both me and my wife have been on anti-depressant tablets but they don't solve the problem, do they? I mean, we are suffering because we are poor. It all comes down to income – the more income you have, your outlook in life expands. You have more choices, broader horizons but what do we have? (Alex, forties, full-time cleaner, £5.88 per hour)

Alex was a full-time cleaner at Wythenshawe Hospital in Baguley. He earned £5.88 per hour, which was less than the Manchester headline living-wage figure of £6.50. Alex admitted he was poor and he knew why. Quite simply his income was not high enough to meet his costs of living. As our conversation unfolded it became clear that he was not extravagant, he just wanted what all parents want: to be able to afford the basics for his children and a little bit more besides. In his words, to 'broaden their horizons'. However, his income, with his wife's, was not sufficient to achieve this. So how does Alex feel about working hard all day, doing an important job and then receiving less than £200 per week after tax? What do Alex and his family go without to make sure that the outgoings match their income? These two questions and the answers given by Alex and other workers like him provide the focus for this section, which provides a flavour of the experience of working poverty in Manchester (for a more detailed account, see Pattison 2007, 2008a, 2008b).

Working for a low income

There was general agreement among those interviewed that their current pay levels were too low to meet the basic costs of living in Manchester, with respondents variously describing their wage levels as constituting 'poverty pay' or 'survival incomes' which were barely enough to make ends meet:

> I get paid monthly but it doesn't last the whole month … there's just enough money in the bank to pay the bills with little left over for living … if things don't change I have a dismal outlook really as I am barely existing on the money I am being paid. (Richard, forties, full-time porter, £5.88 per hour)

This situation was made worse by the perception that bills were rising disproportionately relative to income: 'Prices keep going up and I think well where is it going to end? My wages don't go up at the same rate so each year it gets harder' (Alan, thirties, full-time porter, £5.88 per hour). This was particularly pertinent in 2008, given above-inflation rises in council tax and the rising cost of food and oil.

In addition, 80 per cent of respondents were unhappy with their working conditions and, in particular, the lack of sick pay. For these workers their only sick pay entitlement was Statutory Sick Pay, which was £72.55 per week and was payable from the fourth consecutive day off – for the first three days workers received nothing. This had serious financial impacts on the workers when they were ill, for instance: 'In the past I've had flu but I'll come into work because I can't afford to have the time off ... you have to live off the statutory minimum but how are you supposed to live off that? It won't even pay the rent let alone all of the other bills' (Alex, forties, full-time cleaner, £5.88 per hour).

This placed workers in a financial dilemma. Staying off sick meant losing out on valuable pay and obliterating finely balanced weekly budgets, while coming into work meant getting paid but making themselves feel worse. Aronsson et al. (2000) have termed this 'sickness presenteeism' whereby people turn up to work even though they are ill because they cannot afford to lose valuable income. They note that this is most prevalent at the lower end of the labour market, as it is here that basic protection – such as sick pay – has all but disappeared in an attempt to cut labour costs.

The combined effect of low pay and poor working conditions affected workers psychologically, with several believing that their pay and working conditions reflected their value in society. Over half variously referred to feeling 'small' because of their low wages and the subsequent effects it had on their lifestyle. This led to feelings that they were not respected. The role of respect in the literature as an effect of low income is often downplayed in favour of the effects on standards of living or spending power (see Sennett 2003). Indeed, respect is not a factor in either the absolute or the relative definitions of poverty. Workers cannot eat respect, shelter under respect or spend respect, yet it remained a key issue in the interviews. The combined effect of this lack of respect was to make workers feel undervalued in the workplace in addition to being undervalued in the labour market and society more widely.

These experiences led 40 per cent of the workers interviewed to believe that work did not pay, contrary to the aims of New Labour. Debbie summarizes the feelings of the respondents with her views:

> There is not a benefit to working because you just have to pay more for everything, which takes up any extra money you get from working. When you are working you have to pay your rent, your council tax, your gas, electric, but on the dole you get your rent and council tax paid for ... You know they help the poor but not people that work.

They don't think that you are poor if you are working. I pay for people to be on the dole but I can't afford to buy anything for myself! I am paying for somebody else to have a house when I haven't even got one of my own and I'm feeding somebody else when I scrape by. I feel as though I am getting punished for working. They should be helping you. I mean someone somewhere should be rewarding you for working. (Debbie, twenties, full-time cleaner, £5.88 per hour)

Living on a low income

A lack of income affected those interviewed in a multitude of ways, which often overlapped to exacerbate the experience of poverty. The three main issues emerging from the research were the effects of low pay on food consumption, the ability to acquire decent housing, and being unable to participate in activities and consume at levels which many in Britain take for granted. Here I explore some of the issues relating to food poverty and housing affordability and accessibility (for more details, see Pattison 2007, 2008b).

In the discussion about workers' perceptions of their pay levels, respondents frequently cited how income affected their lives. Attempting to afford even the basic necessities was variously described as 'a constant battle', 'soul destroying' and 'an uphill struggle'. The effects of income on food and housing were always at the forefront of discussions. Low pay affected the ability of households involved in the research to afford and/or access a healthy balanced diet. Shipler (2004) has referred to food as a flexible expenditure item in that it is purchased with the money left over after bills and rent had been budgeted for. For the vast majority of respondents this meant they had less money than they needed for food: 'I always have to cut back on food because of rent and bills … By the time I have paid my bills I am left with £20 a week for food' (Peter, forties, full-time cleaner, £5.88 per hour). This resulted in a minority (18 per cent) of those interviewed having to miss meals because they could not afford sufficient amounts of food to last the week: 'Sometimes I do miss meals because of money … you'll look in the fridge and you think I should have gone shopping but you haven't got the money to go until pay day' (Andy, forties, full-time porter, £5.88 per hour).

However, a much more common problem identified in the interviews was the affordability of fresh and healthy food, which was a problem reported by 78 per cent of respondents. They complained that they could not afford fresh fruit and vegetables, fresh meat and/ or fresh ingredients to make home-cooked meals. They acknowledged the need to eat healthily but were prevented from doing so because of a lack of money. Instead, many relied on a diet of 'cheap calories' (Hitchman et al. 2002) from microwaveable meals, tinned foods and snacks which were high in fat, salt and calories and low in key nutrients: 'The easy option is junk food, you know, microwaveable meals, they are cheap and convenient. If you don't have the money, the only thing you have got is the cheaper option' (Debbie, twenties, full-time cleaner, £5.88 per hour). Often respondents bought economy brands to access the cheapest possible calories. This diet, while keeping hunger at bay, had severe medium- to long-term consequences for the health of the individual, including raising the risk of obesity, diabetes, heart disease and several cancers (see Kempson 1996). Although many of the respondents were aware of the effects of their diet, they conceded that short-term income restraints and the need to avoid hunger outweighed longer term health concerns.

In addition, 28 per cent of respondents noted that they struggled to physically access cheap nutritious food because they could not afford to run a car and as such found themselves living in 'food deserts' (Wrigley 2002; Wrigley et al. 2003). The 'food desert' metaphor represents those areas of a community where 'cheap nutritious food is virtually unobtainable' (Whitehead 1998: 189) within a 500 metre radius of a household. Food deserts have emerged as the retail geography of the UK has changed in the last thirty years with the rise of large out-of-town superstores and the subsequent decline of supermarkets in the inner city (Wrigley 2002; Wrigley et al. 2003). As such, residents without cars found it increasingly difficult to access the superstores and were forced to shop at local stores, which were often more expensive and had limited choice: 'We do have shops that are closer, like Nisa, which is about five minutes away, but it's limited choice and it costs more. You know you are paying double for everything in there, so my mum gets less food for her money' (Miriam, twenties, full-time cleaner, £5.88 per hour). This meant that carless households struggled to access a healthy balanced diet locally.

Issues of affordability and accessibility were also evident in the local housing market. In terms of affordability, problems of supply and demand in the UK housing market more generally have caused house prices to rise disproportionately to income. This has priced many low-income households out of either owning or privately renting housing. In Manchester, average property prices increased by 16.5 per cent to £159,798 in 2007. Although these prices are below the national average, the predominance of low wages in the city has led Manchester City Council (2007: 3) to acknowledge that there is 'a growing affordability problem in the city'. For example, a first-time home in Ardwick in 2002 was 2.3 times median local income, whilst in Baguley it was 3.4 times. By 2006 this had increased to 4.8 times median local income in both areas (Manchester City Council 2007). As such, many respondents said they 'couldn't even dream of owning' their own home on the wages they were receiving as there was no chance of getting a mortgage for £100,000 or more. A lack of housing affordability has had severe consequences for levels of social equality in the city as increasing numbers of the city's population become excluded from home ownership. Over 80 per cent of respondents claimed that they did not believe they could afford to buy a house at current prices on their household income. This can have a profound impact on social mobility as the gulf widens between those with and without assets. For those who could not afford to buy, the private rental sector was seen as just as unaffordable, with respondents being forced to spend a significant proportion of their income, at the expense of other items, because of the cost of private housing and the lack of availability of social housing in the city.

One element of Thatcher's streamlining of the state during the 1980s was the privatization of public housing through the 'right-to-buy' legislation. However, a combination of selling off existing stock with a lack of construction of new units has meant that local demand for social housing has vastly outstripped supply. Ottewell (2006) has noted that in Manchester four social houses are sold off under the right-to-buy policy for every one added to the housing stock. This has manifested itself in long waiting lists, with over 30,000 people waiting for social housing – an increase of almost 100 per cent over the past five years: 'I've been on the waiting list over four years but

I think they've forgot about me!' (Debbie, twenties, full-time cleaner, £5.88 per hour). Similar experiences by other respondents fostered resentment towards the system and exacerbated already existing feelings that work does not pay: 'The irony is if I stopped working and went on the dole I would get a flat off the housing immediately and they would pay the rent. You know, they would be giving me money! But because I have a job and pay my taxes I am put on a bloody waiting list! It's all wrong!' (Richard, forties, full-time porter, £5.88 per hour).

These brief excerpts from the research on the lived experience of working poverty induced by processes of neoliberalism in both the labour market (minimal levels of pay and working conditions caused by outsourcing) and the housing market (the re-regulation of mortgage lending regulations and the privatization of public housing have affected housing affordability and accessibility respectively) have demonstrated how the trans-subjectivities of neoliberalism become inter-subjectivities through the everyday experiences of Manchester's working poor. As such, these processes have been part of the reason for the widening social inequalities and increased levels of working poverty in Manchester. By way of conclusion, I want to return briefly to the concept of social justice and its future in the UK.

Squaring the circle? Local social justice and actually existing neoliberalism

In light of the pernicious effects of neoliberalism on low-paid workers, the perceived inadequacy of the current minimum wage and the rise of the Living Wage concept in US and UK urban areas, the current research aimed to investigate 'actually experienced' neoliberalism in the form of working poverty in Manchester through the lens of the living wage. The living wage is quintessentially a social justice concept. I understand social justice to be about fairness and equality of opportunity. For Harvey (1972) social justice is about the just distribution of income so that the needs of a population can be met, while for Sen (1985) social justice is about capabilities – what people are able to do. However, Kitson et al. (2000: 631) have noted that 'neoliberal economic policies, by lifting the constraints on the exercise of unequal power, increase injustice and trigger a downward economic and social spiral.' The resultant effects on the lives of working poor households are not 'fair' or 'just' and do not allow for equality of opportunity or the attainment of basic needs or capabilities, or the maximization of human potential. The Living Wage movement has attempted to address these social and economic injustices by providing low-wage workers with a wage level which allows them to meet their basic needs and avoid poverty and social exclusion. This is the first step on a long road to allowing low-income households to have access to the same opportunities as the majority of people in twenty-first-century Britain.

However, the living wage is one piece in a broader poverty-alleviation puzzle which advocates an alternative imaginary or agenda for social justice in urban areas through a contestation of current neoliberal practices (Leitner et al. 2007). The movements that have coalesced around the Living Wage concept are also campaigning around issues such as affordable housing, as they recognize that these community issues are part of a wider strategy towards the implementation of social justice and the alleviation of poverty. One of the main successes of groups such as TELCO has been to put issues of poverty, low pay, social exclusion and social justice back on both the local and national political agenda.

However, there are limits to what Living Wage campaigns can achieve, due to the small number of workers covered by the local legislation. This can limit the impacts of such campaigns on overall poverty rates and wider labour market regulation. In a recent response to a Living Wage petition, the UK government stated that it remained committed to tackling poverty through the making work pay strategy of a national minimum wage and Working Tax Credits rather than local living wages. However, current increases in the number of working poor individuals in the UK, coupled with recent problems of tax credit overpayment, has dented the public's confidence in this strategy.[4] If the living wage is not seen as the way forward to help alleviate poverty in the UK by New Labour, then changes need to be made to the making-work-pay strategy to ensure that tax credits top up the wages of low-paid workers to sufficient levels so that they can meet their basic needs.[5]

In sum, in the context of the current neoliberal climate and New Labour's penchant for minimal and diluted labour market regulation, there remain very significant challenges for the pursuit of social justice in the UK labour market. However, given the unsustainability of current levels of poverty and inequality for both national economic success and the local reproduction of labour, it is a challenge which is becoming increasingly important to take up.

Notes

I would like to thank Frank Hont, the regional secretary for Unison North West, for supporting my research with Unison resources; Deborah Littman, the pay-bargaining officer at Unison London, for our discussions; Rena Wood (Unison) and Cllr Brian O'Neill (Woodhouse Park) for their invaluable help with recruiting participants; and my supervisors, Professor Kevin Ward and Dr Neil Coe, for their support and advice. I would also like to thank the editors for involving me in this project. The usual disclaimers apply.

1. Pseudonyms are used to protect the identity of participants.
2. At the time of the research the National Minimum Wage level was £5.35/hour.
3. Working Tax Credits are a payment to top up the earnings of low-paid workers aged 25 and over and working at least 30 hours per week unless they are disabled, over 50 and returning to work or parents, who only need to work over 16 hours per week to qualify. The amount received is based on household income and circumstances.
4. The recent problem of tax credit overpayment has dented the confidence of many low-income households in the system and has put many off claiming (Hencke and Inman 2007). In the last three years nearly £6 billion has been overpaid. The government's attempts to claim this back from low-income households has had disastrous consequences. Hencke and Inman (2007) have noted that hundreds of thousands of households have been overpaid and 'some claimants were forced to sell or remortgage their homes' to afford the repayments. As such, the tax credits system is no longer seen by many as an effective income-maximizing tool. Indeed, Frank Field, MP for Birkenhead, noted in 2006 that 'tax credits are clearly the bluntest of anti-poverty weapons and are the equivalent of attempting delicate keyhole surgery with a hacksaw' (Field 2006, quoted in Branigan and Inman 2006: n.p.).
5. See Cooke and Lawton 2008 for possible policy changes.

References

Abrams, F. (2002) *Below the Breadline: Living on the Minimum Wage*, London: Profile.

Ambrose, P. (2003) *Love the Work, Hate the Job: Low Cost but Acceptable Wage Levels and the 'Exported Costs' of Low Pay in Brighton and Hove*, Brighton: University of Brighton.

Amin, A. (1994) 'Post-Fordism: Models, fantasies and phantoms of transition', in A. Amin (ed.) *Post-Fordism: A Reader*, Oxford: Blackwell, pp. 1–40.

Aronsson, G., K. Gustafsson and M. Dallner (2000) 'Sick but yet at work: An empirical study of sickness presenteeism', *Journal of Epidemiology and Community Health* 54: 502–9.

Barnett, C. (2005) 'The consolation of "neoliberalism"', *Geoforum* 36: 7–12.

Benhabib, S. (1986) *Critique, Norm and Utopia: A Study of the Foundations of Critical Theory*, New York: Columbia University Press.

Brenner, N., and N. Theodore (2002) 'Cities and the geographies of "actually existing neoliberalism"', in N. Brenner and N. Theodore (eds), *Spaces of Neoliberalism: Urban Restructuring in North America and Western Europe*, Oxford: Blackwell, pp. 2–32.

Brenner, N., J. Peck and N. Theodore (2005) 'Neoliberal urbanism: Cities and the rule of the market', draft, July 2005, www.geography.wisc.edu/faculty/peck/Brenner-Peck-Theodore_Neoliberal_urbanism.pdf; accessed 31 January 2007.

Centre for Cities (2007) *Cities Outlook 2008*, London: Centre for Cities.

Cooke, G., and K. Lawton (2008) *Working Out of Poverty: A Study of the Low-Paid and the 'Working Poor'*, London: IPPR.

Craig, D., and G. Cotterell (2007) 'Periodising neoliberalism?', *Policy and Politics* 35: 97–514.

Davies, P., and M. Freedland (2007) *Towards a Flexible Labour Market: Labour Legislation and Regulation since the 1990s*, Oxford: Oxford University Press.

Ehrenreich, B. (2002) *Nickel and Dimed: Undercover in Low-Wage USA*, London: Granta.

Esping-Anderson, G. (1985) *Politics against Markets*, Princeton: Princeton University Press.

Felstead, A., and N. Jewson (1999) (eds) *Global Trends on Flexible Labour*, London: Macmillan.

Giddens, A. (1998) *The Third Way: The Renewal of Social Democracy*, Cambridge: Polity Press.

GLAE (Greater London Authority Economics) (2005) *A Fairer London: The Living Wage in London*, London: Greater London Authority.

GLAE (Greater London Authority Economics) (2006) *A Fairer London: The Living Wage in London*, London: Greater London Authority.

GLAE (Greater London Authority Economics) (2007) *A Fairer London: The Living Wage in London*, London: Greater London Authority.

Grimshaw, D. (2004) 'Living wage and low pay campaigns in Britain', in D. Figart (ed.), *Living Wage Movements: Global Perspective Views*, New York: Routledge, pp. 101–21.

Grover, C. (2005) 'Living wages and the "making work pay" strategy', *Critical Social Policy* 25: 5–27.

Harvey, D. (1972) 'Social justice and spatial systems', in R. Peet (ed.), *Geographical Perspectives on American Poverty*, Worcester: Antipode, pp. 87–106.

Harvey, D. (2000) *Spaces of Hope*, Edinburgh: Edinburgh University Press.

Harvey, D. (2005) *A Brief History of Neoliberalism*, Oxford: Oxford University Press.

Hencke, D., and P. Inman (2007) 'Harsh rules force poor to spurn tax credits', *Guardian*, www.guardian.co.uk/business/2007/oct/09/money.socialexclusion.

Hitchman, C., I. Christie, M. Harrison and T. Lang (2002) *Inconvenience Food: The Struggle to Eat Well on a Low Income*, London: Demos.

Howell, C. (2004) 'Is there a Third Way for industrial relations?', *British Journal of Industrial Relations* 42: 1–22.

Jessop, B. (2003) 'Changes in welfare regimes and the search for flexibility and employability', in H. Overbeek (ed.), *The Political Economy of European Employment: European Integration and the Transnationalization of the (Un)employment Question*, London: Routledge, pp. 29–50.

Kempson, E. (1996) *Life on a Low Income*, York: Joseph Rowntree Foundation.

Kitson, M., R. Martin and F. Wilkinson (2000) 'Labour markets, social justice and economic efficiency', *Cambridge Journal of Economics* 24: 63141.

Leitner, H., E.S. Sheppard, K. Sziarto and A. Maringanti (2007) 'Contesting urban futures: Decentering neoliberalism', in H. Leitner, J. Peck and E.S. Sheppard (eds), *Contesting Neoliberalism: Urban Frontiers*, New York: Guilford Press, pp. 1–25.

Levin-Waldman, O.M. (2005) *The Political Economy of the Living Wage: A Study of Four Cities*, New York: M.E. Sharpe.

Littman, D., and H. Murphy (2006) *A Living Wage for Cardiff*, London: Unison.

Low Pay Commission (2007) *Historical Rates*, www.lowpay.gov.uk; accessed 27 February 2008.

Luce, S. (2004) *Fighting for a Living Wage*, London: Cornell University Press.

Manchester City Council (2007) *Affordable Housing Trends in Manchester and Salford 2007. Technical Report November 2007*, Manchester: Manchester City Council.

Manchester Partnership (2007) *Manchester State of the City Report 2006/2007*, Manchester: Manchester Partnership.

Merrifield, A. (2002) *Dialectical Urbanism: Social Struggles in the Capitalist City*, New York: Monthly Review Press.

Niedt, C., G. Ruiters, D. Wise and E. Schoenberger (1999) 'The effects of the living wage in Baltimore', Economic Policy Institute Working Paper no. 119, www.epinet.org; accessed 9 December 2004.

Ottewell, D. (2006) 'Year-and-a-half wait for home', *Manchester Evening News*, 6 January, www.manchestereveningnews.co.uk; accessed 26 February 2008.

Ottewell, D. (2007) 'City's "growing poverty gap"', *Manchester Evening News*, 5 September, p. 16.

Palmer, G., T. MacInnes and P. Kenway (2007) *Monitoring Poverty and Social Exclusion 2007*, New Policy Institute, www.jrf.org.uk/bookshop/eBooks/2152–poverty-social-exclusion.pdf; accessed 18 January 2008.

Parker, H. (1998) *Low Cost but Acceptable: A Minimum Income Standard for the UK: Families with Young Children*, Bristol: Policy Press.

Parker, H. (2002) *Low Cost but Acceptable: A Minimum Income Standard for Working Households with Children, Living in Swansea, South Wales*, National Centre for Public Policy, University of Wales, Swansea.

Pattison, V. (2007) 'The experience of working poverty in Manchester', *Unison Supplementary Evidence to the Low Pay Commission*, www.unison.org.uk/acrobat/ LPC92007supplementary.pdf; accessed 6 January 2008.

Pattison, V. (2008a) *The Living Wage and Working Poverty in Manchester*, Ph.D. thesis, University of Manchester, www.bwpi.manchester.ac.uk.

Pattison, V. (2008b) *Experiencing Neoliberalism: The Working Poor in Manchester*, Brooks World Poverty Institute Working Paper Series, www.bwpi.manchester.ac.uk.

Peck, J. (1996) *Work-place: The Social Regulation of Labor Markets*, London: Guilford Press.

Peck, J. (2002) 'Labor, zapped/growth, restored? Three moments of neoliberal restructuring in the American labor market', *Journal of Economic Geography* 2: 179–220.

Peck, J., and A. Tickell (2002) 'Neoliberalizing space', *Antipode* 34: 380–404.

Peck, J., and A. Tickell (2007) 'Conceptualizing neoliberalism, thinking Thatcherism', in H. Leitner, J. Peck and E.S. Sheppard (eds), *Contesting Neoliberalism: Urban Frontiers*, New York: Guilford Press, pp. 26–50.

Peck, J., and K.G. Ward (2002) 'Placing Manchester', in J. Peck and K.G. Ward (eds), *City of Revolution: Restructuring Manchester*, Manchester: Manchester University Press, pp. 1–17.

Perrons, D. (2000) 'Living with risk: Labour market transformation, employment policies and social reproduction in the UK', *Economic and Industrial Democracy* 21: 283–310.

Pierson, J. (2005) *A Living Wage? Mapping Low Pay in Birmingham: A Report Written for Birmingham Citizens and Community Union's Living Wage Campaign*, www.birminghamcitizens.org.uk; accessed 18 November 2005.

Powell, M. (2000) 'New Labour and the Third Way in the British welfare state: A new and distinctive approach', *Critical Social Policy* 20: 39–60.

Radcliffe, S.A. (2004) 'Neoliberalism as we know it, but not in the conditions of its own choosing: A commentary', *Environment and Planning A* 37: 323–9.

Rubery, J., K. Ward, D. Grimshaw and H. Beynon (2005) 'Working time, industrial relations and the employment relationship', *Time and Society* 14: 89–111.

Sen, A. (1985) *Commodities and Capabilities*, Amsterdam: North-Holland.

Sennett, R. (2003) *Respect: The Formation of Character in an Age of Inequality*, London: Penguin.

Shipler, D.K. (2004) *The Working Poor: Invisible in America*, New York: Vintage.

Smith, A., and A. Rochovská (2007) 'Domesticating neoliberalism: Everyday lives and the geographies of post-socialist reform', *Geoforum* 38: 1163–78.

Standing, G. (1997) 'Globalization, labour flexibility and insecurity: The era of market regulation', *European Journal of Industrial Relations* 3(1): 7–37.

Tickell, A., and J. Peck (2003) *Making Global Rules: Globalisation or Neoliberalisation*, draft, December, www.nottingham.ac.uk/geography/general/news-events/ Tickell_MakingGlobalRuleslongversion.pdf; accessed 31 January 2007.

Unison (2002) *Justice Not Charity: Why Workers Need a Living Wage*, submission to the Low Pay Commission by Unison and the Low Pay Unit, October, London: Unison.

Veit-Wilson, J. (2004) 'The need for scientific not arbitrary judgements', in

Zacchaeus 2000 Trust, *Memorandum to the Prime Minister on Minimum Income Standards*, London: Unison, Appendix 4.

Walsh, J. (2000) 'Organising the scale of labor regulation in the United States: Service-sector activism in the city', *Environment and Planning A* 32: 1593–610.

Ward, K.G., C. Fagan, L. McDowell, D. Perrons and K. Ray (2007) 'Living and working in urban working class communities', *Geoforum* 38: 312–25.

Weldon, L.S., and H. Targ (2004) 'From living wages to family wages?', *New Political Science* 26: 71–98.

Whitehead, M. (1998) 'Food deserts: What's in a name?', *Health Education Journal* 57: 189–90.

Wills, J. (2001a) *Mapping Low Pay in East London*, report written for TELCO's Living Wage Campaign, www.geog.qmw.ac.uk/staff/pdf/finalreport.doc; accessed 16 December 2004.

Wills, J. (2004) 'Organising the low paid: East London's living wage campaign as a vehicle for change', in W. Brown, E.G. Healy, E. Heery and P. Taylor (eds), *The Future of Worker Representation*, Oxford: Oxford University Press.

Wills, J. (2006) 'What's left? The Left, its crisis and rehabilitation', *Antipode* 38(5): 907–15.

Wills, J. (2007) *A Chronology of the London Living Wage*, www.geog.qmul.ac.uk/livingwage/chronology.html; accessed 29 April 2007.

Wrigley, N. (2002) 'Food deserts in British cities: Policy context and research priorities', *Urban Studies* 39: 2029–40.

Wrigley, N., B. Warm and B. Margetts (2003) *Food Retail Access and Diet: What the Leeds Study Desert Reveals*, www.dolphin.soton.ac.uk/ec2002/desert/html; accessed 18 September 2006.

5

Bargaining with the devil: neoliberalization, informal work and workers' resistance in the clothing industry of Turkey

Ergül Ergün

The pressures of globalization and neoliberal policies have led many countries, including Turkey, to become integrated into the world market. In the early 1980s, Turkey's economic policies shifted from heavily protected import-substitution strategies towards neoliberal policies based on an open market economy and export-oriented production. One of the main industries in which Turkey joined the world market was the textile and clothing industry, which expanded more rapidly than Turkey's overall economic development as exports mushroomed.

This chapter examines how neoliberal policies became embedded at the local level in industrial clothing workshops which flourished in the peripheral neighbourhoods of Istanbul as they became engaged in export-oriented production. The chapter focuses on the influence of neoliberal policies on the employment structure of the clothing industry in Turkey and workers' acts of resistance in industrial workshops. It links these policies to the politics of everyday life by focusing on the ways in which industrial workshop workers have engaged in struggles of their own and the limitations of these struggles within the context of changing production relations, state policies and existing organizational alternatives.

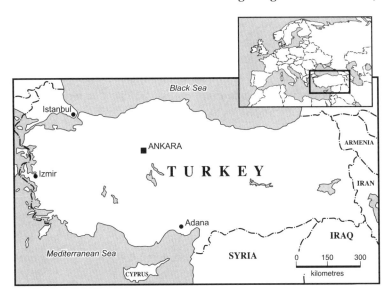

FIGURE 5.1 Map of Turkey

The chapter begins by placing the informal sector within the context of neoliberal policies and the flexibilization of the labour market. It then provides background information on structural adjustment policies in Turkey (Figure 5.1), through which an open market economy and export-oriented production were introduced. It then focuses on how SAPs and changing production relations influenced employment structures, state policies and trade union activities in Turkey. Finally, the chapter examines how these changes affect labour protection and workers' struggles in clothing workshops.

Neoliberal economic policies, labour flexibility and the informal sector

The role of the informal sector in the economy has changed profoundly as a result of neoliberal economic policies through which labour has been flexibilized via subcontracting chains. Growing instability in world markets, fluctuations in demand, and rapid shifts in production designs encourage the emergence of flexible, low-risk production structures with more flexible labour processes (Standing

1989, 2002). These processes also lead companies to reduce the fixed-wage labour force and to use more contract workers, homeworkers and temporary labour (Radcliffe 1999; Boris and Prügl 1996; Benería 1989). In turn, this allows companies to produce with more flexible working hours and to subcontract to small informal enterprises that are not covered by labour regulation.

The informal sector is often defined as involving income-generating activities taking place outside the framework of public regulations (Sassen 1991; Benería 1989; Castells and Portes 1989). The sector is usually characterized by ease of entry and exit, little capital and equipment, low pay, lack of workers' rights, labour-intensive and low-skilled work and no fixed employment contracts (Charmes 2000; Hahn 1996). Early studies identified the informal sector as left over from precapitalist modes of production. Until the 1980s, international organizations such as the ILO, UN, USAID and the World Bank perceived the informal sector primarily as part of a development process and an integral aspect of industrialization in less developed countries (LDCs) (Waldinger and Lapp 1993; Benería 1989). It was assumed that factory mass production would absorb the labour force and informal forms of production would gradually be eliminated. The informal sector was understood as an area of subsistence production that lowered the costs of labour-force reproduction and maintained the surplus population (Hahn 1996; Castells and Portes 1989).

In Turkey, since the 1950s, the informal sector has become a major concern in social science literatures, as rural populations moved to urban areas. The early literature on the informal sector had a similar perspective to mainstream developmentalist theory. The informal sector was analysed within the context of migration and uncertain working conditions. It was often argued that badly paid jobs were brought into the metropolitan areas via migration. For instance, Tekeli (1978) attributed the emerging informal sector in Turkey to rapid rural–urban migration in the 1970s. He suggested that since the rural workforce could not be absorbed in the organized sector in the cities, this workforce directed their economic activities to the marginal sector. Similarly, Şenyapılı (1981) described the informal sector as a marginal part of the economy at the beginning of the 1980s.

These perspectives, however, do not explain the reality of the informal sector today. According to Charmes (2000), informal activities constituted between 20 per cent and 95 per cent of the urban labour force of LDCs during the 1990s. The number of industrial workers in informal activities expanded dramatically in the 1980s in Latin America, forming between 50 per cent and 70 per cent of the urban workforce (Lawson 1992: 16). In Bangladesh, 70 per cent of the urban labour force was informal (Charmes 2000) and 80 per cent of new jobs were in the informal sector in the early 1990s in Guatemala City (Radcliffe 1999). This sector has thus become the central feature of LDCs, rather than being a marginal part of the economy.

The increasing visibility of the informal sector has been emphasized not only in LDCs, but also in more developed countries (MDCs) (Boris and Prügl 1996; Gordon and Sassen 1992). Gordon and Sassen (1992) suggest that core manual jobs offering security and permanent occupations for the unskilled mass of the population are steadily in decline in MDCs. On the other hand, the use of cheaper and more flexible sources of unorganized labour has been increasing and temporary, casual jobs and self-employed forms of work have been growing rapidly.

Informalization is a response of industries to the acceleration of international competition and pressures to cut costs. Subcontracting chains allow firms to change divisions of labour in such a way that lower-skill and lower-wage tasks can take place in small-scale firms in the informal sector. These changes give firms flexibility in the use of capital and labour. On the other hand, they enable the bypassing of state regulations, social legislation and organized labour's control over the work process by shifting low-skill and low-wage tasks to the informal sector (Castells and Portes 1989). Subcontracting chains, which allow parent firms to remain flexible in their usage of capital and labour and avoid fixed commitments to workers, link transnational enterprises to small local firms, workshops and homeworkers. These chains have drawn the informal sector into highly competitive international markets. Small- and medium-sized firms are as active as big organizations and factories within the production model arising from neoliberal policies (Boris and Prügl 1996; Lawson 1992).

Neoliberal policies and structural changes in international capitalism have placed the informal sector and small-scale production at the centre of economic development in LDCs and have transformed 'old forms of production' into new forms in MDCs. While firms operating in the formal and informal sectors have been integrated in the same production process, the border between the two has become blurred. The development of the informal sector is no longer merely perceived as a survival strategy of the urban poor. It is also no longer considered a deviant part of the economy that is expected to disappear when the formal sector becomes large enough to employ the available workforce. In the following sections, I focus on the local dynamics of informal production and workers' strategies in the clothing industry in Istanbul. However, first I elaborate how neoliberal policies were introduced in Turkey and the influence of these policies on the clothing industry.

Structural adjustment in Turkey

In the 1980s, Turkey followed a similar path to many other countries in the introduction of structural adjustment programmes (see North and Olson in this volume), in part to deal with a foreign debt of $18 billion in 1980 (Ahmad 1993) and an economic crisis (Elson 1995; Saad-Filfo 2005; Veltmeyer and Petras 2005; Escobar 1995).[1] Under the advice – or rather pressure – of the World Bank and the International Monetary Fund, SAPs were placed on the agenda in Turkey in January 1980. Turkish foreign debt was rescheduled between 1978 and 1981 and a World Bank structural adjustment loan of $250 million was provided (Ertan-Lemontagne 1991).

The programme aimed to bring down inflation by freeing prices, to reduce public expenditure, to cut back consumption by holding down wages, and to increase exports to enable debt repayments and access to new credits. The policy made a virtue of the necessity for low unit labour costs and also a decrease in domestic demand to make more goods available for external markets. Both of these necessities meant greater control over, and reductions in, wages (Çağatay and Berik 1994; Yeldan 1994). Suppression of wages and the introduction of SAPs resulted in strong social opposition. The attempt to force unionized workers to accept belt tightening was very costly, with 54,000 workers going on strike and the loss of 7.7 million working days between January and September 1980 (Ahmad 1993: 209).

In response to ongoing instability, the civil regime was overthrown by a military coup on 12 September 1980. Parliament was dissolved and the constitution was suspended. Trade unions and civil society organizations were banned. Free collective bargaining and strike activities were suspended (Ahmad 1993). However, the economic stabilization programme remained untouched. Under the highly restrictive environment created by the *coup d'état*, the implementation of SAPs was ensured without any significant social opposition from the press, the unions or the parliament. Following the coup, the architect of the stabilization program in Turkey, Turgut Özal, became deputy prime minister with responsibility for the economy. Özal later commented that if it had not been for the coup of September 1980, the economic programme would not have succeeded (Ertan-Lemontagne 1991).[2]

Since the early 1980s, successive Turkish governments have actively shown their willingness and enthusiasm to allow foreign capital investment. Most of these governments worked as an active partner with the private sector in the search for foreign markets, with incentives given to export firms, and in the creation of infrastructure necessary for foreign and national capital. One of the rising stars of these neoliberal economic policies was the export-oriented textile and clothing industry.

The textile and clothing industry in Turkey

Textile and clothing production is not new in Turkey. In fact, the industry is one of the oldest forms of industrial production in the country. Industrialization started in Turkey during the nineteenth century with the production of consumer goods, such as textiles, clothing and food. However, textile and clothing production was targeted mainly towards the domestic market until the 1980s. The share of manufactured textile products in total exports was very low, whereas textile raw material exports were considerably higher (Ansal 1999; Eraydın 1998).

FIGURE 5.2   A typical peripheral neighbourhood of Istanbul, in which the researcher worked as a garment worker

Alongside the introduction of SAPs, the textile and clothing industry was supported by the state as the main export sector and given incentives. The share of textiles in total exports was only 2 per cent in 1968 but increased to 23 per cent in 1983. Clothing and textile exports increased from $81 million in 1980 to $6.2 billion in 1995 and to $11.8 billion in 2005 (Eraydın 1998; Neidik and Gereffi 2006), while increasing their share in manufacturing output to 43.5 per cent in 1990 (Sönmez 1996). The clothing industry, in particular, has shown a drastic rise accounting for 60 per cent of overall output in the textile and clothing industry in the 1990s (Ansal 1999; Kayasü 1995).

According to the ILO (1996), employment in the textile and clothing industry in Turkey grew by 33.7 per cent between 1980 and 1993.[3] The clothing industry, which employs 1.5 million workers according to official figures, is one of the significant driving forces in Turkey's economy (Bodgener 1997). Consequently, Turkey became one of the top five countries in global clothing exports in 2005 (Neidik and Gereffi 2006).[4]

FIGURE 5.3 Two clothing workshops in Istanbul, hidden in the ground and basement floor of a residential flat

Spatial divisions of labour in the clothing industry and industrial workshops

Production, particularly in the Turkish clothing industry, is mainly based on subcontracting relations. The industry relies heavily on small-scale workshop production and the informal sector (Ansal 1999; Kayasü 1995). Although there are some estimates concerning informal work in the clothing industry in Turkey, they do not provide a clear picture, owing partly to the lack of research in this area and partly to the hidden nature of the informal sector.

One of the reasons for the expansion of the informal sector in the clothing industry is the increasing decentralization of production from large-scale firms in order to compete in international markets. From the mid-1980s, large-scale clothing firms in Turkey encouraged their laid-off foremen to use their redundancy payments to establish subcontractor workshops by guaranteeing access to the market and orders (Duruiz 1995; Atatuz and Atauz 1992). Indeed, interviews with trade-union representatives in Turkey support this argument.[5] For example, a representative of the Textile and Clothing Union (Teksif)[6] stated that since the 1980s some of the large-scale clothing producers have supplied machinery for their experienced workers as redundancy payments. While the parent firms consequently reduced the number of workers in the core company, they shifted some of the stages of production to such smaller workshops, often located in residential areas of Istanbul (Figures 5.2 and 5.3).

The process of production in the clothing industry in Turkey is based around the specialization of individual workshops and firms in particular stages of garment manufacture. However, there is a clear pattern involving the separation of tasks and how particular specialized production locations are spread within an urban area. Work processes requiring 'qualified' white- and blue-collar workers are mainly located in large-scale firms based in industrial zones. Most of the workers in such firms have formal protection, such as a work contract and rights to social security. On the other hand, 'unskilled', labour-intensive and routine tasks, such as sewing and embroidering, are often subcontracted to workshops located in residential peripheries. The small-scale firms contribute to capital accumulation in the export companies by providing them with relatively cheap inputs.

The fragmentation of the work process between different enterprises not only enables flexibility in terms of orders, but also creates the possibility of informality, and therefore decreases the cost and increases the opportunity for competitiveness at an international level. On the one hand, cost reduction strategies are based on cheaper rents in the peripheries and lack of costs for workers' transportation, because the workshops are already located in residential districts. On the other hand, the physical concealment of the workshops in the peripheral neighbourhoods creates the possibility for clandestine activity and informality.

State policies relating to the clothing industry and the informal sector

Although workshop workers officially have rights of equal treatment with other wage earners, none of these rights appears to be implemented within workshop settings. Indeed, laws are system-atically flouted. Formal legislation seems to lose its significance and protective powers for these workers. In many of the garment workshops in which I conducted research there was often no written contract between workers and employers. Work was mainly contracted using verbal agreements. The majority of workers were not covered by either national insurance or social security systems. Formal social regulations such as the right to retire, statutory holidays, maternity rights, limits on overtime, vacation pay, minimum wage levels and regulations in terms of health conditions of the workplace were not applied in the workshop settings.

The lack of application of labour legislation with regard to work-shop workers appears to be closely linked to the informal character of the workshops and their physical concealment in peripheral neigh-bourhoods. Workshops look like domestic residences from the outside, and therefore they easily escape labour inspection teams (Figure 5.3). In addition, incidents mentioned by workers also underline the informality of the workspaces and the difficulty of implementing labour legislation:

> One day two men with smart clothes came to the workshop. As soon as they came in, we knew that they were government officers. The men asked the boss where the employer was. The boss himself said 'the boss is not here, he won't come today. He went to his village for a visit. I am just a worker in the workshop.' The labour inspectors went and did not come again. (Zeynep, worker, aged 18)[7]

As stated by Berik (1987) in her valuable study on carpet workers, the smaller and darker the workshops, the more difficult it is for labour inspectors to detect them and apply labour legislation. Ironi-cally, the worse the working conditions are, the easier it is for employers to avoid sanctions. However, this argument explains only half of the story. Since Turkey is integrated into the international market via its labour cost advantage, the limited profitability rates and instability of workshop production do not lend themselves easily to standard labour regulation. Workshop employers in Istanbul also mention the impossibility of imposing formal social rights under the existing power relations in the market: 'The work is very unstable.

Sometimes, there is no work for six months. How can I hire workers with social security and national insurance, while the future of the work is so insecure?' (The Peak Textile, workshop employer).

State policies relating to the clothing industry have mainly concentrated on increasing foreign exchange inputs, the export potential of the country, and potential employment creation. Informal work, workshop production and workers themselves receive little attention. There were only 650 labour inspectors in the Ministry of Labour to control labour standards in the whole country in the early 2000s. It is estimated that there are 3 million textile and clothing workers in Istanbul alone (Kaya 2000). Clearly, labour standards cannot be controlled with this limited number of labour inspectors even in the garment workshops hidden in the peripheries of Istanbul, let alone in all workplaces in Turkey.

Since the organization of the industry via international subcontracting chains does not lend itself easily to tight regulation, the application of labour standards by increasing labour inspection does not often produce positive outcomes. For instance, State Planning Institute representatives referred to a project that was developed in 1996–97 in the western cities of Turkey. This project was supported by the Ministry of Labour, local governors, police headquarters, municipalities and guilds. It involved imposing certain labour standards in the workshops, such as limiting the maximum amount of working hours, implementing overtime payments, social security systems, compensation payments, official holidays and abandoning child labour. In just one of the cities, Uşak, 10,000 workers were covered by social security as a result of this project. Working hours decreased to 7.5 hours per day with the support of the police force. However, at the end of the year, approximately 40 per cent of the workshops had gone bankrupt.

Trade unions and informal-sector workers in Turkey

The development of international subcontracting chains has had a devastating effect on traditional forms of union organization across the globe. As the direct connection between those with real power in production chains and workers has been broken, the scope of overt collective bargaining over employment conditions has become limited (Hale and Wills 2005; Ergün 2004). The violation of workers' rights and prevention of union activities are more evident in the highly mobile textile and clothing industries. Cases of workers' collective protests and traditional forms of union organizing often result in retail firms sourcing elsewhere and local workers losing their jobs (Hale 2005; Anner and Evans 2004; Cravey 2004; Traub-Werner and Cravey 2002). Research on clothing subcontracting chains also suggests that there is often active hostility among employers to trade-union activities (Kearney and Gearhart 2004; Khan 2002). Traditional trade unions often experience difficulty in taking on board the needs and rights of women informal-sector workers who make up the majority of workers in the clothing industry (Kabeer 2004; Rowbotham and Mitter 1994).

In Turkey, the power of the trade unions has been gradually eroded as a result of macro-level economic and social policies since the early 1980s. The number of trade-union members has been decreasing as result of the decline in employees working in stable jobs. There is also an enormous gap between the number of trade-union members and the number of formal-sector workers. For instance, while the total number of registered workers was 7.4 million in 1992, trade-union membership amounted to only 2.2 million (Türel 1993). Trade unions have been struggling to maintain their existing membership and have therefore been experiencing difficulty in developing new strategies to organize the growing number of informal-sector workers.

Despite the fact that some union representatives are aware of the importance of industrial workshops and the informal sector, particularly in the clothing industry, they do not have significant strategies for targeting workshops. One of the main reasons is the apparent difficulty in organizing industrial workshops. Trade-union representatives suggest that any attempt at organizing can be easily detected and prevented by employers:

> We cannot even get organized in medium-scale workshops, let alone in the small ones. Suppose that we tried to get organized in a workshop with forty workers. The employer has his own friends as workers. If one worker registers with the trade union, s/he would

find him/herself outside the door on the following day [i.e. would be dismissed]. (Hak-iş union representative)

They also refer to the current structure of the industry and informality provoked by the subcontracting chains and international competition:

> Unionization cannot be introduced in the garment workshops because when the workers are unionized they have many social rights, such as the introduction of holiday payments, retirement rights or the control of working hours. The employers of the workshops cannot support this type of workforce. (Hak-iş union representative)

Trade-union representatives also argue that it is more feasible to concentrate their limited efforts on larger workplaces, so that they can obtain a reasonable-sized membership to pay fees, and therefore gain a greater power base. Hence, despite the fact that no limit on workplace size in relation to unionization exists in labour law, trade unions tend to target the workplaces that hire more than thirty workers.

Rather than putting their efforts into the cumbersome and long-term project of organizing small industrial workshops, trade unions often focus on more influential public events, such as organizing demonstrations against the erosion of labour rights and social services. Even though these attempts are crucial and have an indirect effect on informality in terms of widening the awareness of labour rights and preventing the erosion of social security systems, they do not offer opportunities for organizing informal-sector workers.

Conservative influences in the trade unions are another obstacle faced by these organizations. It is often argued that the growth of the informal sector via subcontracting chains is an attack on the social state because the sector decreases labour costs and eliminates labour unions (Koç 1999). Informalization via subcontracting chains is described as a trick to disempower unions by dividing the work process into small units (DİSK-AR 1994). A decrease in the size of workplaces, the clandestine nature of work in residential areas, and the low-labour-cost policies of the clothing industry present difficulties for unions to organize in the informal sector. However, the perspective that sees the informal sector as an attack on unionization also creates a division among workers and presents an obstacle to developing a positive strategy for organizing the informal sector. Those trade unions with conservative influences tend to perceive workers in large-scale factories as 'real' workers and therefore as more central. Furthermore, they either undermine labour in the neighbourhoods or, worse, perceive them as a threat or an obstacle to the organization of factory workers. A trade-union representative recognized this situation:

> The workforce in the informal sector is not even viewed as 'real' workers by many union members. This perspective is adopted not only by trade unions, but also by many factory workers. Some of them see their status as privileged relative to informal-sector workers. They do not perceive these workers' problems as their own problems. This workforce is seen as temporary, apolitical, unorganized or too young to be organized or inexperienced in labour struggle. They are viewed as the 'dregs of the society'. (DİSK, union representative)

In summary, formal labour organizations and state policies provide limited alternatives and protection for informal-sector workers at national, regional and local levels. Bearing in mind the poverty of existing organizing possibilities for informal-sector workers, the next section focuses on garment workers' acts of resistance and their limits.

Bargaining and its limits

Garment workers develop strategies at a local level in an individual and collective way for fairer working conditions, higher salaries and increased control over their workplace. The main disputes in the workshops are related to wages, working hours/overtime and the pace of work. Increasing working hours and the pace of work are linked to the control of labour processes and all these issues are related to the extraction of labour power. The strategies developed by the workers depend on their power to negotiate for fairer conditions. One of these sources of power of garment workers derives from their family and kinship relations. These relations are mobilized by the workers as well as the employers as part of workplace relations. Gender relations are often absorbed and manipulated within kinship and family relations, as these relations are operationalized by the employers and the workers:[8]

There was a disagreement in the workshop where I used to work and I wanted to leave. The boss hadn't given me my wage for the last two months. Previously, my sister and I used to work in the same place. My sister was engaged. She, her fiancé and I used to go out together. When I said to the boss that I planned to give up the job and asked for my payments, he threatened to tell my family that I was going out with men. I went home and told my family what happened in the workshop before the boss could. Then, the boss came to our house to talk with my family. He argued with my father. After this argument, the boss had to give me my salary. Then I gave up the job. (Sibel, worker, aged 18)

As well as operationalizing traditional forms of social relations, workers develop new forms of solidarities created within the industrial workshops. Garment workers often enter the bargaining process, or resist the working conditions together with their co-workers as well as their other family members:

We were on the overtime shift that night. Two girls came five minutes late. The boss asked why they were late. They said 'Our family didn't let us come earlier.' The boss said 'Then tell your family not to let you work, either.' And he fired them. After the girls went, five workers became annoyed and gave up work. The partner of the boss intervened by saying, 'Why do you let the girls go out during the night? They will be frightened. We should go and bring them back.' In the end [so as not to lose seven workers all at once], the employer had to call those two girls back. (Zeynep, worker, aged 18)

The success of bargaining attempts depends on a series of factors such as workers' ability to act together, existing work alternatives, the current needs of the employer, and whether it is easy to replace the worker(s) involved in the bargaining process. Scott (1985) argues that when we distinguish various levels of resistance, such as formal versus informal, individual versus collective, spontaneous and short-term versus organized and long-term, we are actually speaking about the limits of available options framed by the level of repression. From a similar perspective, I suggest that the parameters of resistance in garment workshops also need to be analysed taking into account the context of repression:

There isn't any solidarity in garment work. This is the rule of work-shops, because the workers are compelled to work. When they open their mouths, the boss says the door is over there. We are always under the threat of being fired… When you try to complain about something to the boss, everybody thinks that you are on the edge of being fired or giving up the job. The boss fires anyone who answers him back. I have never tried to bargain with the boss. The only thing that I can do is to give up the job, when the knife touches the bone [i.e. when the conditions become unbearable]. I cannot do anything else. (Berna, worker, aged 19)

In her study of the social agency of flexible workers in the UK, Cook (2000) argues that access to rights is an important aspect of workers' empowerment. The lack of a right to appeal against unfair dismissal – either at legal or application level – may seriously influence workers' power to challenge unfair treatment. She observes that the insecure nature of the work allows the workers very limited power to negotiate their rights. The negotiating power of the workers is also influenced by the low level of engagement by trade unions and NGOs. Similarly, workers often do not have any formal guarantee of work in industrial workshops in Turkey. Their acts of resistance and solidarity are threatened by work insecurity and the constant fear of losing their job. Perhaps for the very same reason, resistance and solidarity in bargaining with the employer have a chance of succeeding when the workers envisage leaving their job.

Conclusion: bargaining with the devil

The clothing industry in Turkey became a successful export industry at the price of pushing the labour-intensive part of production towards the informal sector. The organization of the industry within international subcontracting chains, continuous pressure on prices and the level of flexibility imposed by the international market are the major dynamics of this division of labour. On the other hand, state policies concerned with the clothing industry offer limited alternatives to improve working conditions in the workshops, partly because of their own limitations and partly because of the awareness of the vulnerability of the industry. As a result of the vulnerability of industrial workshops to international fluctuations, the limitations of state protection and the informality of work, workers feel that they are under constant threat of losing their jobs.

Resistance is related to how much bargaining power workers have, whether there is any channel through which demand is transferred, whether any formal organization exists to support resistance, and what the cost of resistance is for the individual worker. Acts of resistance in the workshops are suppressed by the insecurity of the work and the constant threat of job losses. Garment workers develop resistance strategies as part of their local, daily reality. Workers develop these strategies according to the sources of power available to them. However, there are limited formal opportunities and social protection that would help to transform these strategies into long-term solidarities and extend them to a wider context.

Notes

I am grateful to Professor Nina Laurie, Dr Emma Clavering, Lucy Mayblin and the editors for their valuable suggestions and comments. The ORS awards scheme and the School of Geography, Politics and Sociology, Newcastle University, provided scholarships to complete this study.

1. SAPs have attracted many criticisms since they were first introduced. Researchers argue that SAPs have a negative impact on increasing income polarization; identifying development as a social Darwinist process based on ethics of greed, the survival of the fittest in the market without any space for sharing; undermining socio-cultural and historical realities of the societies in which the policies have been applied; causing disastrous effects on the poor of the developing world (Standing 2002; Pilger 2001; Elson 1995).

2. After the initial boom period associated with the SAPs, Turkey found itself in a vicious cycle of fiscal instability and debt-led growth, heavily dependent on inflows of short-term capital, leading to three successive financial crises in 1994, 2000 and 2001. During these crises, thousands of small and medium-sized firms and their workers were affected due to bankruptcies. Massive lay-offs also took place in large enterprises. Debt payments are the largest item in the budget today constituting over half of total government spending (Buğra 2003; Öniş 2006).

3. The report addresses only formal employment. Considering that informal employment is common in the clothing industry, this amount is probably higher.

4. This scenario is not unique to Turkey. Clothing, textile and footwear industries are the main export sectors for many LDCs. The geographical distribution of these industries has changed dramatically in the past thirty years. As the market has been internationalized, these industries have been relocated from more developed countries, where they continue to be consumed, to less developed countries (ILO 1996).

5. The empirical part of this study is based on Ph.D. field research conducted in the peripheral neighbourhoods of Istanbul between May 1999 and Sep-

tember 2000. Semi-structured interviews with workshop owners, focused interviews with female workers and participant observation as a worker in a garment workshop constituted the main sources of data. In total, 21 workshop employers and 50 female workshop workers were interviewed. Supplementary data came from semi-structured interviews with a large number of informants including subcontracting firm managers, trade-union and government representatives.

6. There are three main trade-union confederations in Turkey, namely Trade Unions Confederation of Justice Seekers (Hak-iş), Revolutionary Workers' Trade Unions Confederation (DİSK) and Workers' Trade Union Confederation of Turkey (Türk-iş). Teksif is the textile and clothing branch of Türk-iş.

7. Workshop and workers' names have been changed to maintain anonymity.

8. For a detailed discussion on the operationalization of gender relations by the employers and workers in informal garment workshops, see Ergün 2002, 2004.

References

Ahmad, F. (1993) *The Making of Modern Turkey*, London and New York: Routledge.

Anner, M., and P. Evans (2004) 'Building bridges across a double divide', *Development in Practice* 14(1/2): 34–46.

Ansal, H. (1999) '75 Yılda Başı Çeken Sektörlerden Tekstil', in O. Baydar (ed.), *75 yılda Çarklardan Çiplere*, Türkiye İş Bankası Kültür Yayınları, Türkiye Ekonomik ve Toplumsal Tarih Vakfı, Istanbul, pp. 183–90.

Atauz, S., and A. Atauz (1992) 'Enformel Sektör, Kentsel İşgücü Pazarları, Sosyal ve Ekonomik Yapılanmalar Üzerine Betimsel Tartışmalar', *Planlama*, 9: 4–21.

Ayata, S. (1991) *Sermaye Birikimi ve Toplumsal Değişim*, Ankara: Gündoğan.

Benería, L. (1989) 'Subcontracting and Employment Dynamics in Mexico City', in A. Portes, M. Castells and L.A. Benton (eds), *The Informal Economy: Studies in Advanced and Less Developed Countries*, London: Johns Hopkins University Press, pp. 173–88.

Berik, G. (1987) 'Women carpet weavers in rural Turkey: Patterns of employment, earning and status', *Women, Work and Development* 15, Geneva: International Labour Organization.

Bodgener, J. (1997) 'The clothing industry in Turkey', *Textile Outlook International* 71: 37–59.

Boris, E., and E. Prügl (eds) (1996) *Homeworkers in Global Perspective*, London: Routledge.

Buğra, A. (2003) 'The place of economy in Turkish society', *South Atlantic Quarterly* 102(2/3): 453–70.

Çağatay, N., and G. Berik (1994) 'What has export-oriented manufacturing meant for Turkish women?', in P. Sparr (ed.), *Mortgaging Women's Lives: Feminist Critiques of Structural Adjustment*, London: Zed Books, pp. 78–95.

Castells, M., and A. Portes (1989) 'World underneath: The origins, dynamics, and

1 3 2   *Social justice and neoliberalism*

effects of the informal economy', in A. Portes, M. Castells and L.A. Benton (eds), *The Informal Economy: Studies in Advanced and Less Developed Countries*, London: Johns Hopkins University Press, pp. 11–37.

Charmes, J. (2000) 'Informal sector, poverty and gender: A review of empirical evidence', unpublished paper presented in 'Homeworkers Worldwide International Mapping Workshop', Leeds.

Cook, J. (2000) 'Flexible employment – Implications for a gendered political economy of citizenship', in J. Cook, J. Roberts and G. Waylen (eds), *Towards a Gendered Political Economy*, London: Macmillan, pp. 145–64.

Cravey A. (2004) 'Students and the anti-sweatshop movement', *Antipode* 36(2): 203–8.

DİSK-AR (1994) 'Dünyada ve Türkiye''de Sendikal Hareketin Krizi', *DİSK Araştırma Enstitüsü Aylık Bülteni* 16: 13–20.

Duruiz, L. (1995) 'Gümrük Birliği Arifesinde Türk Hazır Giyim Sanayi: Sanayinin Rekabet Gücü', *DİSK Araştırma Enstitütüsü Aylık Bülteni* 18: 13–15.

Elson, D. (1995) 'Male bias in macro-economics: The case of structural adjustment', in D. Elson (ed.), *Male Bias in the Development Process*, Manchester University Press, Manchester, pp. 164–90.

Eraydın, A. (1998) 'Ekonomik Başarının Yükünü Üstlenenler: Dış Pazarlarda Rekabet Gücü Kazanan Konfeksiyon Sanayinde Kadın Emeği', in F. Özbay (ed.), *Küresel Pazar Açısından Kadın Emeğinde ve İstihdamında Değişmeler: Türkiye Örneği*, Istanbul: İnsan Kaynağını Geliştirme Vakfı, pp. 103–44.

Ergün, E. (2002) 'Understanding the integration of Istanbul's peripheral neighbourhood into the world market: A disclosure of women's labour in the "secure" places', *Boğaziçi Journal: Review of Social, Economic and Administrative Studies* 16(11): 21–33.

Ergün, E. (2004) *Atölye Kızları: A Study of Women's Labour in the Export-oriented Garment Industry in Turkey*, Ph.D. thesis, Newcastle University.

Ertan-Lemontagne, Ö. (1991) *IMF-Supported Programs in Developing Countries and Their Impact on Vulnerable Groups: The Case of Turkey after 1980*, Ph.D. thesis, University of New Hampshire.

Escobar, A. (1995) *Encountering Development: The Making and Unmaking of the Third World*, Princeton: Princeton University Press.

Gordon, I., and S. Sassen (1992) 'Restructuring the urban labour market', in S. Fainstein, I. Gordon and M. Harloe (eds), *Divided Cities: New York and London in the Contemporary World*, Oxford: Blackwell, pp. 105–28.

Hahn, J. (1996) 'Feminization through flexible labour', in E. Boris and E. Prügl (eds), *Homeworkers in Global Perspective: Invisible No More*, New York and London: Routledge, pp. 219–38.

Hale, A. (2005) 'Organising and networking in support of garment workers', in A. Hale and J. Wills (eds), *Threads of Labour*, Oxford: Blackwell, pp. 40–68.

Hale, A., and J. Wills (2005) 'Threads of labour in the global garment industry', in A. Hale and J. Wills (eds), *Threads of Labour*, Oxford: Blackwell, pp. 1–15.

ILO (1996) *Globalization Changes the Face of Textile, Clothing and Footwear Industries*, Geneva: International Labour Organization.

Kabeer, N. (2004) 'Globalization, labour standards and women's rights', *Feminist Economics* 10(1): 3–35.

Kaya, S. (2000) 'Activist round table' organized by Working Group on Women Home-based Workers in Turkey, International Association for Feminist Economics Conference, Istanbul.

Kayasü, S. (1995) *Local Production Organisations Oriented Towards Global Markets: Subcontracting Relationships in Clothing Industry*, Ph.D. thesis, METU, Ankara.

Kearney, N., and J. Gearhart (2004) 'Workplace codes as tools for workers', *Development in Practice* 14(1/2): 216–23.

Khan, S.I. (2002) 'Trade unions, gender issues and the ready-made garment industry in Bangladesh', in C. Miller and J. Vivians (eds), *Women's Employment in the Textile and Manufacturing Sectors of Bangladesh and Morocco*, Geneva: UNRISD/UNDP.

Koç, Y. (1999) 'Sendikacılığın Güncel Sorunları', *Türkiye İşçi Sendikaları Eğitim Yayınları* 40, Ankara.

Laurie, N., and L. Bondi (eds) (2006) *Working the Spaces of Neoliberalism: Activism, Professionalisation and Incorporation*, Oxford: Blackwell.

Lawson, V. (1992) 'Industrial subcontracting and employment forms in Latin America: A framework for contextual analysis', *Progress in Human Geography* 16(1): 1–23.

Munck, R. (2005) 'Neoliberalism and politics and the politics of neoliberalism', in A. Saad-Filho and D. Johnston (eds), *Neoliberalism: A Critical Reader*, London: Pluto, pp. 60–69.

Neidik, B., and G. Gereffi (2006) 'Explaining Turkey's emergence and sustained competitiveness as a full-package supplier of apparel', *Environment and Planning A* 38: 2285–303.

Öniş, Z. (2006) 'Varieties and crises of neoliberal globalisation: Argentina, Turkey and the IMF', *Third World Quarterly* 27(2): 239–63.

Pearson, R. (1992) 'Gender issues in industrialisation', in T. Hewit, H. Johnson and D. Wield (eds), *Industrialisation and Development*, Oxford: Oxford University Press, pp. 222–47.

Peck, J., and A. Tickell (2002) 'Neoliberalizing space', *Antipode* 34(3): 380–404.

Pilger, J. (2001) *The New Rulers of the World: A Carlton Programme for ITV-UK*, Rugby and London: George Over.

Polanyi, K. (2001) *The Great Transformation: The Political and Economic Origins of Our Times*, Boston MA: Beacon Press.

Radcliffe, S.A. (1999) 'Latina labour: Restructuring of work and renegotiations of gender relations in contemporary Latin America', *Environment and Planning A* 31(2): 196–208.

Rowbotham, S., and S. Mitter (eds) (1994) *Dignity and Daily Bread: New Forms of Economic Organising among Poor Women in Third World and the First*, London: Routledge.

Saad-Filho, A. (2005) 'From Washington to post-Washington consensus: Neoliberalism agendas for economic development', in A. Saad-Filho and D. Johnston (eds), *Neoliberalism: A Critical Reader*, London: Pluto Press, pp. 113–19.

Sassen, S. (1991) 'Informal economy', in J.H. Molenkopf and M. Castells (eds), *Dual City: Restructuring New York*, New York: Russell Sage Foundation, pp. 79–101.

134   *Social justice and neoliberalism*

Scott, J.C. (1985) *Weapons of the Weak: Everyday Forms of Peasant Resistance*, London: Yale University Press.

Şenyapılı, T. (1981) *Gecekondu: Çevre İşçilerinin Mekanı*, Ankara: METU.

Standing, G. (1989) 'Global feminization through flexible labour', *World Development* 17(7): 1077–95.

Standing, G. (2002) *Beyond the New Paternalism: Basic Security as Equality*, London: Verso.

Tekeli, İ. (1978) 'Kalkınma Sürecinde Marjinal Kesim ve Türkiye Üzerine Bir Deneme', in İ. Tekeli and L. Erder (eds), *Yerleşme Yapısının Uyum Süreci Olarak İç Göçler*, Ankara: Hacettepe University, pp. 338–62.

Traub-Werner, M., and A. Cravey (2002) 'Spatiality, sweatshops and solidarity in Guatemala', *Social and Cultural Geography* 3(4): 383–401.

Türel, O. (1993) *Ekonomik Büyüme, İstihdam ve Sendikalar*, Ankara: METU Development Studies.

Varçın, R. (1996) *An Analysis of Conflict and Cooperation in the Informal Sector of the Economy in Turkey*, Ph.D. thesis, University of Oregon.

Velmeyer, H., and J. Petras (2005) 'Foreign aid, neoliberalism and US imperialism', in A. Saad-Filho and D. Johnston (eds), *Neoliberalism: A Critical Reader*, London: Pluto Press, pp. 120–26.

Waldinger, R., and M. Lapp (1993) 'Back to the sweatshop or ahead to the informal sector?', *International Journal of Urban and Regional Research* 17(1): 6–29.

Yeldan, E.A. (1994) 'The economic structure of power under Turkish structural adjustment: Prices, growth and accumulation', in F. Şenses (ed.), *Recent Industrialization Experience of Turkey in a Global Context*, London: Greenwood, pp. 75–90.

6

Transitions to work and the making of neoliberal selves: growing up in (the former) East Germany

Kathrin Hörschelmann

Contextualizing risk

A few years ago, the main regional newspaper in the former east German state of Thuringia started a new initiative to help schoolleavers make their first steps into the world of work: it offered them the opportunity to publish a free advertisement in the careers section of the weekend supplement in order to attract employers who might be able to offer a place for vocational training. The published adverts included a passport-sized photograph together with a brief description of qualifications, preferred career, key skills and personality traits. Employers were asked to contact the paper with offers for any of the young people selling themselves and their labour power in this way.

In a situation of high unemployment and severe shortage of vocational training places (Vogel 1999; Lutz 2001), the adverts symbolized most strikingly what is meant by the twin processes of individualization and neoliberalization. Couched in a discourse of choice, opportunity and self-initiative, they reveal the ugly face of labour commodification that makes young people highly vulnerable to exploitation. Their own career ambitions matter little as these young people seek to attract a potential employer, and, since salaries for vocational trainees are low, even those who succeed in gaining

FIGURE 6.1 Map of Germany

a training place through the advertisements will be unable to live without additional financial support from parents or social services.

Finding paid employment is, of course, a major route to establishing independent lives and towards at least partial self-fulfilment for many young people. To talk in terms of exploitation and labour commodification thus risks undervaluing the significance of (paid) work for a young person's sense of self-worth, for achieving a certain material standard of living and for sustaining important social relations. It does, however, draw attention to the unequal power relations that continue to shape young people's lives under the very conditions of individualization that are presented as liberating and pluralizing in neoliberal parlance.

In this chapter, I highlight the pressures that bear on young people in eastern Germany as they search for training and employment opportunities that will enable them to achieve their wider life ambitions. I describe the fractured nature of trajectories into work that ensue from difficult labour market conditions and aim to show how young people negotiate them. The chapter is based on interviews with 101 young people in the Saxon city of Leipzig (Figure 6.1).[1] Participants were recruited in youth clubs and interviewed in group discussions that were held over five weeks in 2003. Most of the young people were between 12 and 18 years of age and of mixed gender and educational background, but in some friendship groups younger and older participants joined the discussions (Table 6.1).

As might be expected, the issue of work and post-16 education was most relevant to those nearing the end of secondary school – that is, from about 14/15 years of age onwards. Although the research focused primarily on identity effects of young people's engagements with transnational youth cultures, questions of employment and material security figured large in the discussions with older participants, who drew strong connections between their lifestyle options and career opportunities. While the diversity of their interests in music, fashion and media could easily be said to mirror postmodern youth cultures elsewhere (Epstein 1998; Miles 2000), the material insecurities that many of the participants in this project encountered limited the extent to which they could revel in 'conspicuous consumption' and meant that diverse cultural styles did not necessarily translate into more fragmented identities embracing instability and flux (Hörschelmann and Schäfer 2005; Hörschelmann 2008). On the one hand, interviewees prioritized finding a (fulfilling) long-term career over other options and aimed to establish trusting social relations, strong friendships, belonging to peer groups and good relations with their families. On

TABLE 6.1   Summary of focus groups in the Leipzig study

	Activity[a]	Ages	Gender	Education[b]	Parents[c]
A	Unsupervised club	10–13	4 female 1 male	Special needs students: 4 lower, 1 medium grade	2 unemployed 1 blue-collar 2 service 3 unknown
B	Drawing course	11–14	3 female 2 male	4 higher grade, 1 medium grade	2 blue-collar 2 service 4 professional
C	Photography course	19–23	2 female 3 male	4 university students 1 nursing student	1 unemployed 3 blue-collar 1 service 4 professional
D	Unsupervised club	10–19	2 female 6 male	5 medium grade 2 lower grade 1 vocational college	4 unemployed 1 housewife 3 blue-collar 6 service 2 unknown
I	Model-building course	10–13	4 male	2 higher grade 1 medium grade 1 lower grade	1 unemployed 3 blue-collar 4 service
E	Unsupervised club	14–18	3 female 6 male	8 medium grade 1 vocational college	2 unemployed 2 housewives 1 early retired 1 retraining 4 blue-collar 6 service 2 unknown
F	Privately funded club, running club café	13–16	4 female 1 male	2 medium grade 3 higher grade	1 blue-collar 2 service 6 professional 1 unknown
G	Arts club	15–17	4 female 3 male	1 medium grade 6 higher grade	7 service 6 professional 1 unknown
H	Supervised weekly club	15–19	12 female	7 higher grade 4 vocational college 1 unknown/no grade	3 unemployed 4 blue-collar 14 service 2 professional 1 self-employed

Notes

a Some of the groups met regularly for specific courses; others met daily or weekly and were either completely unsupervised or supervised by a youth worker, who would occasionally run activities with them.
b Lower grade = Hauptschule; medium grade = Mittelschule/Realschule; higher grade = Gymnasium.
c Blue-collar includes unskilled to skilled factory workers and those working in artisanal production (butchers, bakers). Service workers include low-skilled cleaners as well as skilled office workers, public service workers, nurses and health workers. Professionals include teachers, university lecturers, engineers.

the other hand, collective identities were articulated through 'old' ethnic, nationalistic and regional categories that excluded and worked to scapegoat others, particularly immigrants. Individualistic lifestyles were more characteristic of older participants from higher-level schools, who were better educated and from predominantly wealthier family backgrounds. Younger participants and those with lower levels of educational attainment rarely departed from the dominant style of their peer group.

While some embraced the greater choice of lifestyles that neoliberalization potentially entails, most worried about employment insecurities and saw such insecurity as a major threat to their livelihoods. In a situation where two-thirds of the working-age population are either long-term unemployed or constantly moving between temporary employment, shorter periods of unemployment and (re)training measures (Vogel 1999; Lutz 2001), it should not be surprising that many young people opt to vote 'with their feet', planning to move to western Germany or abroad in the future in order to gain (better) employment (Dienel 2005; Förster 2004). Mobility combines with a range of other measures of 'governing the self' (Rose 1996, 1999) to meet the perceived requirements of an unstable labour market, such as being resourceful, entrepreneurial, and able to adapt to change at short notice (Kelly 2006; Burchell 1996).

Individualization and governmentality

One way to conceptualize how young people in eastern Germany respond to the difficult economic situation is through the theory of individualization developed by Ulrich Beck in his work on 'risk society' (Beck 1986, 1993; Beck and Beck-Gernsheim 2002). Beck's key argument is that industrialized societies have produced a wide range of new risks that erode confidence in the effectiveness and validity of existing political, economic, scientific and technological mechanisms. He develops a framework that relates the emergence of new global risks to changes in social structures, arguing that individuals are affected increasingly equally by risks and that their responses are shaped less and less by traditional solidarities such as those of class. Greater wealth no longer protects against some of the risks produced by industrialized society and there is thus less polarization between those affected or not affected by risks than used to be the case in class society. Beck argues that social inequalities have not disappeared but that the general level of wealth has increased with the welfare state and has, as a consequence, eroded the basis for class solidarity. Unemployment is one of the issues he focuses on, which, while recognizing that some marginalized groups are more severely affected, he describes as a temporary process, a life phase (or several) that more and more people encounter at some stage in their lives. Beck (1986, 1993) recognizes the persistence of social inequalities, but sees them as increasingly untied from class structures and as forming temporary phases during an individual's life course. As a consequence, individuals increasingly see inequalities as caused by personal characteristics and actions rather than by societal conditions and social structures (Beck and Beck-Gernsheim 2002). Individuals are thus forced to make themselves into the centre of their life plans:

> As the range of options widens and the necessity of deciding between them grows, so too does the need for individually performed actions, for adjustment, coordination, integration. If they are not to fail, individuals must be able to plan for the long term and adapt to change; they must organize and improvise, set goals, recognize obstacles, accept defeats and attempt new starts. They need initiative, tenacity, flexibility and tolerance of frustration. (Beck and Beck-Gernsheim 2002: 4)

Beck's work is based on analyses of the west German, post-war welfare state. It assumes the existence of a welfare state with its dual effects of, on the one hand, universalizing rights, opportunities, and access to basic material necessities, and, on the other hand, treating its citizens as individuals with responsibility for using those rights and opportunities (Beck 1993). He recognizes the need to differentiate between different forms of risk society, but offers precious little insight into how to analyse such differences and how to understand social conditions in other parts of the world. Beck mentions the possibility of 'poverty individualization', but offers few detailed insights into its causes and conditions. He also underestimates the continuing importance of social structures for placing individuals unequally in risk society. Individualization pressures may indeed come to bear on individuals from all backgrounds, but how they are able to respond to them and how severely they may be affected by taking the *wrong* decisions differs significantly between social groups.

This has been a central point of critique for many commentators. Evans (2002: 262) has thus challenged 'the simplistic application of the concept of "individualization" in different socioeconomic and cultural environments, in ways which assume unilateral trends within undifferentiated contexts of "modernization"', while authors such as Furlong and Cartmel (1997), Roberts (1995), Bynner et al. (1997) and Isengard (2003) have highlighted the continued significance of socio-economic differences in young people's lives. Yet, a more critical engagement with the ethnocentric assumptions of Beck's work and the exploitative consequences of individualization for those most disadvantaged by unequal global socio-economic conditions has been a long time coming. Cross-cultural researchers are beginning to challenge the former (see Amit-Talai and Wulff 1995; Ansell 2005), while the latter is most explicitly addressed in recent work on governmentality and subjectivity that follows a Foucauldian framework (Foucault 1988; Rose 1996, 1999; Kelly 2006; Walkerdine 2003) as well as in historical materialist critiques of neoliberalism (Brenner and Theodore 2002; Harvey 1999, 2005; Bourdieu 1998).

I draw explicitly on these critical engagements in the following discussion in order to move beyond a purely descriptive account of individualization processes, for which Beck's work is indeed valuable, towards highlighting the less voluntaristic aspects of neoliberal subjectivities, the continuation of unequal power relations and the significance of context (Walkerdine 2003). An important issue is not to underrate young people's active participation in the making of their lives, their creative engagements with present circumstances (James et al. 1998; Jenks 1996), and the benefits that they derive from the diversity of lifestyles that current market societies potentially offer them (Miles 2000). Remembering this is especially important in the post-socialist east German context in which this research is placed. Young people here certainly enjoy a greater variety of biographical options, political views and cultural identities than their parents and grandparents did. Yet it could be argued that this increased choice is a surface illusion and that the material securities which socialism offered in return for political conformity allowed more freedom for creative self-expression and active participation in social life.

While at first sight many of the responses detailed below seem to match Beck's arguments on individualization, they differ in one important respect: the individualization strategies that most participants described were not an end in themselves, but a means to achieve more predictable, stable livelihoods and biographies. Further, while Beck argues that risk society creates new structures of inequality that can affect everyone at various stages of their lives, thus making class less and less relevant, the young people interviewed in this project had very different resources at their disposal to meet the demands of individualization. Growing up in a structurally disadvantaged region also made their lives more precarious and risky. Socio-economic, contextual conditions affected their individual opportunities and the strategies they would need to adopt to respond to risks arising from their particular geographical location (Cartmel 2004; Jentsch and Shucksmith 2004; Bynner 2005; Walther et al. 2005). Longitudinal research conducted between 1987 and 2004 by Förster (2004) on young east Germans' experiences of societal change shows clearly the extent of structural disadvantage and its effects on people's evaluation of market society. By 2004, two-thirds of the 31-year-old interviewees had already experienced unemployment and 34 per cent had been out of work more than once. Förster concludes that unemployment runs through the whole population and affects not just those who are made redundant, but also those who have indirect experiences of it through families and friends, creating a collective sense of disadvantage that limits people's identification with the current social order.

Such findings very clearly run counter to Beck's more optimistic anticipation of the opportunities for self-fulfilment that a work-poor, time-rich society may be able to offer (Beck and Beck-Gernsheim 2002). They point to the need for a more thoroughly cross-cultural and situated approach, which informs critique rather than just describing an assumed universal condition that, on closer inspection, turns out to be very particular indeed. For this, we need to turn to the work of anthropologists, sociologists and geographers of youth and childhood who develop context-specific, relational accounts of age and social reproduction (Katz 2004; Skelton and Valentine 1998; Ansell 2005; Talai and Wulff 1995; James et al. 1998). Marxist critiques of what Harvey (2005) calls 'dispossession by accumulation' and Foucauldian analyses of processes of governing the self (Rose 1996, 1999) are further helpful for understanding why expressions of individualization are not simply to be equated with laissez-faire, postmodern, plural lifestyle options. Foucauldian perspectives approach individualization as a discourse rather than as a factual consequence of socio-economic and cultural changes and as such allow a better insight into the relations of power and knowledge that produce individuals *as* entrepreneurial selves. As Kelly (2006: 8) has argued,

> certain psychological discourses articulate with (Neo)Liberal views of enterprise to produce a view of the Self as the entrepreneurial Self. (Neo)Liberalism emerges, not only as a means of governing the State, the economy, and civil society, but also as a means of governing in these domains via the rational, autonomous, responsible behaviours and dispositions of a free, prudent, active Subject we can identify as the entrepreneurial Self.

The subjectivities thus created are characterized by major contradictions between the demand for flexibility, on the one hand, and the requirement for coherent, stable selves that are able to deal with constantly changing demands, on the other hand. Walkerdine (2003: 241) describes this cogently:

> It is argued that these times demand a subject who is capable of constant self-invention. Such a subject is presumed by, as well as being the intended product of, contemporary forms of education and training, and is a subject who is propped up and supported by a whole array of psychological support, most particularly forms of counselling and therapy ... While self-realisation is what is expected of the life project and one in which success is judged by the psychological capacities to succeed, the ability to handle uncertainty, the never knowing where work will come from etc., in fact produces an almost inevitable failure that will be lived as a personal failure ... [T]he subject is supposed to be able to choose who they are from a myriad offerings, who can make themselves. But, this subject is actually also supposed to be sustained by a stable centre, an ego capable of resilience.

The following analysis shows how these contradictions play out in practice for young east Germans in their search for meaningful future life trajectories. First, I examine how they view their future employment prospects and what possibilities and constraints they anticipate. This is followed by a discussion of 'techniques of the self' that have become a primary strategy for managing entry into the labour market. I highlight the extent to which individualization is embraced by participants as something they *can* do (especially in a post-socialist context where revolutionary politics are thoroughly discredited), but also show the important effects of uneven access to resources such as social networks, cultural capital and (parental) material security on young people's ability to tackle biographical risks.

Tackling uncertainty

Like other states in East Central Europe, eastern Germany adopted a neoliberal, 'shock therapy' approach to the transition from state socialism to capitalism that assumed 'that transition is a relatively unproblematic implementation of a set of policies involving economic liberalisation and marketisation alongside democratisation' (Smith and Pickles 1998: 2; Bradshaw and Stenning 2004). Yet eastern Germany's particular path differed from other post-socialist states due to the decision to unify Germany in 1990 via the route of annexation, which led to the wholesale adoption of western Germany's economic and political system in the former GDR (Dunford 1998; Behrend 1995). Practically overnight, east German businesses were faced with competition from their more efficient western counterparts, had to adapt to radically new regulations, management practices and trade structures, respond to shifting consumer demands, and sell their products at the same price levels and to the same markets as western firms. This led to 'an unprecedented recession only compensated by huge transfers from West Germany' (Dunford 1998: 100). Manufacturing and mining output declined drastically and unemployment levels soared. Transfers from the west to the east prevented the steep increase in poverty that has been witnessed in other post-socialist states and led to rising incomes for those in work, while also securing pensions at relatively generous levels (Hörschelmann 2004). Yet unemployment levels have remained high and social inequalities have increased notably over the last twenty years. They are set to rise further in the coming years as a result of recent changes in the German welfare legislation which curtail redundancy benefits and other forms of social wage (Paugam 2004).

One key indicator of structural inequalities between social groups and the German regions is child poverty. The rates of relative child poverty, measured as the percentage of children growing up in families with less than 50 per cent of the national median income, is substantially higher in all of the east German states than in their west German counterparts (21 per cent compared with a national rate of 17 per cent (Bertram 2006: 38). Since incomes continue to be lower in eastern Germany, however, the rate of relative child poverty measured against the median income of the eastern federal states only is lower at 14 per cent (compared with 16 per cent for the west German states (Bertram 2006)). Income inequalities are thus still somewhat less pronounced in eastern than in western Germany, but high rates of unemployment and lower incomes mean that children and young people in eastern Germany experience significantly higher levels of deprivation, and this in turn affects their education, health, social inclusion and future employment prospects.

Just as rates of deprivation and inequality have increased, state funding for welfare programmes and for other means of enhancing children's and young people's social well-being have been reduced and continue to be cut or privatized. There are few remaining publicly funded leisure facilities and social clubs, and those located in the most deprived areas of cities such as Leipzig tend to be underfunded and have few trained staff. This, together with the difficult situation of parents who may not be able to support their children either with financial resources or through social networks and informed career advice, produces a highly uneven terrain of opportunity for young people facing competition in a tight job market. Those most in need of diversifying their training and, if necessary, moving to western Germany to find employment are often those with the fewest resources to support them. Not only do they thus start out from a more risky position, but they also face greater future risks, since they have fewer resources to fall back on and tend to enter lower-paid,

FIGURE 6.2   Regenerated turn-of-century housing in Leipzig's South East (Südvorstadt)

less stable employment that becomes a trap rather than a temporary stage in the life cycle.

In the project discussed here, a majority of participants had already experienced unemployment in their families or among friends and worried a great deal about how it might affect them in the future. They described not just the material effects of joblessness but also social and psychological impacts such as declining self-respect, depression, withdrawal from social life and constant worries about the future. In 'Leipzig East', an old working-class district not far from the city centre, we interviewed a mixed-gender group of special needs students between the ages of 12 and 14, who were particularly disadvantaged by their low levels of educational attainment and their families' difficult socio-economic situation. They met on a daily basis in the club and mostly came from the neighbourhood, in most cases living only a few doors away. The club offered some organized activities like a cooking class and board games, but they mainly just 'hung out' there and used the club as their main meeting space. Staff at the club made it clear that they did not have the

FIGURE 6.3   High-rise area in Leipzig West (Grünau)

capacity to offer much more than their presence and looking after the facilities. This was a chronic feature, particularly of publicly funded youth centres and clubs. They had only a few fully paid members of staff (normally just one or two) and were otherwise run by untrained volunteers and temporary workers on job-creation schemes. The services that young people, especially from poorer backgrounds without finance to pay for leisure activities, encountered were thus often insufficient to meet their needs, if not in terms of the provision of space and facilities then in terms of trained staff input and offers for organized activities that participants from wealthier backgrounds took for granted. Further, the city authorities placed emphasis on sports, which in practice privileged particular hegemonic masculinities and excluded many girls, for whom special groups were then organized by some clubs.

Discussion with the group in 'Leipzig East' frequently centred on the question of jobs and education, despite the fact that we focused primarily on their leisure interests. When asked whether they knew any people who were unemployed, all but one of the participants cited a parent. They disagreed on the psychological effects of joblessness, but identified work as essential for material wellbeing:

> Interviewer: Do you know any people who are unemployed?
> Bettina:[2] Yes, my mum.
> Sabine: Yes, my mum too. She has a back problem.
> Nick: My dad is also unemployed. But I won't tell you why …
> Interviewer: If you know people who are unemployed, what's that like?
> Sabine: Hmmm.
> Bettina: They just sit at home and don't do anything proper.
> Sabine: No, my mum doesn't do that.
> Bettina: Well, my mum does.… She tries to get work every now and then but she doesn't get any.
> Interviewer: Well, it's not that easy, is it?
> Bettina: She's trying to retire now…
> Interviewer: Do people change when they become unemployed?
> Bettina: Yes.
> Sabine: Well, my mum hasn't changed. She's still the same.
> Bettina: They sit around and drink more…
> Interviewer: But is it important to have work?
> Sabine: Yes, it is for the money.
> Bettina: Well, we all want to have more and more, but without money, you can't do anything. (Group A)

Not far from this club, we met another group in a youth cultural centre who were in the same age range, but from higher-level schools. Although they were in the main from more privileged backgrounds and only one of them had a parent who was unemployed, they also highlighted the significance of work for material security and prestige:

> Karin: I would say that people who like to work, OK, it's always stressful, but I think everybody would rather work than sit at home and, I mean, what do you want to do all day at home? It can make you quite depressed after a while, I would say. I don't think I could do that…
> Interviewer: So why is it so important for people to work?
> Karin: Well, to earn money and not be at home all day, and I think people who are unemployed are more likely to become losers [*Absteiger*] generally.
> Marcel: Yes, prestige, to put it like that. (Group B)

Paid employment in a meaningful occupation was thus still seen as crucial for self-identity, social respect and fulfilment in life. Rather than embracing possibilities for alternative lifestyles based on a minimum social wage, even those of our participants who had experienced and enjoyed aspects of this aimed for paid employment and a long-term career in order to gain both self-confidence and the respect of others. The issue of 'respect' was raised particularly by male participants, who worried about their chances of finding a partner if they were financially insecure and without a stable career. Failing to get work thus threatened not only their material situation but also their chances of having a family and of 'fitting in' with general social norms:

> Interviewer: Is unemployment an issue that you worry about every now and then? Work, finding work?
>
> Andy: I was unemployed once for two months and I worried about it then.... For me it was like, I couldn't get unemployment benefit, had to live off income support, I mean, it was only for two months but after those two months I was pretty depressed.
>
> Nadja: Really? Why?
>
> Andy: Well, I mean, getting income support!
>
> Nadja: OK, well.
>
> Interviewer: Can you tell me why you were feeling so depressed?
>
> Andy: Well, back then I didn't have any prospects. That was straight after my social service year [replaces military service]. I hadn't got a training place and I had to pay my rent somehow and it didn't look like something was going to come up anytime soon, or, anyway, I didn't have an aim in front of me. And that's why those two months were pretty hard.
>
> Interviewer: Why is that so difficult? I mean, couldn't you have said, okay, the rent, I'll get the money together somehow. Why is it so bad to be without work? Why is work so important?
>
> Andy: It's not important. I mean, if I had the money, I could imagine living quite well without work. I think I would be able to keep myself busy. I think it's in order to have something to do. I mean, you don't just get less money, you also get a worse, well it's stupid to say reputation, whether you deserve that or not, but in any case it's bad to say you are unemployed. The feeling that you are achieving something, I mean, that also gives you a sense of inner satisfaction, or at least that's how I feel at work. (Group C)

'Flexibility' was very much a means to an end rather than an end in itself. While opportunities to travel and to experience different lifestyles were embraced by some (particularly better-educated) participants, most aimed for material security and continuity in their social bonds and identities:

> Interviewer: So, if you had more money, what would you do more?
> Robert: Well, put the money away somewhere and that's that.
> Peter: Yes.
> Robert: As far away as I can.
> Stefan: On the account, that would be best.
> Tom: To save for something.
> Stefan: Yes, to save for something.
> Interviewer: For what?
> Stefan: Don't know.
> Peter: A house.
> Stefan: Yes, a house.
> Peter: So you might be better off at some point, better than if you spend it all at once. In the end you have, maybe you have a new house. And then you can also live cheaper, still have work...
> Interviewer: To have a house, is that a dream for you, a goal?
> Peter: Yes.
> Stefan: Yes, of course.
> Peter: But then I would also want to have a family. I wouldn't do it without a family. (Group D)

Where participants' parents were unemployed, they described not only how the mood in their families had changed, but also how pressures to live more frugally affected their self-esteem and position in school peer groups, especially as they could not participate in the types of consumption that would mark them out as fashionable and cool. One of our youngest participants, 11-year-old Steffen, described this indirectly as he talked about a friend whose parents were unemployed:

> I really don't care what somebody wears. For instance, one of my friends is poor. The parents don't have work and so he doesn't wear the newest clothes. He just wears older clothes and so on, but he is still my best friend. (Group I)

Participants who had already finished school often described unpredictable, fractured or unsuccessful pathways into paid

FIGURE 6.4   Shopping street in the centre of Leipzig

employment and further education. Their search for work included not only extensive numbers of applications, but also seeking further training through (normally unpaid) placements that, in many cases, did not lead to a job. Again and again, participants worried that they may have exceedingly high expectations and would need to revise their standards in order to get work. The following quotation from group D shows this clearly. The group consisted mainly of boys who were about to leave, or had already left, school. Only one of them had found an apprenticeship with the local tram company through family contacts, after his grandmother had paid for his driving licence. The others had either applied unsuccessfully or gone from one temporary job to another:

> Interviewer: Do you worry about unemployment?
> Christina: Yes.
> Robert: I worry about that every day.
> Interviewer: But you have a job now, don't you? …
> Robert: Yes, but you never know for how long.
> Interviewer: What sort of job would you like to do?
> Robert: I'd do anything, like I said. Whatever comes along, I'll take it. As long as the money's right …

Stefan: I would do almost anything. But at the moment my results are so poor that, and with the job interviews now, that's really not my thing.

Interviewer: Have you had to go to any interviews yet?

Stefan: No, so far it's only been rejections and so on...

Interviewer: And where have you applied?

Stefan: Well, as a shop assistant or something like that.

Interviewer: OK, but you don't think you've got much of a chance?

Stefan: (shakes his head)

Interviewer: No. In that case, I'll cross my fingers for you.

Stefan: Because, in the past, all you had to do was to go there, 'yes, OK, we'll take you', and that's just not the way it is anymore.

Peter: Well, it used to be ...

Stefan: All those tests and all that. They really test you ... I never get as far as the job interview. I only get as far as buying the stamp, sending it off and waiting for an answer, which is a rejection.

Nick: But that's just the way it is.

Peter: Same here.

Robert: It's hard to find a job nowadays.

Stefan: They go more by your looks nowadays.

Robert: Yes, that's bad nowadays.

Interviewer: Stephan, have you ever done a placement or something like that?

Stefan: Hm.

Interviewer: Yes?

Stefan: Yes, I really quite liked it and that's why I came up with the idea to do something like that. That was in the DIY store, and I really wanted to apply there again, but they don't take anybody on. (Group D)

Participants who had not yet found an apprenticeship were anticipating needing to complete a 'preparation' or 'social' year. They criticized these schemes as a waste of time that did not help them to develop useful skills and qualifications. They felt stigmatized rather than enabled by such state measures to keep young people in education and off the unemployment register. The risks to their future development were significant. Without recognized career training, their only option would be to take on unskilled, low-paid jobs, and they were unlikely to find more stable and skilled employment even if they moved to other parts of Germany. This system thus risks producing a permanently excluded class of young workers, who, at the same time, are less and less able to rely on state benefits to prevent them from slipping into poverty.

Governing the self

Despite their frustrations, few of the young people that were interviewed questioned the structural causes of unemployment and economic decline. Instead, they focused on their own failings through lack of effort or 'messing up' at school and, as above, worried about their appearance and mannerisms, thus emphasizing issues of style, embodiment and cultural capital that are gained through techniques of self-government and personal effort. Few reflected critically on the ways in which family background and social networks can impact on such apparently 'personal' characteristics (Bourdieu 1984, 1999; Côte 2002). Their responses were strikingly similar to those presented by Evans (2002) in her summary of findings from an Anglo-German project. Evans (2002: 262) highlights how,

> despite feelings of lack of control in the least advantaged groups and disbelief in some of the principles of individualism and meritocracy, most research participants attached considerable importance to individual effort and expressed the belief that if people worked hard and achieved suitable qualifications then they should be able to follow their own independent pathway in adult life. Social connections, forging them and 'making them work for you', as well as the importance of image and self-presentation were much emphasized. They are certainly not blind to the influences of economic and social structures, but the least advantaged emphasized that they have to be 'realistic' in their individual aspirations and goals.

Similarly, participants in our project primarily focused on their own efforts and the need to 'try harder', even in the face of seemingly insurmountable obstacles. Thus the group of boys below remained adamant that finding an apprenticeship was mainly a matter of time and effort, despite having made their first disappointing experiences with failed applications:

Interviewer: Right. So is that a problem then, to find an apprenticeship here?
Paul: Yes.

Adam: Yes.

Tilo: Not really.

Interviewer: So is that something you are having to think about now?

Adam: Yes.

Tilo: I mean, it's not really a problem. You just have to achieve something in school and then apply often enough. For instance, I know somebody who didn't have the best school results, but he got offered four places for an apprenticeship. He just tried hard, early on, and applied a lot.

Interviewer: Have you sent off any applications yet?

Paul: Yes.

Adam: Of course.

Interviewer: And how is it going?

Paul: Shit.

Interviewer: Really?

Paul: Well, yes.

Tilo: I don't have a place at the moment…

Jonas: The problem of most young people is that they go to the job centre, but if you've finished school, you need to go from firm to firm and ask, because the job centre doesn't have all the training places. I know that from my own experience.… I made the mistake of not going round asking. And that's what many people do wrong. They think, well, I have my school-leaving certificate, I'll get something anyway…

Tilo: Firms demand a lot more and if you don't achieve that then you can't be surprised that you don't get a training place and then you can't just say that there aren't any training places. I think that's complete nonsense.

Jonas: They just don't want to have a training place.

Tilo: Precisely. I mean, when I see that some of them only apply five or six times. That's not enough! You have to apply sixty, seventy times…

Interviewer: So have you done that, sixty, seventy? I find that quite a lot.

Tilo: Well, it is a lot, between thirty and sixty is a lot. I also haven't sent many off. I have sent about fifteen. I'll honestly say, I was lazy and now I have, I am forced more or less to go to FE college [*Fachoberschule*]. But that doesn't bother me. (Group E)

Failure at school was identified as a key obstacle to gaining (desirable) employment and participants were highly critical of their own or their friends' difficulties of achieving the required results in school for particular occupations. They were highly aware of the premium placed on good qualifications. For those from lower educational backgrounds, the dominant question was one of achieving a school leaving certificate that would allow them to train for their desired occupation (see group A below), while for those who were already at higher-level schools the issue was one of combating grade inflation (Bourdieu and Passeron 1977) and adding additional skills and experiences to their CV (see group F below):

Ines: I want to finish school and then I'll try to do my *Abitur* [higher-level certificate].

Sabine: But at the moment it looks like you will need to repeat the year!

Ines: What?

Sabine: It already looks like you will need to repeat the year. Everybody in our class looks like they need to repeat the year...

Interviewer: Would you say you have better chances with an *Abitur*?

Sabine: If you have a good middle-school qualification, that's enough, because you have better marks, you know more about stuff, so you can get a better qualification. Then I would say, if you have a grade 9 [lower] qualification, I would still go studying, that would be the best thing. Or a grade 10, and would go studying for a couple of terms. (Group A)

Interviewer: Do you feel like it's possible to achieve what you want to achieve?

Anne: Of course. For instance, I went to comprehensive school [*Realschule*] and the first major goal that I have had to work really hard for was that I would get accepted at the Evangelical School and I worked really hard for that, tried to do that and, yes, now I have been accepted ... I think, if you really try hard and you really want it and make some compromises for that, then it's going to work out OK...

Sarah: [If you want to go abroad], then you have to prepare really early for that. For instance, I haven't decided what I want to do yet, I mean I know what I want to do, but it'll change over the next three years. Like, for instance, this English Certificate. That's not like you can sit there and think, OK, now I have this English thing, in three years *Abitur*, and leave it at that. You have to carry on with that, like, if you just do school it's not enough. You always have to do a little bit on top of that. (Group F)

In virtually all of the groups interviewed, individual ways of tackling the difficult job situation were emphasized over and above calls for a sustained political response. The discourses clearly followed an individualistic rhetoric of self-governance, emphasizing the need to persevere, to be flexible and geographically, as well as downwardly, mobile. Nonetheless, some participants highlighted the exasperation of those who had failed to find employment despite enormous dedication. Circumstances beyond individuals' control that were highlighted as 'unfair' included age and gender discrimination and the severe shortage of employment opportunities in 'the East'. Their answers again emphasized individual solutions such as temping, retraining and, most of all, moving to the west of Germany:

> Interviewer: Do you worry about not getting a job?
> Andy: Well, you still have the choice to go somewhere else, don't you? I mean, somewhere where there is work.
> Interviewer: Where is that?
> Nadja: In the West...
> Interviewer: So would you say that opportunities are unevenly distributed?
> Karl: No, why?
> Interviewer: Because you have to go to the west to get work?
> Andy: Well.
> Karl: That's your choice. I mean, the opportunities are equally distributed. You can go where you want to go. You always have that opportunity.
> Interviewer: And if you want to stay here?
> Andy: Then you have to be a bit flexible. (Group C)

Most of our participants were prepared to move to western Germany for a training place or job. Some saw this as a great opportunity and looked forward to the possibility of gaining new experiences. This applied particularly to better educated participants, for whom mobility meant searching for the best career chances and developing exciting new lifestyles. We also interviewed young people from poorer backgrounds, however, for whom moving to the west or even just to another city was a chance to 'get away', to escape from difficult circumstances (Hörschelmann and Schäfer 2007). Apart from these cases, mobility was seen as a necessity rather than a 'free' choice and something that involved high emotional costs (also see Jones 1995). The risk of losing connections to friends and family as well as leaving a city that they enjoyed living in were some of the reasons why the prospect of having to move away worried many of the young people we interviewed:

> Interviewer: Would you go to the west or would you rather stay in the east?
> Kara: Yes, I would.
> Hannah: Yes.
> Maria: Well, I don't know, I think...
> Susanne: Well, I don't have anything against them.
> Hannah: If I got a good job in the west that I'm happy with and if people are OK, then I don't have a problem with that. That's the same as if I had a stupid job in the east, where I don't like people, don't know, then I would also go to the west.
> Tina: And if you got a better offer in the west, then of course you would go. (Group G)

Independent of their education, gender and class status, our participants actively participated in building lives commensurate with risk society. Their strategies included better education and, for the privileged, accumulating socio-cultural capital in their leisure time, spatial mobility, flexibility, trying harder/making more of an effort and revising their expectations. While this may be disappointing for social theorists interested in more revolutionary, collective responses to the structural inequalities that neoliberal economies perpetuate, from the perspective of many young people there is no alternative. 'Governing the self' is the one thing they can do here and now. It involves no major leaps of faith and no going back to the 'good old days' of socialism, which in eastern Germany remains largely discredited, despite the electoral successes of the 'left' party. This is not to say, however, that young people embark on their strategies of individual 'risk management' from the position of a level playing field. In addition to different possibilities for gaining cultural capital through higher and extra-curricular education (or, as Côte 2002 puts it, identity capital), social capital in the form of networks and family support systems makes a major difference to the risks that individuals take (also see Jentsch and Shucksmith 2004; Evans 2002; Lehmann

2004). Strategies of relying on family support and networks included the (unpopular) option of living at the parents' expense, getting help from a parent to find information about future career opportunities and using their connections to particular businesses. In some cases, parents were setting up small businesses (like shops) in order to provide future possibilities for their children:

> Sabine: Well, I want to be a vet or...
> Ines: I don't know.
> Sabine: I want to be a vet or, there was something else I wanted to be, shop assistant, normal doctor or something like that.
> Ines: Pet shop assistant, like.
> Interviewer: Like a carer?
> Sabine: No, my parents want to open a pet shop ... or an animal shelter. (Group A)

While participants rarely articulated a critique of structural inequalities, negotiating the demands of individualization led some to look for collective scapegoats that could be blamed for the difficulties they encountered. Contrary to what may be expected, this did not contradict their attitudes towards self-discipline, flexibility and hard work. Rather, they blamed immigrants for receiving social benefits for little effort, for not fitting in with the logic of individualization that they themselves allegedly pursued. They wildly exaggerated both the numbers of immigrants living in Leipzig and the benefits available to them. Xenophobic hostilities were raised by both male and female participants from a range of backgrounds, though more radical opinions were expressed by lower-educated, poorer young men:

> Robert: I don't hate foreigners who work, who do everything like us Germans. So, if they work ... There are foreigners who arrive at the social office with a Mercedes! Yes, that's awful. They wait for five minutes at the social office, get a cheque and go home.
> Michael: They get everything for nothing.
> Robert: That's awful. You should have a look at my flat and then look at the flat of a foreigner.
> Interviewer: So you think they have more?
> Robert: Well, of course. And expensive, and expensive!
> Michael: They have five video recorders, three cameras...
> Robert: And my flat is nearly falling to pieces...
> Michael: ...ten mobile phones.

Robert: ...because I can't afford anything...

Michael: The other day, when I went to the job centre, I saw a foreigner with the absolutely latest mobile phone. I would really like to know where they get the money for that. I haven't had as much money as they have in my whole life!

Robert: I'll have to earn that kind of money first, that they get. (Group D)

Such xenophobic views were, however, challenged in several of the groups, especially by those who valued alternative lifestyles, who had themselves experienced discrimination and/or who, like Doreen below, saw similarities between their own need to be mobile and the situation of immigrants to Leipzig:

Anna: Sure, there are some [foreigners] that work hard here and provide for their family and pay their taxes and so on. I don't mind those, but you know, those that just move here somehow stupidly, well, they can do that elsewhere, they can do that in their own country...

Doreen: But what would you do, if for instance, assume you get a super cool job abroad. You said yourself that you could imagine working abroad...

Anna: Yes.

Doreen: And then they will think the same about you. Do you know how that will make you feel?

Lydia: Yes, but there are some here that just don't adapt themselves. (Group H)

'Individualization' does not in itself lead to greater openness towards others and a decline in racial, ethnic and national identities. It can, in fact, reinforce the competitive logic that underlies much revanchist, chauvinist politics. Yet, at the same time it offers the possibility of greater empathy and cosmopolitan 'openness' due to similarities of experience.

Conclusion

Rather than adopting universalizing *de facto* descriptions and theories of individualization, we need to remain alert to the processes of social differentiation that place individuals unequally along various axes of risk distribution (Mythen 2005; Green et al. 2000; Isengard

2003). Risks are historically, geographically and socially differenti-ated (in type, cause and effect) and experienced and perceived *from particular positions, in particular contexts.* While the responses of young people reflect individualization *discourses,* the research presented in this chapter suggests that we may more usefully think about indi-vidualization through a historical-materialist and Foucauldian lens in three interrelated ways:

- as an institutional (structural) requirement,
- as a political discourse,
- as a form of self-governance employed by young people to succeed in risk societies, entailing both compulsion and opportunity.

Such an approach keeps in focus *non-voluntaristic* aspects of indi-vidualization and offers a starting point for critique that recognizes socio-economic and political pressures bearing on individuals who seek viable biographical pathways through a situation that displays some strikingly stable features in terms of social structure. It retains a focus on young people's agency without ignoring the social context in which their actions unfold and against which they plan for the future (Lehman 2004; Evans 2002).

'Risks' may be unpredictable and distributed along axes that are no longer primarily determined by social status and location, but it is a step too far to proclaim therefore universal exposure to, and experi-ence of, them. The research presented here shows that young people require substantial cultural, social and economic capital to reduce the threat of failure in post-socialist risk societies. Yet in Germany the sources of these forms of capital are highly unevenly distributed between eastern and western parts of the country and within post-socialist eastern Germany itself. This places many young people in a position of far greater risk than their more affluent counterparts. Those who, because of the difficult structural situation and their already disadvantaged position, fail to gain long-term employment or further education after school enter a vicious cycle of temporary, dead-end jobs, periodic retraining or complete economic inactivity that fast decreases their future life options. They need enormous amounts of resilience, perseverance and sheer luck in order to break that cycle, since the harsh new welfare regime offers them few steps 'back on the ladder'. 'Governing the self' in line with neoliberal demands for flexibility, mobility and self-reliance may appear as the only option for young people whose bases of social support have been eroded, yet it will not tackle the underlying social inequalities that set them on such uneven paths into the future. For this, greater political commitment, solidarity and continuity are needed, none of which is forthcoming in the current climate of welfare cuts and 'tightened belts'.

Notes

1. The project was funded by the Economic and Social Research Council (Ref. R000223955) and focused on 'Globalisation, cultural practice and youth identity in former east Germany'.
2. All interviewee names have been changed to protect anonymity.

References

Amit-Talai, V., and H. Wulff (1995) *Youth Cultures: A Cross-Cultural Perspective*, London: Routledge.

Ansell, N. (2005) *Children, Youth and Development*, London: Routledge.

Beck, U. (1986) *Risikogesellschaft. Auf dem Weg in eine andere Moderne*, Frankfurt: Suhrkamp.

Beck, U. (1993) *Die Erfindung dea Politischen. Zu einer Theorie reflexiver Modernisierung*, Frankfurt: Suhrkamp.

Beck, U., and E. Beck-Gernsheim (2002) *Individualization: Institutionalized Individualism and its Social and Political Consequences*, London: Sage.

Behrend, H. (ed.) (1995) *German Unification: The Destruction of an Economy*, London: Pluto Press.

Bertram, H. (2006) 'Overview of child wellbeing in Germany: Policy towards a supportive environment for children', Innocenti Working Paper no. 2006–2, Florence: UNICEF Innocenti Research Centre.

Bourdieu, P. (1984) *Distinction: A Social Critique of the Judgement of Taste*, Cambridge MA: Harvard University Press.

Bourdieu, P. (1998) *Acts of Resistance: Against the New Myths of Our Time*, Cambridge: Polity Press.

Bourdieu, P. (1999) 'Site Effects', in P. Bourdieu (ed.), *The Weight of the World: Social Suffering in Contemporary Society*, Cambridge: Polity Press, pp. 123–9.

Bourdieu, P., and J.-C. Passeron (1977) *Reproduction in Education, Society and Culture*, London: Sage.

Bradshaw, M., and A. Stenning (eds) (2004) *East Central Europe and the Former Soviet Union: The Post-Socialist States*, London: Pearson.

Brenner, N., and N. Theodore (eds) (2002) *Spaces of Neoliberalism: Urban Restructuring in North America and Western Europe*, Oxford: Blackwell.

Burchell, G. (1996) 'Liberal government and techniques of the self', in A. Barry,

162   *Social justice and neoliberalism*

T. Osborne and N. Rose (eds), *Foucault and Political Reason: Liberalism, Neo-Liberalism and Rationalities of Government*, London: UCL Press, pp. 19–36.

Bynner, J., E. Ferri and P. Shepherd (eds) (1997) *Twenty-Something in the 1990s: Getting On, Getting By, Getting Nowhere*, Aldershot: Ashgate.

Bynner, J. (2005) 'Rethinking the youth phase of the life-course: The case for emerging adulthood?', *Journal of Youth Studies* 8(4): 367–84.

Cartmel, F. (2004) 'The labour market inclusion and exclusion of young people in rural labour markets in Scotland', in W. Mitchell, B. Bunton and E. Green (eds), *Young People, Risk and Leisure: Constructing Identities in Everyday Life*, London: Palgrave Macmillan, pp. 73–93.

Côte, J. (2002) 'The role of identity capital in the transition to adulthood: The individualization thesis explained', *Journal of Youth Studies* 5(2): 117–34.

Dienel, C. (ed.) (2005) *Abwanderung, Geburtenrückgang und regionale Entwicklung. Ursachen und Folgen des Bevölkerungsrückgangs in Ostdeutschland*, Wiesbaden: VS Verlag.

Dunford, M. (1998) 'Differential development, institutions, modes of regulation and comparative transitions to capitalism: Russia, the Commonwealth of Independent States and the former German Democratic Republic', in J. Pickles and A. Smith (eds), *Theorising Transition: The Political Economy of Post-Communist Transformations*, London: Routledge, pp. 76–114.

Epstein, J.S. (1998) *Youth Culture: Identity in a Postmodern World*, Oxford: Blackwell.

Evans, K. (2002) 'Taking control of their lives? Agency in young adult transitions in England and the new Germany', *Journal of Youth Studies* 5(3): 245–69.

Förster, P. (2004) *Ohne Arbeit keine Freiheit. Warum junge Ostdeutsche rund 15 Jahre nach dem Susammenbruch des Sozialismus noch nicht im gegenwärtigen Kapitalismus angekommen sind*, Leipzig: Rosa-Luxemburg-Stiftung.

Foucault, M. (1988) 'Technologies of the self', in L.H. Martin, H. Gutman and P.H. Hutton (eds), *Technologies of the Self: A Seminar with Michel Foucault*, Boston MA: University of Massachusetts Press, pp. 16–49.

Furlong, A., and F. Cartmel (1997) *Young People and Social Change: Individualization and Risk in Late Modernity*, Buckingham: Open University Press.

Green, E., W. Mitchell and R. Bunton (2000) 'Contextualizing risk and danger: An analysis of young people's perceptions of risk', *Journal of Youth Studies* 3(2): 109–26.

Harvey, D. (2005) *A Brief History of Neoliberalism*, Oxford: Oxford University Press.

Harvey, D. (1999) *The Limits to Capital*, London: Verso.

Hörschelmann, K. (2004) 'The social consequences of transformation', in M. Bradshaw and A. Stenning (eds), *East Central Europe and the Former Soviet Union: The Post-Socialist States*, London: Pearson, pp. 219–46.

Hörschelmann, K. (2008) 'Politics, lifestyle and identity: The story of Sven, east Germany', in C. Jeffrey and J. Dyson (eds), *Telling Young Lives: Portraits in Political Geography*, Philadelphia: Temple University Press, pp. 81–96.

Hörschelmann, K., and N. Schäfer (2005) 'Performing the global through the local: Young people's practices of identity formation in former East Germany', *Children's Geographies* 3(2): 219–42.

Hörschelmann, K., and N. Schäfer (2007) '"Berlin is not a foreign country, stupid!" Growing up "global" in eastern Germany', *Environment and Planning A* 39(8): 1855–72.

Isengard, B. (2003) 'Youth unemployment: Individual risk factors and institutional determinants. A case study of Germany and the United Kingdom', *Journal of Youth Studies* 6(4): 357–76.

James, A., C. Jenks and A. Prout (1998) *Theorizing Childhood*, Cambridge: Polity Press.

Jenks, C. (1996) *Childhood*, London: Routledge.

Jentsch, B., and M. Shucksmith (2004) *Young People in Rural Areas of Europe*, Aldershot: Ashgate.

Jones, G. (1995) *Leaving Home*, Buckingham: Open University Press.

Katz, C. (2004) *Growing Up Global: Economic Restructuring and Children's Everyday Lives*, Minneapolis: University of Minnesota Press.

Kelly, P. (2006) 'The entrepreneurial self and "Youth at-risk": Exploring the horizons of identity in the twenty-first century', *Journal of Youth Studies* 9(1): 17–32.

Lehman, W. (2004) '"For some reason I get a little scared": Structure, agency, and risk in school–work transitions, *Journal of Youth Studies* 7(4): 379–96.

Lutz, B. (2001) 'Im Osten ist die zweite Schwelle hoch. Fehlende Arbeitsplätze und Nachwuchsstau vor den Toren des Arbeitsmarktes', *Forschungsbericht aus dem ZSH*, 01–02, Halle.

Miles, S. (2000) *Youth Lifestyles in a Changing World*, Buckingham: Open University Press.

Mythen, G. (2005) 'Employment, individualization and insecurity: Rethinking the risk society perspective', *Sociological Review* 53(1): 129–49.

Paugam, S. (2004) 'Armut und soziale Exklusion: Eine soziologische Perspektive', in H. Häussermann, M. Kronauer and W. Siebel (eds), *An den Rändern der Städte. Armut und Ausgrenzung*, Frankfurt: Suhrkamp, pp. 71–96.

Roberts, K. (1995) *Youth and Unemployment in Modern Britain*, Buckingham: Open University Press.

Rose, N. (1996) 'Governing "advanced" liberal democracies', in A. Barry, T. Osborne and N. Rose (eds), *Foucault and Political Reason: Liberalism, Neoliberalism and Rationalities of Government*, London: UCL Press, pp. 37–64.

Rose, N. (1999) *Governing the Soul*, London: Free Association Books.

Skelton, T., and G. Valentine (eds) (1998) *Cool Places: Geographies of Youth Cultures*, London: Routledge.

Smith, A., and J. Pickles (1998) 'Introduction: Theorising transition and the political economy of transformation', in J. Pickles and A. Smith (eds), *Theorising Transition: The Political Economy of Post-Communist Transformations*, London: Routledge, pp. 1–24.

Vogel, B. (1999) 'Arbeitslosigkeit in Ostdeutschland. Konsequenzen für das Sozialgefüge und für die Wahrnehmung des gesellschaftlichen Wandels', *SOFI–Mitteilungen* 27.

Walkerdine, V. (2003) 'Reclassifying upward mobility: Femininity and the neoliberal subject', *Gender and Education* 15(3): 237–48.

Walther, A., B. Stauber and A. Pohl (2005) 'Informal networks in youth transitions in West Germany: Biographical resource or reproduction of social inequality?', *Journal of Youth Studies* 8(2): 221–40.

7

The emergence of a working poor: labour markets, neoliberalization and diverse economies in post-socialist cities

Adrian Smith, Alison Stenning, Alena Rochovská and Dariusz Świątek

Since the collapse of state socialism in East-Central Europe (ECE) there has been an extensive process of labour market transformation. Relatively secure and singular employment in state-owned enterprises has given way to greater labour market differentiation and uncertainty and increased unemployment. Labour shedding from former state-owned industries has been extensive as deindustrialization has proceeded (Smith 2000). But industrial decline has been accompanied both by the growth of new forms of employment and by increasing non-participation in the labour market (Rainnie et al. 2002). Sectoral restructuring has been connected to an expansion of service-sector activity, particularly in the major cities where it has created new jobs in both the highly paid finance and other intermediary sectors and a raft of less secure and low-paid employment in lower-status sectors. Many of these new growth sectors have been allied to changes in employment contracts and security, resulting in increasing insecurity in the labour market. Much of this labour market transformation has been associated with the neoliberalization of ECE societies as post-socialist transformation programmes have focused on restructuring the role of the state, increasing the emphasis on individualized responsibility and ethics, and extending the commodification of everyday life, from health care to public transportation and education.

These transformations have exacerbated the segmentation of ECE labour markets, creating several distinct labour markets characterized by very different pay, employment and status conditions and reinforcing social divisions. This chapter examines the growing phenomenon of insecure, poor-quality, contingent labour (Peck and Theodore 2001), the diversification of work among poorer households in post-socialist cities, and the implications for social justice. We explore the ways in which labour market restructuring and the precariousness of household livelihoods lead those who would traditionally have been seen as workers into a diversity of class positions (Gibson and Graham 1992; Smith and Stenning 2006). These workers negotiate formal and informal employment, domestic and other unpaid labour and forms of self-employment and entrepreneurship. These shifting forms of labour remake the materialities and subjectivities of class, as the meanings of work are also remade (see, for example, Bauman 1998; McDowell 2003; Stenning 2005b), and create a precariousness to livelihoods undermining commitments to social justice.

Whilst labour market segmentation and change are well documented in North America and Western Europe (Peck 1996), they are a more recent and less researched phenomenon in the post-socialist world. In this chapter, we explore the diverse forms of labour market integration in two major central European cities – Kraków, Poland, and Bratislava, Slovakia – and examine the ways in which those who find themselves in, or on the margins of, contingent and insecure labour markets, sustain their livelihoods. We ask how such workers and their households negotiate the segmentation of the labour market, the erosion of employment security and the emergence of in-work poverty, and explore the diverse economic practices of those for whom formal employment does not provide sufficient income to ensure social reproduction. In this way, we assess the articulations between labour-market participation and other spheres of economic life, including informal and illegal labour, household social networks, state benefits and the use of material assets.

The chapter is organized as follows. In the next section we examine the key labour market dynamics in the post-socialist countries of

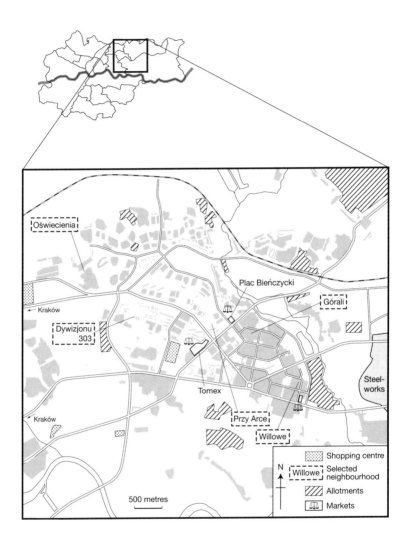

FIGURE 7.1 Map of Nowa Huta, Kraków, Poland

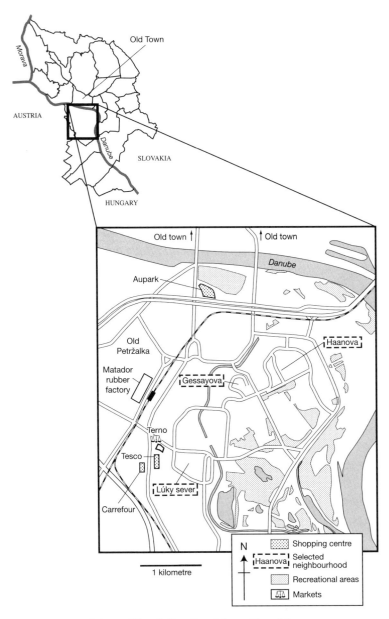

FIGURE 7.2 Map of Petržalka, Bratislava, Slovakia

FIGURE 7.3   Osiedle Przy Arce, one of Nowa Huta's neighbourhoods

ECE, highlighting increasing segmentation and neoliberalization. We then discuss the dimensions of these changes in the context of the labour markets of the two cities in which we have conducted our research. The third section explores the working lives of residents in two housing districts. After exploring the experience of employment insecurity and the emergence of a 'working poor', we document the ways in which households engage in informal and illegal employment, combine multiple jobs within the household, and connect their employment to other spheres of their household economies. We highlight the need to understand the complex articulations between households' labour market positions and their wider economic practices in order to appreciate fully how they struggle to create sustainable livelihoods in the face of dramatic employment change.

The research draws upon fieldwork in two of the largest 'socialist-era' housing districts in Central Europe: Nowa Huta in Kraków, Poland, and Petržalka in Bratislava, Slovakia (Figures 7.1 and 7.2). Built during the post-war period, these housing districts became home to largely in-migrating populations of relatively young families, who had continuing connections to rural and (later) wider-city economies alike. Both districts were established at the height of Central

FIGURE 7.4 View of Petržalka from the old town quarter of Bratislava

European state socialism, and both are located adjacent to primary urban centres. In this sense they offer exemplary case studies of urban settlements established during the state socialist era (Figures 7.3 and 7.4). The research has used a multi-method approach. While resources and accurate population records prevented the undertaking of a fully random representative sample survey, our approach was to select 'representative' neighbourhoods in each district on the basis of a range of criteria, including relative levels of social exclusion (from analysis of census and housing authority data), detailed field observation, location and accessibility in relation to the main city, and age of construction. Within each neighbourhood, individual housing blocks were chosen to reflect the range of socio-economic situations, including levels of poverty, block size and demographic composition. Within each selected block we then, first, undertook a face-to-face questionnaire with a total of 350 randomly selected households. A selection of around 70 households were then identified for follow-up, in-depth interviews. We used a number of intersecting criteria to identify such households, starting with household income to ensure a range of household material positions. Interviews lasted between forty-five minutes and two hours, and many were conducted with more than one household member. The questionnaire and interview work was complemented with ethnographic research, including observations in street markets, soup kitchens, homeless hostels, pensioners' clubs, allotments, playgrounds and other key community sites, and with ninety semi-structured interviews, carried out with key informants in state and other institutional settings to explore issues of social exclusion, policy measures and institutional responses.

Transformation and the neoliberalization of labour markets

While the experience of work and employment restructuring varies geographically across ECE, a number of common labour market trends are identifiable (Rainnie et al. 2002). High levels of relatively secure employment under state socialism gave way to widespread official and/or hidden unemployment; job security has been replaced by greater job insecurity and employee representation has weakened as political settlements shifted and trade unions declined; dependency on state-owned enterprises to provide not only a monetary wage, but also social amenities in kind (the social wage; Domański 1997), was replaced by greater differentials in the value of formal wages and, for the unemployed, reliance on low-value state benefits and on informal legal and illegal income-generating activities. What appeared previously as relatively singular labour markets, with an extremely dominant state sector and some additional activities on the margin (Smith and Stenning 2006), have become much more diverse and fragmented.

Four main interconnected processes have operated in the labour markets of the post-socialist world. First, post-socialist labour markets are characterized by a much more distinct set of segmentation processes than their state socialist predecessors (Pailhé 2003), although segmentation also existed under the previous system (Domański 1990). Labour market segmentation is occurring both between sectors and within them, leading to the emergence of a number of relatively distinct worlds of work. Segmentation between sectors is occurring as a result of the deindustrialization of the economies of ECE and the attendant growth of financial, producer and basic service employment,

TABLE 7.1 Average wages in Slovakia and Poland (€/month gross)

	Slovakia (2005)	Bratislava (2005)	Poland (2006)	Kraków (2006)
Average wage	485	700	652	600
Financial services	947	1,049	1,254	971
Hotels and restaurants	360	428	501	384

Source: Calculated from data provided by the Slovak Statistical Office and the Polish Central Statistical Office.

particularly in major cities. Segmentation also involves an increased differentiation of the conditions of and remuneration for work within sectors, reflected in a polarization of income (Milanovic 1999) and exemplified by average monthly wage levels in Slovakia and Poland (Table 7.1). In both countries, financial services is the highest paid sector, whilst the lowest paid is hotels and restaurants. Both activities are increasingly concentrated in major urban areas – such as those we focus on here – leading to wage polarization in cities.

Labour market segmentation has also been accompanied by a reconfiguration of gender and age differentials within the labour market. Women were often first to lose jobs and have found it more difficult to find new work, experiencing longer periods of unemployment (Hardy and Stenning 2002; Pine 1998). Generational differences have also emerged – at both ends of the age spectrum. Unemployment has been persistently high among young people, including graduates, such that many of the young unemployed have never held formal employment. Large numbers of older workers (over 50) have also been laid off, more often through early retirement than redundancy (Cazes and Nesporova 2003a; Surdej 2004), and have found it difficult to re-enter the labour market (Junghans 2001; Stenning 2005a, 2005b, 2009).

Second, post-socialist labour markets have also become increasingly precarious as the commitment to full employment has given way to individualized employment relationships, the decline of collective representation, instability in working time and, in some cases, greater casualization (Cazes and Nesporova 2003b; EIR Online 2002). Recent attempts to regulate temporary work and the appearance of global staffing agencies in the region (Coe et al. 2006) suggest that this form of contingent labour will become more significant. Moves to increase labour market flexibility have also been associated with instability of job tenure, particularly in the new service sectors, and considerable levels of 'multiple job holding'.

Third, non-participation, through labour market withdrawal and persistent unemployment, has increased (Cazes and Nesporova 2003b). Estimates vary but suggest that around 19 million jobs were lost in the early years of transition (Smith 2000). More recently, the return to positive economic growth has led to greater degrees of employment creation, but most economies in ECE have been unable to create jobs sufficient in number and location to balance employment losses. Indeed, there has been a general failure to tackle serious problems of long-term unemployment (Burns and Kowalski 2004). In 2005, in Poland, Hungary, the Czech Republic and Slovakia between 46 per cent and 68 per cent of the registered unemployed had been out of work for more than twelve months (OECD 2006: 269). In most countries, unemployment benefits are limited to between six and twelve months such that coverage rates are often as low as 25–30 per cent of those unemployed (Cazes and Nesporova 2003b: 116). The limiting of unemployment benefit is just one of the factors behind a marked growth in people leaving the workforce, either to become officially 'inactive' or to exchange non-existent unemployment benefits for pensions or incapacity benefit. Echoing experiences in old industrial regions in the United Kingdom (Beatty and Fothergill 2002), withdrawal from the labour market has become a key feature of labour market dynamics across ECE.

Fourth, persistently high levels of unemployment have provided a context for the neoliberalization of labour market regulation and social welfare systems aimed at promoting flexibility (Jurajda and Mathernová 2004; Smith and Rochovská 2007; Surdej 2004). As a World Bank study has argued:

> EU countries may need to err on the side of greater flexibility and lower security. This may be the case for newer EU members in particular, because they have much poorer business environments, lower

employment rates, and far greater disparities in employment. (Rashid et al. 2005: 59)

The report goes on to argue that any employment, even in low-paid jobs, is worthwhile, not least because 'low paid workers are often secondary earners whose earnings complement incomes of other family members. If this is the case, low pay does not necessarily imply poverty' (Rashid et al. 2005: 64), although the authors give no evidence to support this claim. High levels of unemployment at the national scale have therefore encouraged governments in the region to focus their attention on job creation without considering the quality of employment, in an echo of Western 'work first' policies (Peck and Theodore 2000).

In Poland and Slovakia,[1] the focus has been on reducing unemployment rates by cutting benefits, providing 'incentives' to work, and labour market liberalization through labour law reforms. This has been most clearly captured in the 'work pays' slogan and liberalization programme of labour market and social welfare reform of the former neoliberal Dzurinda government in Slovakia (Barancová 2006; Fisher et al. 2007; Smith and Rochovská 2007), and the Polish government's 2002 'Entrepreneurship, Development, Work' programme, including its 'First Work' initiative and its plan to ease the Labour Code (Chancellery 2002), making it easier to both hire and fire workers. In Poland, whilst successive governments, on the left and right, did move to make the Labour Code more flexible and to control government spending, this was associated, in the 2003 Hausner Plan,[2] with attempts to target key social benefits more successfully (Millard 2006) and to develop more effective labour market institutions (EIR Online 2004). More recently, elections in both Poland and Slovakia have encouraged a tempering of welfare reductions and labour market flexibilization as new governments have focused on a partial rejection of the singularly neoliberal state (Millard 2006; Smith and Rochovská 2007).

In the urban areas that form the focus of this research, the key labour market issue has not, however, been unemployment – in Bratislava and Kraków unemployment rates were 3 per cent and 7 per cent respectively in 2006, compared to national rates of between 13 per cent and 15 per cent. Rather, the key issue has been the quality and security of employment, connected to the emergence of in-work

TABLE 7.2   Sectoral employment change, Bratislava and Kraków, 1993–2005

Bratislava	1993	1995	2001	2005
Industry	41,671	39,121	32,557	33,325
Construction	15,850	13,911	9,249	8,141
Trade and repair	13,543	12,289	15,782	19,901
Hotels and restaurants	3,519	3,172	3,506	3,495
Transport, storage, communications	24,407	24,339	23,088	23,077
Financial services	5,815	10,139	14,881	16,603
Retailing	23,552	20,754	19,950	26,980
Public administration and defence	12,925	14,905	17,274	21,461
Education	27,045	23,789	21,991	20,249
Health and social work	17,765	17,100	16,097	14,416
Other community and social services	14,572	14,605	13,331	11,594

Kraków	1993	1995	1999	2004
Industry	67,300	78,914	77,709	48,744
Construction	38,800	33,670	32,929	17,856
Trade and repair	20,700	29,984	36,739	36,079
Hotels and restaurants	6,700	6,160	6,075	6,547
Transport, storage, communication	14,600	19,584	22,518	15,936
Financial services	7,000	8,656	10,432	8,545
Real estate rental and business activities	16,100	24,363	29,011	30,077
Public administration and defence	6,100	7,606	11,053	14,759
Education	36,900	31,296	32,648	34,478
Health and social work	25,900	31,114	31,481	22,495
Other community and social services	14,800	10,145	8,894	8,344

Source: Slovak Statistical Office; Polish Statistical Office.

poverty. The 'working poor' is a relatively new phenomenon in the post-socialist world, and a largely urban one, reflecting the segmentation of urban labour markets. In both cities, there has been a notable process of labour market restructuring since the early 1990s (Table 7.2). This has involved a decline in employment in manufacturing and construction and a dramatic growth in tertiary sectors.[3] Particular growth was witnessed in retail and wholesale and in financial services and real estate. These growth sectors are characterized by markedly different wage levels (see Table 7.1).

The emergence of secondary labour markets with pay levels far below the labour market average raises critical questions about the ability of neoliberalization programmes and new jobs in these occupations to provide a living wage and to sustain household livelihoods on the basis of formal employment alone, particularly in such high-cost cities. In order to understand how social reproduction is attempted within poor households, all forms of labour need to be explored, taking analysis into wider realms of commodified and non-commodified work.

Negotiating segmented labour markets and the emergence of in-work poverty

Despite the existence of low levels of unemployment in Bratislava and Kraków, exclusion from the labour market remained an important issue for many households involved in this research. In 2005, unemployment levels among surveyed households averaged 11 per cent of the total sampled population in Petržalka and 9 per cent in Nowa Huta, higher than the cities' averages. The incidence of unemployment was significantly higher among those living in surveyed households with equivalized incomes below 60 per cent of the regional median (a typical measure of households 'at risk' of poverty), and much lower in the highest income group (Table 7.3). Consequently, unemployment is very closely related to poverty. Not only are benefit levels generally very low, but in most instances are only paid for the first six months of unemployment. In Petržalka, 31 of the 150 surveyed households had at least one unemployed household member, yet just 4 households had income from unemployment benefit and in Nowa Huta, 35 of the 200

TABLE 7.3 Employment structure of households in Petržalka and Nowa Huta relative to 'at risk' of poverty levels (% of household members in each income group)

	Below 60% of median income	61–100% of median income	101–140% of median income	Over 140% of median income
Petržalka				
Employed	32.4	45.4	58.8	72.2
Self-employed	2.8	5.7	5.0	6.1
Carer	0.0	0.0	0.0	0.0
Not working for health reasons	2.8	0.6	0.0	0.0
Maternity/paternity leave	5.6	5.7	1.3	3.5
Studying	12.7	9.8	7.5	4.3
Unemployed	31.0	8.0	5.0	0.9
Retired but working	2.8	2.3	5.0	4.3
Retired	5.6	16.7	15.0	2.6
Studying and working	0.0	1.7	0.0	5.2
Other	4.2	4.0	1.3	0.9
Total (n)	(71)	(174)	(80)	(115)
Nowa Huta				
Employed	27.5	44.0	48.0	55.7
Self-employed	0.0	7.8	2.9	8.6
Carer	0.0	1.7	2.0	0.0
Not working for health reasons	11.7	6.0	7.8	3.8
Maternity/paternity leave	2.0	0.9	1.0	1.6
Studying	3.9	3.4	11.7	3.8
Unemployed	39.2	12.9	2.9	2.2
Retired but working	0.0	0.9	0.0	4.3
Retired	9.8	19.8	20.6	16.2
Studying and working	0.0	0.9	0.0	3.2
Other	5.9	1.7	2.9	0.5
Total (n)	(51)	(116)	(102)	(185)

Source: Household survey 2005.

FIGURE 7.5 Occupational profile of household members relative to relative poverty risk levels, Petržalka and Nowa Huta, 2005

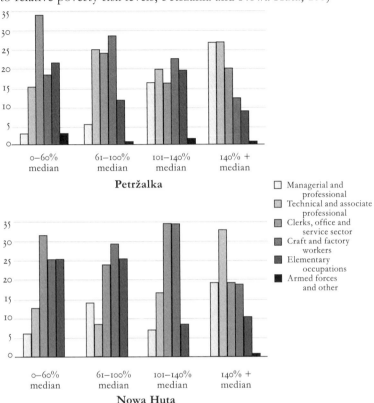

Source: Household survey 2005.

surveyed households had at least one unemployed household member, yet just 6 households had income from unemployment benefit.

Around one-third of members of households 'at risk' of poverty (with equivalized incomes below 60 per cent of the regional median) were in employment in both Petržalka and Nowa Huta, suggesting the existence of high levels of 'in work poverty' (Table 7.3). Those 'at risk' of poverty tend to occupy jobs characterized by low pay in lower skill, lower status service-sector and elementary occupations (cleaners, security guards etc.). Over half of adults living in surveyed households in both districts with the lowest incomes, and therefore

TABLE 7.4   Average monthly income for households with different employment structures (€ equivalized)

	Petržalka	Nowa Huta
Managerial and professional	480	471
Technical and associate professional	380	374
Clerks, office and service sector	368	270
Craft and factory workers	363	276
Elementary occupations	359	230

Source: Household survey 2005. Data for 'other' households are not included because of the low count.

at risk of poverty, worked in basic service-sector jobs and elementary occupations (Figure 7.5). At the other extreme, over half of adults living in surveyed households in the highest income group worked in managerial, professional and technical jobs. Average monthly equivalized household income was lowest among surveyed households in both Petržalka and Nowa Huta with members employed in elementary occupations, clerks, office and service sector jobs, and craft and factory worker occupations (Table 7.4).

Labour market segmentation and the emergence of in-work poverty are also associated with the feminization of certain sectors of the labour market (Domański 2002). While the proportion of women in higher status jobs (managerial and professional, and technical and associate professional occupations) was slightly above the average in the two urban districts, there was a marked concentration of women in office and service sector occupations (retailing and hotels/restaurants) (Table 7.5). While some of these jobs may be of the kind referred to as 'secondary earners' by Rashid et al. (2005), many are prime earners in a context in which male household members are out of work, or simply not present due to family break-up. For example, of the 41 per cent of employed women in Petržalka who worked in basic service and elementary occupations, 36 per cent of these women were living without a male partner in the same household. There is also marked evidence of particular problems experienced

TABLE 7.5   Gender and occupational structure in Nowa Huta and Petržalka (%)

	Nowa Huta		Petržalka	
	total	*women*	*total*	*women*
Managerial and professional	14.4	15.9	14.5	16.9
Technical and associate professional	22.0	26.9	24.9	28.9
Clerks, office and service sector	24.4	31.7	23.3	33.1
Craft and factory workers	24.7	12.4	22.4	8.4
Elementary occupations	14.1	13.1	13.6	11.4
Armed forces and other	0.3	0.0	1.3	1.2
Total (n)	(291)	(145)	(317)	(166)

Source: Household survey 2005.

by young people within the labour market such as concentration in service and elementary occupations characterized by low pay levels and insecurity (69 per cent of those 18–24 year olds living in Nowa Huta who were working).

Consequently, unemployed household members involved in our research tended to be either older men and women whose skills no longer matched the demands of the labour market or younger people who had struggled to make the transition from education to employment. In Nowa Huta, for example, Mrs Kwiatek[4] explained that her husband, a trained electrician, had been unable to find work because of the increasing conditions attached to employment: 'an electrician always finds work but they're always putting conditions, if it's not age, then a driving licence, if not a driving licence then a computer'. Mr Kowalik, in his mid-twenties, was typical of the younger unemployed worker: 'I've been registered with the labour office for two years … When they make an offer, because I'm without an occupation … then I go to the place of work and it turns out someone else has already started.'

The experience of long-term unemployment was common – for those with particular barriers to employment, such as single mothers and those with disabilities, unemployment occasionally stretched for five or more years. For the majority, unemployment benefits had long since ceased – older workers waited desperately for when they could start receiving their pensions and younger workers were forced to rely on their families, one-off emergency benefits or informal work (see below).

Others found themselves slipping between unemployment and insecure employment. Mrs Modzelewska, a single mother in her thirties living in Nowa Huta and currently out of work, explained:

> For now I don't work, for some time, because it's hard to find work. And before, yes, it worked well for me ... then I worked as a sales assistant in a small bar, for more than a year, then I had my child and for maybe five years I was out of work. I worked in [a second-hand clothes shop], but that was really brief. And I cleaned in a shop here in Huta. That was more that more than five years ago ... it was very casual work.

Mrs Zajacová, a 50-year old female respondent living in Petržalka with her partner, her adult son and her former husband, represented another typical experience of more unstable work patterns:

> I changed [my job] a lot. I lost my job in Pozemne Stavby [a construction company] in 1991, when the enterprise was closed. I got a redundancy payment and I was then registered at the labour office. Then I was employed in a kindergarten. I worked there for four years, but it was a very poor salary, so I decided to go to [work for a] private entrepreneur. ... He went bankrupt after half a year, [and] he didn't pay me. He still owes me SKK10,000 [€263] and also a redundancy payment. Then I was unemployed for half a year after which I went to [work at] Minigril. It was also a private enterprise and they also went broke ... so I had to leave and I was at the labour office again for around two months. I met the director who works in the kindergarten. She told me they have a vacant position ... and she asked me if I wanted to come back. So I am there.

Yet the pay levels at the kindergarten remain very low and Mrs Zajacová is forced to supplement her income by working in a second job as a cashier at a hypermarket. Such employment trajectories mean that household members negotiating the low-wage service economy rarely experience a stable career path. They invariably move from one low-paid, insecure job to another, to periods without work, and

FIGURE 7.6   Arcelor Mittal in Nowa Huta (formerly the Lenin Steelworks), still employing approximately 6,000 workers

back again, combining multiple jobs during periods of employment in order to earn enough to ensure basic social reproduction.

Even for those in work, pay and conditions are rarely stable. Recent years have seen the withdrawal of in-work benefits – the 'social wage' provided in addition to monthly wages (Domański 1997). Reported levels of in-work benefits tended to be higher in Nowa Huta than Petržalka, reflecting the continuing role of the former Lenin Steelworks, now Arcelor Mittal Poland (Figure 7.6), as a major employer (Stenning 2005a). A significant number of households continued to have access to free or subsidized food at work, to subsidized holidays and, occasionally, subsidized transport and medicines. In Nowa Huta, 44 per cent of surveyed households also had access to very cheap or even interest-free loans through their employers, contrasting with just 9 per cent in Petržalka (see Stenning et al. 2007). In Nowa Huta, interviews suggested that access to loans through the workplace was a very important means of managing household budgets.

Articulations beyond the formal labour market

The precariousness of the formal labour market forces poorer households to engage with a number of other economic practices to attempt to sustain household livelihoods (Gibson-Graham 2006; Smith and Stenning 2006; Williams and Round 2007). Our research indicates that whilst income from primary employment was the most important source, on average, for all households (see also Clarke 2002), it was considerably less important in households at risk of poverty (Table 7.6). To supplement income from formal employment, poorer households drew not only on other forms of informal and illegal labour, but also on their other assets – housing, land, citizenship rights and social networks (Smith and Stenning 2006).

In recent years, there has been a growing emphasis on documenting and explaining the diversity of economic practices negotiated in the construction of livelihoods (Gibson-Graham 2006; Leyshon et al. 2003; Smith and Stenning 2006). For many, these have been centred on attempts to think differently about the nature of economic practices, placing an emphasis on diversity and dynamism, seeing within and alongside capitalist social relations a myriad other economic forms (Gibson-Graham 1996, 2006) that do not 'belong to capital's life process' (Chakrabarty 2000: 63). For some, this kind of approach has been operationalized through the livelihoods concept such that

> Livelihoods are understood not only in terms of income earning but a much wider range of activities. These include gaining and retaining access to resources and opportunities, dealing with risk, negotiating social relationships and managing social networks and institutions within households, communities and the city. (Beall and Kanji 1999: 1)

Our emphasis here is on the ways in which such assets and practices work in combination with the neoliberalization of the formal capitalist labour market and are articulated with wider social relations. In addition to exploring these articulations, we also recognize that diverse economic practices draw workers into a variety of class positions (Gibson and Graham 1992) within and beyond the capitalist class processes of post-socialism. These include diverse forms of

TABLE 7.6 Average proportion of income derived from various sources (% of household income relative to household income groups)

	Main job	Other jobs	Pensions	Child benefit	Unemp. benefit	Other social benefits	Other sources
Petržalka							
Below 60% of median	54.9	4.8	19.6	2.6	1.6	3.4	8.9
61–100% of median	58.4	4.1	28.0	2.2	0.4	0.6	4.6
101–140% of median	70.1	0.9	21.0	0.7	0.0	3.5	3.1
Over 140% of median	91.7	2.6	3.6	0.4	0.0	0.0	1.2
Total	69.8	3.3	18.0	1.4	0.4	3.8	2.8
Nowa Huta							
Below 60% of median	32.5	0.8	11.2	8.3	15.4	2.9	29.4
61–100% of median	52.2	6.5	27.3	0.8	0.8	0.2	12.4
101–140% of median	55.5	3.9	28.1	0.2	0.3	0.4	11.8
Over 140% of median	72.0	5.9	18.3	0.1	0.0	0.9	2.8
Total	58.5	4.9	21.6	1.4	2.3	0.9	10.5

Source: Household survey 2005.

entrepreneurship and self-employment – largely informal, domestic and other unpaid labour, and reciprocal labour, amongst others.

Informal and illegal employment

One of the main ways in which household members attempt to secure a livelihood in the context of low-paid work is through combining several jobs, a kind of 'portfolio employment', either in the formal economy, or through work in informal employment. Indeed, engaging in additional and informal employment is often not a choice but is widely seen as a necessity to enable individuals to secure a living wage. Mrs Senecka, for example, a single woman in her thirties living in Nowa Huta, has formal employment as a caretaker in a neighbouring housing block. In addition, she earns a supplementary income from doing odd jobs (shopping, cleaning, caring) for an elderly couple living in the block where she works, sometimes takes on extra shifts to cover for her colleague, and in her spare time, as a trained seamstress, takes in small sewing jobs from friends and acquaintances in the neighbourhood – many of whom she knows from her caretaking work – for which she 'charges' anything from a cup of coffee to a few złoty. Like many individuals engaging in secondary work, and in an echo of socialist practice (Kalleberg and Stark 1993; Smith and Stenning 2006), such additional income-earning opportunities are often founded on the basis of the skills, knowledge and contacts acquired through primary paid work. This is exemplified by a female respondent, Mrs Cukrikova, in Petržalka, living in a 'working poor' household with a male partner employed as a carpenter, who suggested: 'In fact this moonlighting of my husband is very important. He gets paid SKK 100 [€2.60], sometimes SKK 200, which we save so that we will have at least something to buy things with for Christmas, otherwise I don't know what we would do.'

Many individuals and household members – especially in the poorer households – were actively engaged in work in the informal economy that involved 'illegal' practices. Often, informal work was seen as an alternative to being registered as unemployed. The increasingly low level of state benefits, coupled with a desire to avoid state surveillance, acts as a disincentive to register, especially in Slovakia where the neoliberal state had been doing its utmost to monitor labour market participation and benefit payments.

For those not eligible to receive social assistance benefits, informal work provides a small but important additional income supplement. For example, the Bombová household in Petržalka, comprising one retired woman and her middle-aged son, supplemented the pension income they received with income from the son's periodic informal work cleaning windows and flats. This accounted for about one-third of their monthly income of SKK17,000 (€447). For others, the margins of informal employment are a means to manage flows of benefit and employment income. A typical example of this is the Lastovičková household in Petržalka, comprising a woman in her thirties and her young son, living with her parents and her single brother. The woman is formally unemployed and receives some state benefits for herself and her child, yet she works informally in a kitchen for three to four hours a day. She has no contract for this work. Rather, her retired mother has the contract of employment, which allows the daughter to continue to claim benefits and the employer to avoid tax and insurance payments, a clear articulation of commodified informal labour and citizenship assets, which we explore in more detail below.

In other cases, the benefits from illegal employment are not mutual: the husband of Mrs Brestovicová, one Petržalka respondent, works as a barman in the city centre and receives irregular salary payments from his employer. The household can never be certain how much money they will have and, as a consequence, often have to borrow money to meet their costs. Officially Mr Brestovic is paid the minimum wage and is given the rest cash-in-hand. This enables his employer to pay lower taxes, but means that he will never have sufficient 'official' income to access a mortgage from a bank. In Nowa Huta, Mrs Kowalik, a young woman with an unemployed husband, recently attempted to formalize her employment contract:

> Yes, for now I have a contract, but I worked for this woman for almost a year without a contract, but I asked for a contract because of my child. ... She said to me, you're a young woman, you have time to earn for your pension ... so I asked again for a contract, and now I have a contract for a year, but I don't know what will happen ... I used to earn more, but when I got a contract ... she had to cut my wages because she had to pay for [social] insurance.

In some cases, informality had been imposed by employers 'sub-contracting' employment and transferring workers to positions of self-employment. However, the experience of self-employment varies according to the position in the labour market. Whilst some encounter insecurity, long hours and the loss of in-work benefits, others see advantages in the opportunities for additional work and greater autonomy. In one Petržalka household, Mr Senzo, a former employee at the local rubber enterprise, Matador, was told by the management of the privatized former state-owned enterprise that he either had to become self-employed or he would be made redundant. He now has to find work on his own, one consequence of which is that he works very long hours (sometimes up to eighty per week) and experiences periods without work. Consequently, the household's income is insecure and remains reliant on the female partner's income from her relatively low-paid job as a secretary, belying the argument that female workers are secondary earners in household budgets. In a contrasting example from Nowa Huta, Mr Wolak, a qualified accountant, was required to work freelance so that his former employer could avoid paying his social insurance and pension contribution. Yet, despite some months of real insecurity, he had more recently seen his income increase as he was able to work both for his former employer and for other firms, and informally for friends and acquaintances.

Households and labour migration

For some the flexibility and temporality of employment were linked to opportunities for labour migration to western Europe. We identified – particularly in Nowa Huta (reflecting prevailing patterns of labour migration in the two countries) – several cases of household and family members working overseas, either currently or in the recent past. In some cases, this had involved periods of temporary work, and for others labour migration had been a feature of socialist work too, with contract work in 'friendly' states and working holidays in Europe and North America providing means for major purchases.

However, bearing in mind that this research was carried out as labour migration to the old EU member states (particularly to the UK, Ireland and Sweden) was rapidly growing, we also identified households where, during the course of our research, members had migrated within Europe for short periods.[5] Whilst for some this was about individual earning and return migration, for others the household connection to labour migration came through remittances providing short-term but crucial support for household budgets. For many households, especially in Nowa Huta, short-term labour migration is a regular option within the breadth of economic strategies considered. Of course, such opportunities are structured by household characteristics (age, skill, independence, etc.) and thus not equally available. Labour migration, then, though an option, was not unproblematic.

Combining multiple jobs within households

These examples demonstrate that many households combine multiple jobs – legal and illegal, full-time and part-time, local and international – in the attempt to sustain livelihoods. The difficult experience of multiple job holding is very real, as households try to balance work and domestic responsibilities to increase the number of hours worked, and thus the income received. The creation of 'portfolios' of employment experience, both simultaneously and consecutively, appears to be a key means of maintaining household livelihoods, as workers have been forced to engage in multiple employment strategies.

For some households, increasing the number of household members is used to increase the size and number of jobs in a single (extended) household. One example of such struggles is found in the case of the Brestovicová household in Petržalka, comprising three generations of seven people living in a three-room apartment. All three adult women were unemployed at the time of interview, although each pursued occasional informal work. The two adult men (the father and husband of the respondent) both worked in low-pay service sector jobs in Bratislava. Their combined household livelihood is based on the articulation of the wages of the two men, occasional irregular and informal work of the women, and regular short-term borrowing from a network of family members living in the neighbourhood (Stenning et al. 2007). This enables the household to survive month by month but provides no income to enable savings and little prospect of the couple with a young child to access their own apartment. In other examples, a number of poorer households pointed to the fact that their younger members – schoolchildren and full-time students – took on part-time and casual work in order to supplement household incomes. Multiple job holding in large households thus plays a critical role in sustaining livelihoods, with the benefits often disseminated through kinship networks.

Social and kinship networks

The importance of kin and friendship networks extends through a number of spheres of household economic activity. The most direct connection is the use of social networks to access work. The failure of job centres to offer reasonable work means most find work through acquaintances and recommendations. For the self-employed, too, contacts provided by friends and neighbours are crucial for continuity of income, and in the sphere of informal work such contacts are often the only means to secure work. For example, Mrs Bombová, referred to above, used her personal networks to find work for her 42-year-old son. He was trained as a machine engineer in a Bratislava factory, but never secured permanent work. He is unemployed but receives no unemployment benefit; rather, he works in cleaning and maintenance jobs for local households to supplement the household budget and accesses this work largely through the social networks of his mother. At the other end of the income scale, Mr Wolak, the self-employed accountant introduced above, also relied on networks of friends and acquaintances to access book-keeping work to supplement his regular earnings.

For others, family and kinship networks provide a source of childcare and enable access to the labour market. The most common version of this relationship involves grandparents caring for their grandchildren whilst their adult children, usually daughters, work. In Nowa Huta, Mrs Fabian, after some twelve years on the margins of the labour market, works as an office cleaner but limits her working hours each morning in order to take care of her grand-daughter whilst her daughter works. In other instances, shifting labour market opportunities have resulted in a reversal of working responsibilities and the remaking of non-commodified labour in the home. Whilst Mrs Kwiatek in Nowa Huta continues to go to work, her husband – an unemployed electrician discussed above – stays at home to take care of their daughter and to maintain the home.

In other cases, social networks formed at work prove particularly useful for other spheres of life. In Nowa Huta, Mrs Sedlak, employed in local government, used networks established through workplaces to access scarce services:

I went to work and I said that [my daughter] had to go [to hospital] because something was wrong with her eye, and selflessly my colleagues called and said, listen, but E___, that's her son-in-law, he works somewhere and he has this acquaintance who's a doctor … And later I got a [business] card, and I went to that woman, and she already knew on whose recommendation, and so it was…

Yet this use of work networks may also serve to reinforce exclusion. Poorer households are disadvantaged not only by limited funds for bribes and gifts, but also by the fact that they have less access to the kinds of contacts (whether through professional spheres or with the 'right person') which might be useful. Consequently, they are less likely to use such contacts to access services. As one of our Nowa Huta interviewees, Mrs Kowalik, living on a very low income and employed in marginal jobs, suggests: 'No, we don't do things in that way, because we do not have the sort of acquaintances who have access [to services].' In contrast, in both districts the use of professional contacts to access services and employment opportunities among the most affluent households is very common – reflecting the way in which such households can use job-based networks to further consolidate labour market position and access to services.

Citizenship assets

For some, the small flows of income within extended families and social networks, outlined above, rest on the presence of one or more secure, if small, sources of income from the state, most often in the form of a pension. Following Burawoy et al. (2000), such state benefits can be conceptualized as 'citizenship assets'. We argue that despite the relative decline in the value of and the liberalization of pensions in several countries (Muller 2002, Smith and Rochovská 2007), they continue to be an important source of money income (Table 7.6).

For many households, citizenship assets provide a small but stable income base and articulate in complex ways with various forms of employment. Here we highlight two examples of these mechanisms. The first is where pensions provide a relatively stable income that is redistributed through kinship and extended family networks. For example, a Petržalka household comprising a divorced middle-aged woman, Mrs Uhlíková, living on invalidity benefit with her school-age daughter, receives a regular financial contribution from her pensioner parents living elsewhere in Bratislava since she lost her job due to health problems: 'I pay SKK3,000 [€79] for my flat and my parents pay the rest (SKK4,500) [€118]. But they won't [continue to do that anymore], when my daughter finishes school.… They have helped me for many years in this way.'

The second is where pension or other benefit income provides a basis for the running of very small businesses or the taking on of part-time insecure work (see Cellarius 2004). In labour markets where restructuring has led, through early retirement programmes, to significant numbers of young retirees, this kind of combined pension/employment strategy is quite common. In Poland, early-retired pensioners can earn 70–130 per cent of the average monthly salary with a concomitant reduction in pension payments.[6] In Nowa Huta, one of our respondents, Mrs Idziak, attempts to sustain a living through a couple of informal activities – she gives massages and copies paintings to order – but until recently struggled financially. However, she recently qualified for a disability pension and explains that her financial situation has 'improved a bit because I have this permanent allowance and it's secure, because I used to be without money and it lasted up to three months'. Household members therefore combine employment with benefit income and, in some cases, use their citizenship status as pensioners to negotiate contract and benefit situations. Yet, while for some pension incomes provide a small but stable base on which to attempt to sustain livelihoods, the neoliberalizing pressures outlined above, restricting state expenditures and cutting back on benefit incomes, raise questions about the continuing potential for this kind of combination.

Material assets: land, home and other income-generating activity

A household's home space and other material assets, such as garages and cellars, can also enable additional employment and earning. Not only does available space in the home allow households to increase in size and incorporate more income-earners (see above) but it also enables both more and less established 'entrepreneurial' activities, from starting small businesses to ad hoc work. In addition to the examples of home-based casual work mentioned above, a Nowa Huta couple runs a successful publishing business from a spare room and are starting up a manicure business from the home of the wife's mother, and a Petržalka woman runs a small second-hand clothing shop from her cellar. Whilst some of these activities are wholly commodified, others negotiate a boundary which sees charges being levied for strangers, but being lowered or waived for friends and family (in an echo of socialist-era practice; see Pawlik 1992). In all, our survey demonstrated that 15 per cent of 'other jobs' (that is, any additional jobs beyond the 'main job') were located in the home in Petržalka, and 12 per cent in Nowa Huta. All of this highlights the centrality of domestic space in household economic practices (see also Burawoy et al. 2000).

In addition to employment in home-based enterprise, a significant number of households involved in this research also engaged in work on the land, either on their own or family plots or in labour offered reciprocally to friends and neighbours (Smith 2002; Smith and Rochovská 2007). This labour is rarely commodified, even when employed on other people's land, but more often than not involves some kind of exchange, either through the receipt of vegetables, meat and fruit or through the provision of other forms of non-commodified labour (such as painting and decorating, repairs or childcare). This kind of reciprocal labour is often enacted by the very household members who are the least productive in the formal economy (pensioners, teenagers, unemployed workers), and involves skills developed previously in the workplace. In one Nowa Huta household, for example, the husband, a retired steelworker, regularly does welding on his friends' and neighbours' allotments. In this way, the attempt to sustain livelihoods through work involving commodified wage labour is also articulated with a range of reciprocal practices of unpaid and 'self-employed' labour on the land (Cellarius 2004; Smith 2002).

One further way in which household production of food articulates with the capitalist labour market involves households bypassing the monetary economy, and reducing their dependence on cash income (see also Smith and Rochovská 2007, Smith and Stenning 2006). The Slamková household in Petržalka provides a clear example. The household receives a regular, but low (SKK15,500 [€408]), income from Mrs Slamková's work as a kindergarten teacher. Her daughter, a university student, works regularly in a variety of short-term and informal jobs, to supplement the household budget – sometimes even up to thirty hours in a week. Yet they receive up to 70 per cent of their food consumption needs from a family plot some 60 km from Bratislava in exchange for reciprocal labour offered in looking after the house and land. The Slamková household uses its stable income from employment on essential items, such as housing, but also is integrated into the kinds of reciprocal labour exchange systems outlined above (Smith and Rochovská 2007).

Conclusion

This chapter has explored the neoliberalization of labour markets in Slovakia and Poland. In doing so, it has developed a number of themes common to accounts of neoliberal transformations and their impacts on social justice. First, the national contexts in which this research was carried out reflect the varying ways in which the agendas of the IMF, the World Bank and other international institutions have been implemented and developed in East-Central Europe. The accounts of labour market de- and re-regulation in Slovakia and Poland have demonstrated how such agendas have been taken on board – domesticated – by national politicians. Slovakia's portrayal as 'neoliberal market paradise under the Tatra mountains' (Smith and Rochovská 2007) testifies to the strength of local enthusiasm for the neoliberal project. Yet, in both Poland and Slovakia, the wholehearted pursuance of deregulation and marketization in the late 1990s and early 2000s has been somewhat tempered by an apparent preference, on the part of much of the electorate, for greater labour market security, for protected pay and conditions, and for the legislative expression of solidarity. Thus, the adoption of neoliberalizing labour market policies is not an uncontested process – such policies must be adopted and implemented within the domestic political environment, which reflects more than the wider global narrative of neoliberalization.

Nevertheless, even acknowledging the countervailing pressures for employment security and protection, the changes wrought in Polish and Slovak labour markets have driven a reduction in security, an absolute loss of workplaces, increasing pressure on wages in the less skilled segments of the labour markets and a persistent, even growing, informal sector. These trends have, in turn, fed a marked segmentation of urban labour markets, a process which has been characterized by a dramatic polarization of income and the emergence of a working poor alongside the boom in highly paid sectors such as finance, insurance and real estate. At the same time, reforms in the benefits systems have reduced the safety net for those on the margins of the labour market – in precarious and contingent work – such that the threat of poverty for those falling in and out of work, in and out of the formal sector, is very real. In these ways, the neoliberalization of urban labour markets in Poland and Slovakia has done little to improve social justice outcomes – and has apparently broken the link between the possession of work and decent social reproduction.

In this chapter, we have argued that those who struggle to make a living through formal employment are impelled to rely on *more than* capitalist labour processes, to engage in a diversity of income earning and livelihood activities with which to supplement their formal earnings. These diverse economic practices rest not solely on households' formal labour market position but also on a wide range of social and economic assets – social networks, land and property, and claims on the state – which are employed in attempts to develop alternatives or complements to formal employment and integrate not only commodified labour, but also domestic and reciprocal labour. These practices cross the boundaries between the formal and informal, the legal and illegal, and the capitalist and non-capitalist, and demonstrate the need to conceive of capitalist labour market activities as articulated with a range of 'outsides'.

Drawing attention to these other economic practices and their myriad relations to capital leads us to argue two points. First, with these often demanding, sometimes desperate, occasionally ingenious practices, urban households in Bratislava and Kraków domesticate neoliberalism; that is, they bring it home, connect it to the other spheres of their everyday life and try, not always successfully, to make it tolerable. They thus demonstrate the ways in which neoliberalism must be seen and explored in the places where it is lived, since this perspective enables us to understand the everyday construction of neoliberalism, to decentre the more global read-ings of this powerful project. Second, we argue that neoliberalized labour markets are but one of the spheres through which house-holds construct their everyday economies. Other practices are also present, practices which reflect and enact other economies and other motives. Thus we can see, for example, the persistent importance of the redistributive economies of the state in allowing pension and other benefit income to make other riskier labour market strategies possible, alongside the centrality of social and kinship networks of reciprocal labour. These networks not only enable, in some cases, formal labour market participation, but also reinforce community and familial ties and create spaces for labour which is not only driven by the need for social reproduction. These spaces lead us to ask, with Gibson-Graham (1996: 244), 'what it might mean to call the countries of eastern Europe "capitalist"'.

Yet these articulations often reinforce the inequalities of the formal labour market – the social networks of those in precarious employ-ment are rarely as 'productive' as those accessible to households with strong labour market positions, and persistent exclusion from formal labour markets can diminish the secondary earning opportunities on which many rely. Thus, the impact of labour market neoliberalization and precarious work can be seen as cumulative, and attempts to domesticate neoliberalism are rarely more than partially successful.

The commodification of everyday labour and life has produced a dramatic transformation in the nearly two decades of post-socialism. Yet, the diverse labour which we have documented, produced through the neoliberalization and segmentation of the formal labour market, is often rooted in the experiences of state socialism. Many of the practices – from moonlighting to self-provisioning – developed in the shortage years of socialism, often on the legacies of earlier rural practices (Smith 2002). In post-socialism, however, they work in articulation with newer forms of labour, neoliberalized welfare systems and the growing transnational worlds of work to construct a very particular set of labour processes which for increasing numbers of people raise questions over the ability to ensure social reproduction and promote social justice.

Notes

This chapter arises from research conducted as part of a project funded by the Economic and Social Research Council on 'Social exclusion, spaces of economic practice and post-socialism' (award RES-00023–0695). A slightly different version of the text was published in *Antipode* (2008) and we are very grateful to Blackwell for granting permission to reprint the paper in a revised form here. Previous versions of the chapter were presented at the Annual Conference of the Royal Geographical Society (with the Institute of British Geographers), London 2006, and at the Institute of Human Geography, Johann Wolfgang Goethe-Universität, Frankfurt, 2007. Our thanks go to all those who provided comments on the chapter, to our research participants for spending time to discuss their labour market experiences, and to Ed Oliver for drawing the maps.

1. The analysis here draws on the period before the loss of power in 2006 of the neoliberalizing Slovak government led by Mikuláš Dzurinda (see Smith and Rochovská 2007), which was the period during which the main fieldwork was undertaken. Since 2006, the new populist and more social-democratic government has introduced a partial reform, not least increasing the minimum wage level. In Poland, the research was undertaken during a post-Communist but also neoliberalizing government (see Shields 2007; Millard 2007). Since then, Poland has had two new governments: from September 2005 to October 2007 a populist and largely protectionist one led by Prawo i Sprawiedliwość (PiS, Law and Justice) and from October 2007, a more liberal one led by the centre-right Platforma Obywatelska (Citizens' Platform).

2. Named after the then minister for economy, labour and social policy, Jerzy Hausner.

3. Two important changes in the enumeration of employment in Kraków are reflected in the data in Table 7.2. First, in 2000 employment in firms with more than nine employees was included, compared to firms with four employees before that. Second, since 2004 employment at the major industrial employer (the steelworks) was re-registered to the Katowice region where the owner of the plant, Mittal Steel, has its headquarters in Poland.

4. All names have been changed to ensure anonymity.

5. For more on the emergent forms of migration from Poland to the UK, see May et al., in this volume, and Eade et al. 2006.

6. Those earning over 130 per cent have their pension payments suspended (ZUS 2006: 30).

References

Barancová, H. (2006) 'EU adhesion of the Slovak Republic and the development of employment legislation', *Transition Studies Review* 13(1): 9–12.

Bauman, Z. (1998) *Work, Consumerism and the New Poor*, Buckingham: Open University Press.

Beall, J., and N. Kanji (1999) *Households, Livelihoods and Urban Poverty*, Urban Governance, Partnership and Poverty, Theme Paper 3, London School of Economics, www.idd.bham.ac.uk/research/Projects/urban-governance/resource_papers/theme_papers/3_households_livelihoods.pdf.

Beatty, C., and S. Fothergill (2002) 'Hidden unemployment among men', *Regional Studies* 36(8): 811–23.

Burns, A., and P. Kowalski (2004) *The Jobs Challenge in Poland*, Economic Department Working Paper 414, Paris: OECD.

Burawoy, M., P. Krotov and T. Lytkina (2000) 'Involution and destitution in capitalist Russia', *Ethnography* 1(1): 43–65.

Cazes, S., and A. Nesporova (2003a) *Towards Excessive Job Insecurity in Transition Economies?* Geneva: ILO, www.ilo.org/public/english/employment/strat/download/ep23.pdf.

Cazes, S., and A. Nesporova (2003b) *Labour Markets in Transition*, Geneva: ILO.

Cellarius, B. (2004) *In the Land of Orpheus: Rural Livelihoods and Nature Conservation in Postsocialist Bulgaria*, Madison: University of Wisconsin Press.

Chakrabarty, D. (2000) *Provincializing Europe*, Princeton: Princeton University Press.

Chancellery of the Prime Minister (2002) *Information on the Polish Government Programme 'Entrepreneurship – Development – Work' – A Strategy for the Economic Development of Poland*, www.kprm.gov.pl/english/3585–5290.html.

Clarke, S. (2002) *Making Ends Meet in Contemporary Russia*, Cheltenham: Edward Elgar.

Coe, N., J. Johns and K. Ward (2006) *Flexibility in Action: The Temporary Staffing Industry and Labour Market Restructuring in the Czech Republic and Poland*, The Globalization of the Temporary Staffing Industry Working Paper Series, University of Manchester, www.sed.manchester.ac.uk/geography/research/tempingindustry/download/wp_1.pdf.

Domański, B. (1997) *Industrial Control over the Socialist Town,* Westport CT: Praeger.

Domański, H. (1990) 'Dynamics of labor market segmentation in Poland, 1982–1987', *Social Forces* 69(2): 423–38.

Domański, H. (2002) 'Is the East European "underclass" feminized?', *Communist and Post-Communist Studies* 35: 383–94.

Eade, J., S. Drinkwater and M. Garapich (2006) *Class and Ethnicity: Polish Migrants in London*, ESRC End of Award Report, University of Surrey, www.surrey.ac.uk/Arts/cronem/polish/polish_final_research_report_web.pdf.

EIR Online (2002) 'Temporary work under debate', 10 October, http://eurofound.europa.eu/eiro/2002/10/inbrief/pl0210104n.html.

EIR Online (2004) 'New labour market legislation adopted', 7 June, http://eurofound.europa.eu/eiro/2004/05/feature/pl0405105f.html.

Eurostat (2006a) 'One in six workers self-employed', *Eurostat News Release* 133/2006, 5 October.

Eurostat (2006b) 'Regional unemployment rates in the EU25 ranged from 2.6 per cent to 30.1 per cent in 2005', *Eurostat News Release* 150/2006, 16 November.

Fisher, S., J. Gould and T. Haughton (2007) 'Slovakia's neoliberal turn', *Europe–Asia Studies* 59(6): 977–98.

Gibson, K., and J. Graham (1992) 'Rethinking class in industrial geography', *Economic Geography* 68(2): 109–27.

Gibson-Graham, J.K. (1996) *The End of Capitalism (As We Knew It)*, Oxford: Blackwell.

Gibson-Graham, J.K. (2006) *A Post-Capitalist Politics*, Minneapolis: University of Minnesota Press.

Hardy, J., and A. Stenning (2002) 'Out with the old, in with the new?', in A. Smith, A. Rainnie and A. Swain (eds), *Work, Employment and Transition*, London: Routledge, pp. 99–116.

Junghans, T. (2001) 'Marketing selves: Constructing civil society and self-hood in post-socialist Hungary', *Critique of Anthropology* 21(4): 383–400.

Jurajda, Š., and K. Mathernová (2004) *How to Overhaul the Labor Market: Political Economy of Recent Czech and Slovak Reforms*, Washington DC: World Bank.

Kalleberg, A., and D. Stark (1993) 'Career strategies in capitalism and socialism: Work values and job rewards in the United States and Hungary', *Social Forces* 72: 181–98.

Leyshon, A., R. Lee and C. Williams (eds) (2003) *Alternative Economic Geographies*, London: Sage.

McDowell, L. (2003) *Redundant Masculinities?*, Oxford: Blackwell.

Milanovic, B. (1999) 'Explaining the increase in inequality during transition', *Economics of Transition* 7: 299–341.

Millard, F. (2006) 'Poland's politics and the travails of transition after 2001', *Europe–Asia Studies* 58(7): 1007–31.

Millard, F. (2007) 'The 2005 parliamentary and presidential elections in Poland', *Electoral Studies* 26: 210–15.

Muller, K. (2002) 'From the state to the market? Pension reform paths in central-eastern Europe and the former Soviet Union', *Social Policy and Administration* 36(2): 156–75.

OECD (2006) *OECD Employment Outlook 2006*, www.oecd.org/document/23/0,2340,en_2825_495670_36786071_1_1_1_1,00.html.

Pailhé, A. (2003) 'Labour market segmentation in central Europe during the first years of transition', *Labour* 17(1): 127–52.

Pawlik, W. (1992) 'Intimate commerce', in J. Wedel (ed.), *The Unplanned Society: Poland During and After Communism*, New York: Columbia University Press, pp. 78–94.

Peck, J. (1996) *WorkPlace*, New York: Guilford Press.

Peck, J., and N. Theodore (2000) '"Work first": Workfare and the regulation of contingent labour markets', *Cambridge Journal of Economics* 24: 119–38.

Peck, J., and N. Theodore (2001) 'Contingent Chicago: Restructuring the spaces of temporary labor', *International Journal of Urban and Regional Research* 25(3): 471–96.

Pickles, J., and A. Smith (eds) (1998) *Theorising Transition*, London: Routledge.

Pine, F. (1998) 'Dealing with fragmentation: The consequences of privatisation in rural central and southern Poland', in S. Bridger and F. Pine (eds), *Surviving Post-Socialism*, London: Routledge, pp. 106–23.

Rainnie, A., A. Smith and A. Swain (2002) 'Employment and work restructuring in "transition"', in A. Smith, A. Rainnie and A. Swain (eds), *Work, Employment and Transition*, London: Routledge, pp. 7–34.

Rashid, M., J. Rutkowski and D. Fretwell (2005) 'Labor markets', in N. Barr (ed.), *Labor Markets and Social Policy in Central and Eastern Europe*, Washington DC: World Bank, pp. 59–87.

Royal Institute of Chartered Surveyors (2007) *European Housing Review 2007*, London: RICS.

Shields, S. (2007) 'From socialist Solidarity to neo-populist neoliberalisation? The paradoxes of Poland's post-communist transition', *Capital and Class* 93: 159–78.

Smith, A. (2000) 'Employment restructuring and household survival in "post-communist transition"', *Environment and Planning A* 32(10): 1759–80.

Smith, A. (2002) 'Culture/economy and spaces of economic practice: Positioning households in post-communism', *Transactions of the Institute of British Geographers* 27(2): 232–50.

Smith, A., and A. Rochovská (2007) 'Domesticating neoliberalism: Everyday lives and the geographies of post-socialist transformations', *Geoforum* 38(6): 1163–78.

Smith, A., and A. Stenning (2006) 'Beyond household economies: Articulations and spaces of economic practice in post-socialism', *Progress in Human Geography* 30(2): 190–213.

Stenning, A. (2000) 'Placing (post-)socialism: The making and remaking of Nowa Huta, Poland', *European Urban and Regional Studies* 7(2): 99–118.

Stenning, A. (2005a) 'Re-placing work: Economic transformations and the shape of a community in post-socialist Poland', *Work, Employment and Society* 19(2): 235–59.

Stenning, A. (2005b) 'Where is the post-socialist working class?', *Sociology* 39(5): 983–99.

Stenning, A. (2009) 'Work, place and community in socialism and post-socialism', in A. Herod, S. McGrath-Champ and A. Rainnie (eds), *Handbook of Employment and Society*, Cheltenham: Edward Elgar.

Stenning, A., A. Smith, A. Rochovská and D. Świątek (2007) 'Household financial practices and the changing landscapes of credit and finance in east central Europe', paper presented at Institute of British Geographers Annual Conference, London, August.

Surdej, A. (2004) *Managing Labor Market Reforms: Case Study of Poland*, Washington DC: World Bank, http://siteresources.worldbank.org/INTWDR 2005/Resources/bp_poland_labor_market_reform.pdf.

Tarkowska, E. (1996) 'Unequal distribution of time: A new dimension of social differentiation in Poland', *Polish Sociological Review* 2(114): 163–74.

Wedel, J. (1986) *The Private Poland*, New York: Facts on File.

Williams, C., and J. Round (2007) 'Re-thinking the nature of the informal economy: Some lessons from Ukraine', *International Journal and Urban and Regional Research* 31(2): 425–41.

ZUS (2006) *Social Insurance in Poland*, Warsaw: Zakład Ubezpieczeń Społecznych, www.zus.pl/files/english.pdf.

8

Difference without dominance: social justice and the (neoliberal) economy in urban development

Colin Marx

Understandings of 'the economy' are never far from the surface in conceptualizations of socially just approaches to urban development in developing countries. In these approaches, what 'the economy' is considered to be is seldom explicitly examined (Beall 2002; Devas 2004) and, in practice, policymakers tend to equate 'the economy' with those activities that are identifiable as capitalist and amenable to measurement (Rakodi 1995). Thus, in practice, there are currently two prevailing understandings of 'the economy' and the promises of wealth creation and assumed conditions for success that are associated with each. In the first, capitalist economic activities are the primary source of social injustices because they are exploitative in various, often brutal, ways. In the second, these same economic activities are considered to be part of a solution because they generate the resources through which social injustices can be addressed more effectively. The key point to note is not just that these two understandings coexist, but, more importantly, that 'the economy' is considered to be almost entirely coextensive with capitalist economic activities in both of them. As I will argue, the tendency for both of these opposing understandings to share a common view of 'the economy' restricts attempts to achieve socially just urban outcomes.

But, as the opening statement also hints, understandings of 'the economy' – despite their power – can simply remain subterranean and relatively unexamined. There are two reasons why 'the economy' needs to be addressed when thinking about social justice. The first is that both of the prevailing understandings outlined above disregard other representations of 'the economy' and assume that capitalist activities are always dominant (Gibson-Graham 2002). Perhaps this would not be such a problem if more diverse understandings of the economy were valued. However, as Gibson-Graham (1996, 2002) so systematically argues, the assumption that capitalist activities are always dominant invests undue power in capitalist actors and processes, whilst simultaneously disempowering those economic actors considered to be marginalized or exploited by capitalism.

The second reason is because understandings of 'the economy' tend to become associated with particular parts of cities. Consequently, 'the (capitalist) economy' tends to refer to central or (industrially) productive areas of the city and informal or residential areas are parts that are represented as being of much lesser economic importance. In the context of post-apartheid South Africa, these spatial referents have specific implications for social justice when the historical, inequitable spatial divisions between races coincide with understandings of where 'the economy' is located. In broad terms, 'the economy' is to be found in central and formal industrial areas of historical privilege while the vast majority of poor people live on the periphery of the city (eThekwini Municipality 2001). Progressive post-apartheid governments already find it difficult to contain the momentum of racially and spatially skewed urban development in favour of the economic 'centre'. This means that the added stridency of neoliberal perspectives on urban development only makes it more difficult to realize socially just outcomes. For these neoliberal perspectives encourage, if not compel, city governments to prioritize their 'productive' infrastructure and accessibility to global markets (Monitor Group 2000) rather than favour more redistributive and equitable forms of public investment. For the purposes of this chapter, neoliberalism is broadly understood as an attempt to reorganize social relations to the benefit of those who already hold economic and financial power (Mitchell 2002). In this sense, neoliberalism is antithetical to more immediate

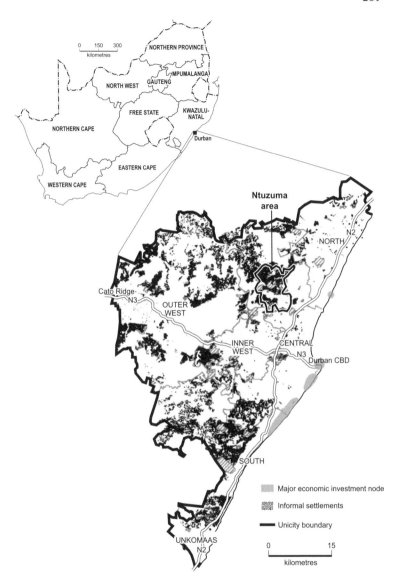

FIGURE 8.1 Map of Durban showing the Ntuzuma district

forms of social justice. But the main argument made here is that part of the process of resisting neoliberalism is not to presuppose that any particular economic activities are inherently confined to particular geographic areas of the city or are always necessarily dominant, but to be able to pay attention to where and when they are.

In relation to this argument, I draw on the example of the city of Durban, which like many other cities in the developing world has felt the keen edge of global economic adjustments (Morris et al. 2000) (Figure 8.1). Examples of parts of Durban's economy that have undergone significant change include the clothing industry (Skinner and Valodia 2003), investments in the port infrastructure (Jones 2002), and pressures on the local government to privatize public services (Desai 2002). However, there is nothing inevitable nor uniform about the effect of global economic pressures and, simultaneously, Durban's local government has set out an impressive and redistributive agenda for the pursuit of achieving social justice on a wide range of fronts (Freund 2002a). These include addressing tangible inequalities in service provision and access to housing and more intangible inequalities such as participating in the governance and development of the city (eThekwini Municipality 2001). These achievements are worth celebrating.

The aim of this chapter is to use the example of poor people's economic activities in one of the poorest areas in the north of Durban to show that these activities are part of a single diverse economy, where outcomes are more open-ended and actors are not preordained to play particular roles (Boggs and Rantisi 2003; Bathelt 2006). In this regard, I suggest that the potential to see poor people's economic activities as part of an economy lies in admitting difference in the economy *and then* resisting any temptation to ascribe any inherent quality to a particular set of activities, such as dominance to those economic activities categorized as neoliberal.[1] Although these two moments are intricately related, I insist on the need to hold them apart analytically. To avoid any misconceptions about my argument, there are clearly times when neoliberal processes dominate poor people's economic activities and these processes can be exploitative and marginalizing. Similarly, considering economic activities as interdependent is not the same as suggesting that benefits and services are distributed equally in Durban, as the vast disparities in living standards (Nicholson 2000) and inequality (Casale and Thurlow 1999) show.

I begin by underlining the political importance of developing new economic subjectivities before presenting the complex geographies of poor people's economic activities in view of a more diverse economy. Following my insistence on keeping the analytical moments between difference and dominance apart, I then focus on some of the attributes of 'the (capitalist) economy' that are considered to account for its dominance for the purpose of decentring and dislodging the assumed inherent dominance of neoliberal economic activities. The conclusion returns to consider how thinking about difference without dominance informs strategies to resist neoliberalism.

Economic subjectivities

The city of Durban is among the top three most important economic areas in South Africa. It is a port city with a population of approximately 2.5 million people and contributes nearly 60 per cent of the province of Kwazulu–Natal's gross geographic product (EDD 2001). Despite this productivity, approximately 44 per cent of the city's population live below the poverty line (eThekwini Municipality 2002), creating the basis for significant inequalities. Commentating on the post-Apartheid period, Freund (2002b: 154) remarks that in Durban

> the African National Congress-dominated metropolitan government has moved effectively to try to distribute amenities more fairly throughout, but this is not, of course, the same as distributing economic activities or creating a more accessible field for accumulation available to much larger numbers of people.

It is with these 'facts' that dominant accounts of Durban's economy are constructed and within this context that I drew upon a strategy of developing new economic subjectivities in conducting the research that informs this chapter. Gibson-Graham (2004: 417) suggests that disrupting dominant accounts of the economy 'entails not only new understandings but new ways of talking, of being in the world, and thus new subjects, co-created along with a different "objectivity"'. One approach to this issue is to displace dominant discourses by talking about other ways of being in order to yield new possibilities of subjectivity and action (Gibson-Graham 2004). Here I pay particular attention to the subjectivities of the research participants in the field site.

Relevant here is the concept of an 'authentic poor and unemployed voice' that informs approaches to poverty and economic growth, which, in turn, frames the ways in which economic marginalization and forms of adverse incorporation in the economy are represented. I suggest that the appeal to an 'authentic voice' ultimately misrepresents the relationship of poor, unemployed people to the economy by suggesting that they somehow exist beyond discourses of poverty and unemployment. For example, in relation to poverty, Meinhof and Richardson (1994: 14) observe:

> poverty is not now, nor has it ever been, just a matter of material existence for poor people. It is, too, a symbolic state, a state that must be appropriately embodied in its representatives. The bodies and accoutrements of the poor must bear direct, 'true' witness to their poverty – just as much on the streets as on television or in the press.

I propose that we could equally add 'research' to this list of 'streets', 'television', and 'the press'. In this view, then, it was not surprising that on my initial entry to the Ntuzuma[2] area in the north of Durban (Figure 8.1), and with a small group of community leaders, the framing of my research as focusing on 'the economy' generated very specific subjectivities among both researcher and researched. These subjectivities were enacted through behaviours and responses in which all economic activities apart from full-time, permanent employment in the formal economy were erased. Since a fair proportion of people in Ntuzuma were not in full-time, permanent employment,[3] economic activities in general tended to disappear from view. Fortunately, I was able to adjust the way in which the research was framed before it was introduced to the wider community and the participating households. Perceiving poverty and unemployment as multidimensional, discursive and material conditions means that specific subjectivities can be triggered in many ways. Consequently, care was taken to minimize the use of the term 'the economy', which triggers particular subjectivities. What counts as 'the economy', what an 'economic activity' is, and how this is expressed are part of bigger discourses about 'unemployment', 'poverty' and 'development'. As Friedland and Robertson (1990: 27) remark, people's ideas, preferences and understandings 'are formed not simply in response to the opportunities that are available, but through the discourse through which people understand what choices are available, what is legitimate or socially appropriate to want, and according to the particular metric in which its costs and benefits are to be evaluated'. As such, 'the economy' and what counts as an economic activity is intricately imbued with all manner of values, behaviours and attitudes (Gudeman 1986; Kaneff 2002). To minimize the ways in which this could influence participating households, the research invoked a discourse of 'valuing what people do'. To achieve this, the methodology drew on a time-use survey technique to record the activities that participants engaged in over the previous twenty-four hours. Participants then identified their most important activity during the recorded period and were asked a tailored set of in-depth questions based on, but not limited to, a prepared list. The data generated the following insights about the interconnections and interdependencies of economic activities in Durban.

Seeing difference in the economy

To begin to see difference in the economy, beyond the singular capitalist economy defined by neoliberal accounts, it is necessary to reconceptualize the relationship between (poor) economic actors and the larger economic structures and processes into which they are (voluntarily or involuntarily) drawn. The introductory section to this chapter drew attention to the problems associated with emphasizing the dominance of economic structures and processes. Equally problematic, however, at the opposite extreme is resorting to a methodological individualism that treats economic actors as atomistic units (Boggs and Rantisi 2003). Within broader social theory, an emphasis on 'practices' has been one way in which analysts have attempted to navigate between these two problematic extremes (de Certeau 1984). 'Practices', in this line of thinking, are the social sites where actors simultaneously make sense of the broader social processes and forces that they are part of, and provide the basis for relating and connecting to other actors. A focus on 'practices' therefore makes it possible to keep both structure and agency in view without necessarily privileging either. Smith and Stenning (2006) have applied and built on this broader 'practice turn' in their work on post-socialist economies to analyse the relations and interconnections that articulate different economies. For Smith and Stenning (2006), practices also point towards the regularities of economic life that sustain livelihoods and the sociality of economic life.

While the concepts of relationality, interconnectedness and diversity that characterize this work on post-socialist economies are all themes that I draw on in this chapter, in my view the task in South African urban economies is slightly different because the policy distinctions between 'the economy' and 'non-economy' are stark and firmly entrenched. It is therefore necessary to recognize that poor people's economic activities are integral to the functioning of a single economy. In order to achieve this recognition it is necessary not just to add poor people's economic activities to the existing dominant understanding (Cameron and Gibson-Graham 2003). The strategic aim is therefore to start with units of analysis – economic activities – that are considered common both within 'the economy' and outside of it or inconsequential to it. By showing the relationships between activities within and without 'the economy' it becomes possible to bring a different sense of a single economy into view. With a different sense of a single economy it will be possible to see more clearly when neoliberal practices are exploitative. A more precise understanding of when neoliberal practices are exploitative is fundamental to more effective forms of resistance and greater effectiveness in achieving social justice.

In this sense, Gibson-Graham's (1996) original intention in focusing on activities was to make the simple yet powerful point that non-capitalist activities that include unpaid work, reproductive work, cooperative work and so on, far outnumber activities that take place within what is considered to be 'the (capitalist) economy' – even if these are not considered to produce as much financial profit. Retaining a focus on economic activities also starts to point towards ways in which poor people's economic activities can be made statistically comparable (Jhabvala et al. 2003).

Relational economic activities

I begin by demonstrating how economic actors in Ntuzuma understand their economic activity as being *co-constituted* by other economic activities. The understanding of an economic activity in relation to other activities suggests that economic activities are dependent on each other without necessarily being caused by each other.

It is useful to begin with the 'value chain' form of analysis that has been adopted by policymakers in Durban as a means of connecting different economic activities in Durban's municipal Informal Economy Policy (EDD 2000). The analysis of connections between economic activities serves to erase a supposed formal/informal economy 'divide' and, consequently, promotes the view of a single economy of which poor people are a part. I propose to build on eThekwini Municipality's[4] 'value chain' analyses by showing how economic actors understand their activities in relation to other activities is contingent rather than predefined and that the economic activities that co-constitute each other do not necessarily have their wellspring in neoliberal economic impulses.

To demonstrate this contingency, I turn to the example of Mr B's investments in moulds to make concrete lintels that are used in the construction of doors and windows. For the moment, I focus on his activities of producing and selling the lintels. In recalling that he 'felt that this place will have demand for this thing [lintels]', he is acutely aware that his production of lintels is related to the activity of selling. In terms of selling lintels, he notes that 'people are getting used to it now' and making 'sense' of purchasing from him. He is 'the only one doing this' and it is clear that this *absence* of other local producers and merchants is important in customers 'telling each other' about his activities. The meaning of his productive activities is also related to other forms of exchange such as bartering 'a lintel for a window frame because you have to work hand-in-hand with people'. To draw together the points of this example, Mr B's productive activity is contingent on whether it is related to the absence of other producers, selling, or bartering. In this way, the contingent relation

FIGURE 8.2   Informal economic activities in Ntuzuma district

between different activities co-constitutes both economic activities,
The difference inheres in the relationship between the activities and
thus difference *binds* diverse activities together across the city such
that relational proximity is more important than spatial proximity
(Boggs and Rantisi 2003).

The 'value chain' approach draws attention to the complex ways
in which different activities are connected, but tends to do this along
one axis. However, it is not just that economic activities connect along
a 'ladder' of the informal/formal spectrum. They are also always
inevitably traced back to the formal centre of the 'real' (neoliberal)
economy. I turn to consider a different example from Ntuzuma,
which builds on the 'value chain' approach, but seeks to illustrate how
activities are related in many different directions and not necessarily
always back to the formal (capitalist) economy.

Mr H has been selling fruit and vegetables next to bus and
minibus taxi ranks for about ten years and supports a household of
six people through this activity. He recently obtained a formal stall,
developed by the eThekwini Municipality at a nearby shopping centre
precinct. He takes pride in listing his product range as including:

'cabbages, potatoes, tomatoes, onions, apples and oranges' according to their seasonal availability. He usually purchases new stock from the wholesale Clairwood market located in the south of the city and sometimes directly from farmers or suppliers who bring their products to the shopping centre precinct. In this way, his supply chain is conventional and is replicated by many other informal fruit and vegetable traders throughout the city (Witt 2000). The fruit and vegetable sellers face continual storage problems, have no access to refrigeration, and theft is a constant concern (Witt 2000; Cross et al. 2001). Consequently, Mr H and the other fruit and vegetable sellers rely on continually replenishing their stock. This, in turn, generates a daily need for a means of transporting the new stock. Apart from generating this need for transport, what is perhaps more interesting is that Mr H cooperates with a number of the other fruit and vegetable sellers around the shopping centre to hire a van to pick up the day's supply of stock. This cooperation extends to the collective preparation of lunch among the traders and the way in which Mr H's economic activities are entangled in relationships among the fruit and vegetable traders.

A 'vertical' value chain analysis of Mr H's economic activity draws attention to the ways in which the fruit and vegetable traders are 'trapped' in an activity that does not earn enough income to propel them into higher-earning activities (Posel 2001). Extensive analysis of the informal fruit and vegetable trade has confirmed that many fruit and vegetable sellers neither know their daily profits nor earn enough income to escape seemingly desperately overtraded market conditions (Cross et al. 2001; Skinner 2005). However, the example of Mr H's 'collective' pricing system for selling tomatoes suggests that economic activities can co-constitute other economic activities 'horizontally' as well as 'vertically'.

According to Mr H, the best time for sales is 'in the afternoons'. Mr H understands that his activity is related to the formal shops in the shopping centre. He and his fellow traders compete for sales with the formal shops. That is, the competition is not his fellow traders who are selling more or less the identical items at similar prices in the stalls immediately next to him and around the shopping centre. Not surprisingly, it is very difficult to differentiate prices when there is a common source of supply among the traders. Therefore, the prices at which Mr H sells tomatoes are determined by their quality. Thus, the traders tend to collaborate so that the price remains more or less the same and the quantity of tomatoes at that price is adjusted according to the quality. The better the quality, the lower the quantity offered for the same purchase price. In a context where storage of a perishable item is an issue, the economic activity of selling is differentiated according to quality/freshness. It follows that widening the range of tomatoes for sale to suit different household budgets will depend on differentiating the quality of the tomatoes. The greater the differentiation, the greater the choice and more likely it will be to attract a wider range of customers and thus, in turn, support a wider range of sales.

Indeed, if the location of the fruit and vegetable sellers next to the shopping centre and bus/minibus taxi rank is taken into account, there are ways in which the selling of fruit and vegetables is more tangibly related to the public transportation 'sector' than to the formal fruit and vegetable wholesale market in the value chain. The location of the fruit and vegetable traders reflects interdependence with the spatiality of township residents' lives and their travel needs. The widespread lack of private transport means that it is difficult for individual households to buy fruit and vegetables in bulk. When the fruit and vegetable customers have to walk long distances it is neither easy nor comfortable to walk far with heavy purchases. At the same time, these customers do not want to purchase goods too early in their journey in case they spoil or are required to pay for an extra seat in the taxi for their purchases. Even if households could afford to transport their fruit and vegetables in greater quantities, they would then be faced with the requirements to store the produce securely and to minimize deterioration. This problem is overcome by purchasing the fruit and vegetables in smaller amounts. The ideal point at which to purchase vegetables is therefore where the mode of transport changes and the customer is close to their final destination. The location of the fruit and vegetable sellers shows a keen awareness of this spatiality and of people's daily rhythms across a city that remains geographically fragmented and racially segregated. The existence of the market reinforces the area as a point to which bus and minibus taxi customers are attracted and where taxis converge and depart. In drawing attention to the perishability of tomatoes (their materiality), the location of the economic activity of selling (at the rank) and the times (in the afternoons and seasonal changes in supply). I start to anticipate other ways in which poor people's economic activities in Ntuzuma are interconnected and overlap with other activities in the city.

In sum, I have suggested that the research participants understand that their activities exist in relation to other activities and actors (see also Smith et al. in this volume). The differences between activities are contingent on the interactions between these activities and inhere in the perceived relationship rather than in an understanding of the activities as independent and preformed. It follows that understandings of economic activities are diverse and cannot be bounded. Difference, in this sense, binds activities together in networks of interdependence that do not necessarily have their locus in the formal (capitalist) economic register. This yields a view of Durban's economy where activities, even very small ones such as those in Ntuzuma, are a 'constitutive power' of the economy (Community Economies Collective 2001). Burt (1995) argues that new economic activities are generated when agents can get between overlapping networks of activities. Following this line of thinking it is possible to hypothesize that the greater the diversity of economic activities in Durban, the greater the possibility of economic actors to generate new economic activities.

Overlaps and interconnectedness

All the economic actors who participated in the research draw attention to at least three different elements of their economic activities. They talk about the *material* qualities or physical attributes of the objects they produce or work with. Examples include the weight of concrete lintels, making them difficult to steal; the speed of assembling items such as sewing church uniforms; the perishability/durability of commodities; and the tools and equipment needed to dig trenches. They also remark upon the *spatial* distance they have to walk/travel to obtain inputs for their activities, such as liquid petroleum gas, the places and boundaries of their operations both inside the neighbourhood and further away in the centre of the city or rural towns, the location of suppliers typically in the central city. Finally, they relate their activities to the *times* of the day, week or month, with their durations, frequencies, suspensions or disruptions. Examples include the best times to sell, how the rhythms of the school day and year affected activities, and how activities fluctuated according to the seasons and annual cycles within the year.

The ways in which economic activities have a materiality, spatiality and temporality, and how these aspects overlap and interconnect, demonstrate another way that poor people's economic activities are part of the city and a single diverse economy. I turn to the example of Ms J's production and sales of *iziqeda* (ice lollies).[5] As a number of scholars have pointed out, economic activities such as Ms J's provide a convenient service in poor areas due to their accessible location in the immediate neighbourhood (Cross 2000; Markewicz English et al. 2000). However, the production and sale of *iziqeda* is related to more than spatial proximity to a market. The physical properties of the *iziqeda* (they must be frozen) are an important part of this convenience that contributes to their production and sales. The quick freezing property of the flavoured mixture minimizes the amount of electricity required and the availability of free municipally supplied water means that the barriers to entry for this type of economic activity are low. Since the *iziqeda* must be frozen (and remain frozen) they must generally be distributed or sold from a house or structure with affordable electricity and a freezer. In instances where Ms J packs her *iziqeda* into a cooler box and sells at the local bus stop or football match, she must be sure of relatively quick sales in a big enough market on a hot enough day. Equally, the long travel times in the searing temperatures of Durban's summer means that it is very difficult for people to purchase these items from 'formal'/industrial sources of ice lollies and transport them home for their children. Industrial suppliers appear unwilling to invest in a distribution system in peripheral township areas, possibly because of a general fear of crime (Harrison et al. 1997). The spatial distance and widespread lack of private transport means that industrially produced ice lollies purchased in a formal shop are unavailable in Ntuzuma. Even if people could transport *iziqeda* home, they are likely to face a storage and/or refrigeration problem. Home-made production is similarly constrained by the lack of refrigeration. This means that children buy *iziqeda* on demand. The temporality of *iziqeda* production and sales extends beyond the time it takes to make the items or the seasonal changes in sales volumes.

The sale of *iziqeda* relies on the amount of cash circulating through the activities that make up Durban's economy (Cross et al. 2001). This is evident as Ms J's sales peak cyclically at the end of the month when workers in the formal economy are paid. Nevertheless, other factors beyond a focus on the amount of cash circulating also influence her activities. These include the school calendar that determines the availability of her primary market of schoolchildren. Thus the seasons and school calendar cycles overlap and intersect in different ways to produce peaks and troughs of sales in relation to the monthly flows of cash generated in 'the economy'. In this case, Ms J's activities are intertwined with, and follow, the infrastructural networks of roads, electricity and energy, water and sanitation. This underscores Amis's (2004) observation that it is much easier for urban governments to destroy livelihoods through the non-provision of infrastructure than create employment.

The material, spatial and temporal aspects of Ms J's economic activity are neither reducible to each other nor fixed. This suggests that both her economic activities and others in Durban result from the combination of these aspects that are at times uneven, fleeting, enduring or even contradictory. The overlaps and interconnections emerge as the activities share spaces, infrastructures, seasons, cycles, daily rhythms and enable Ms J to engage in economic activity. Equally, however, these same issues prevented home-made and industrial production from occurring in Ntuzuma. This raises a more general issue about how the material, spatial and temporal aspects of activities might displace, supplant, isolate or insulate particular economic activities from others, even though they overlap or are interconnected, and how the lack of infrastructure enables certain economic activities (Benjamin 2000).

It follows from the notions of overlap and interconnectedness that economic activities can be *multiply* related to other activities and their associated materialities, spatialities and temporalities (Simone 2004).

Attentiveness to how these different aspects relate and combine arguably enhances the efficiency and effectiveness of economic activities
(Callon 1998; Miller 2002). This in turn hints at the complexity of
how economic activities are interrelated but also provides a different basis for starting to think about how the 'exploitative' dynamics
of neoliberalism might be produced and 'transmitted' or sustained
across the city.

Networks of interdependencies

When considering Mr B producing lintels, earlier in the chapter, I
deliberately restricted attention to a singular relationship with other
economic activities, even though the example threatened to overflow
the limits I was imposing. I did this to draw attention to the way that
the understanding of relational difference binds economic activities
together. Now I more fully represent the way in which the research
participants understand their economic activities as being multiply
related to other economic activities. Indeed, it is difficult to think
of an example of the understanding of an economic activity only
being related to one other economic activity. Drawing on a different
example this time, of Ms M's activities of selling hats, scarves and
socks, I illustrate how economic activities are multiply related to other
activities and how this is important for allowing Ms M to elaborate
many different stories within the city and beyond. The implication
of activities being multiply related is that such an understanding
proliferates the possibilities for overlaps, interconnectedness and
interdependencies of activities that make diverse economic activities
possible in the first instance.

 Ms M started selling hats and socks in the absence of similar
activities, when she did not observe anyone else selling these items
in Ntuzuma. Her economic activity of selling hats, handkerchiefs,
scarves, umbrellas and socks is related to her part-time employment
as a domestic worker (two days per week). In an environment where
people spend a great deal of time outdoors (walking or waiting for
public transport) sometimes on unmade roads, hats that offer 'protection from the sun and the cold, and sometimes go with a style', and
socks, which wear out quickly, have a ready market. Small items such
as socks are also subdivisible from the bulk packs in which they are

found in shops and can therefore be offered on a more affordable and accessible basis to people as the seller goes door to door. The affordability and accessibility are more likely to ensure a cashflow for the seller (Cross et al. 2001). She notes, 'people don't have money in the middle of the month, so they pay me at month end.' Ms M knows that credit and convenience are important aspects that co-constitute her activity and will 'let people buy on credit' if it will help her make a sale. Selling these items from door to door has a specific temporality because the best time for sales is the 'afternoons and weekends' when people are more likely to be at home. Her ability to offer credit and convenience; however, is restricted to 'around Ntuzuma and [adjacent] B-Section' where it is easy to locate customers in networks and follow up for payment. She is not restricted by previous sales because the same person 'might like to buy for someone else, or want another colour'. She started selling socks and so on from door to door with a capital of R100[6] and in a good month has a turnover of 'between R350 and R400'. This contributes nearly half of an overall monthly household income of between R800 and R1,200. However, she prefers domestic work and is always seeking to secure additional work of this type. For this reason her activity of selling hats and socks and her domestic work are simultaneously related to her acknowledged *inability* to engage in another economic activity selling perishable commodities such as 'vegetables [which] can get rotten'.

It follows from this view that economic activities are part of networks of interdependencies with other economic activities, and their materialities, spatialities and temporalities. Thus, activities can simultaneously have multiple meanings and, consequently, can overlap. Given that this interdependence is co-constituted it is difficult to bound the processes of interaction. Nonetheless, the process of establishing the identity of economic activities is not infinitely boundless. Although in theory the establishment of relationships between activities could proliferate endlessly, the meaning of economic activities is stabilized to make categorizations possible. Understandings of activities are restricted, confined, channelled and ranked in many ways (Gudeman 1986; Graeber 2005). One of the ways that understandings of economic activities are contained is in the categories of production, consumption, investment, services and exchange/selling. Another is through the generation and maintenance of different economic registers of value. The research participants in Ntuzuma have sensitivity to these different categories and registers and operate within and across the multiple understandings that can be generated. They realize the importance of making sense of difference and sustaining difference. Usually these registers are ranked in prestige (Graeber 2005). It appears that it is just as important to engage in activities that move up the hierarchy as it is to secure a material output. The hierarchies of prestige vary in space and time but commonly circulate around kin, religion, care, culture or 'the market'. The research participants choose when to activate them, rank them in different ways and convert activities up the rankings according to different social and personal criteria. They do not try to flatten the differences into a single economic register as ostensibly sought by neoliberalism but, instead, provide a basis for new forms of difference to emerge. The difference is critical to being able to have multiple meanings, elaborate different stories and generate new activities and bring to mind the 'interlocking potential' of diverse activities (Simone 2005).

Having generated a view of Durban's economy that consists of proliferating relationships binding activities together through networks of interdependencies, with entanglements of interconnections and overlaps, the task remains to ensure that 'the economy' does not remain locked within the neoliberal capitalist aspect of this differentiated spatial economy that is starting to come into view.

Dislodging and decentring the perceived location of generative economic activities

Before poor people's economic activities can be written into a broader understanding of a single economy, it is necessary to dislodge and decentre the activities that are assumed to be generative and productive from a singular capitalist economic register and specific (confined) central locations within Durban. For the purposes of the argument, I assume that these generative and productive activities can be grouped together under the concept of economic growth. This has the advantage of closely matching the rhetorical and political use of the concept, but does not do justice to the complexities of processes associated with economic growth. I aim to show that activities such as innovation and productivity that conceptually underpin economic growth can potentially occur anywhere within the networks of inter-dependencies, overlaps and interconnections in Durban.

I undertake the task of dislodging and decentring growth from the spatial and conceptual confines of a capitalist aspect of Durban's economy in two progressive steps. The first step works from the existing and dominant understandings of economic growth and sets out the means of disrupting these understandings. The second step looks to the role of the relations and interconnections among different activities and how these relate to innovation and productivity and in so doing start to shift our understanding of the basis of economic growth.

Unsettling economic growth

It is worth recalling that neoliberal understandings of 'the economy' focus on the different ways in which the levels and combinations of capital, labour and technology can increase productivity and innova-tion. The understandings, in turn, are based on a conceptualization of activities that are generative, propulsive and/or innovative, and, importantly, confined within particular physical spaces and 'spaces' of homogenous rationalities or logics. However, I have suggested ways in which diverse economic activities are interdependent and interconnected. Economic activities throughout the city (and beyond) are bound together by (discontinuous) differences and the diverse interconnections that arise through the sharing of infrastructures and overlaps of the material, spatial and temporal aspects of economic activities. Therefore, there is an argument to be made that all eco-nomic activities are less pure and singular than they are made out to be and cannot be captured through a binary understanding of the economy as capitalist/non-capitalist.

Since it is virtually impossible to limit or determine the point at which the interdependencies, interconnections and overlaps of economic activities end – either physically or in terms of meaning – it is possible to suggest that the activities associated with economic growth are less bounded, internally coherent and independent than they are represented as being in dominant accounts of economic growth. If different economic activities are in fact related, then this suggests that it is certain configurations of activities which are responsible for economic growth and it is more difficult to identify a single (neoliberal) activity as the locus of economic growth with any certainty or precision. It is within configurations of activities, rather than through the isolation of single activities, that it would be possible to identify propulsive or generative activities, for example.

This is an important first step in dislodging and decentring economic growth from its perceived current location in particular formal, well-developed spaces of the city and within the rationality of the capitalist economic register. The limitation of this view is that it suffers from what Cameron and Gibson-Graham (2003) describe as an 'added-on approach'. Thus, while the approach suggests ways that diverse economic activities are endlessly linked, the linkages remain conceived within the existing dominant systems of representing and measuring economic growth. As a result poor people's economic activities remain marginalized because they are perceived as too small, fragmented, lacking in equipment, credit and so on to be measured, and hence to contribute to economic growth that is considered to emerge only from neoliberal aspects of the economy (Monitor Group 2000). It is necessary to take a further step.

Reconceptualizing innovation and productivity

A concept/phenomenon such as neoliberal economic growth can be reconceptualized in many ways. Here I look to the relations and interconnections of economic activities and how they make economic growth 'visible'. To arrive at a view of the economy and economic growth which is based on a new understanding of productivity requires stripping away the concepts that buttress the dominant view.

I begin by distinguishing between profitability and productivity to offer possibilities for measuring economic growth beyond a capitalist register of profitability. I continue by focusing on the dominant argument that economic growth is spatially confined and bound by a homogeneous rationality/logic. It is the view of a bounded space of economic growth that this dominant argument marshals that offers the possibility of reconceptualizing innovation and productivity, and, ultimately, the means by which poor people's economic activities can be considered as contributing to economic growth. By not taking this bounded view of space for granted, it emerges that economic growth (as dominantly conceived) has as much to do with the extra- or non-economic power to fix, immobilize, isolate, and lock in advantage across spaces in the city, as it does with innovation and productivity.

One way in which to reconceptualize economic growth is to widen the registers in which economic growth is measured by broadening the current singular focus on 'profitability'. Castells and Portes (1989) observe that poor people's economic activities in informal economic networks have contradictory effects on the growth of capital, labour and productivity. Thus, they introduce doubt to the view that poor people's economic activities cannot be profitable and, hence, contribute to economic growth. They point out that, on the one hand, the productivity of poor people's labour may be lower because the production technologies they utilize are less advanced, and it is suggested that poor people's economic activities are over-represented in consumer-type services where gains in growth tend to be lower. On the other hand, poor people's productivity of capital may be higher because their overheads and labour costs are lower (Castells and Portes 1989). Consequently, to dismiss poor people's economic activities *tout court* appears unwise. However, Massey (1996) takes the argument a step further and makes the point more clearly – although productivity and profitability are related, they are not the same.

In neoliberal accounts of the economy, profitability is generally regarded as an 'engine of growth'. Capitalism as arguably one of the most efficient means of generating profit has therefore come to be seen as the most effective way of ensuring increases in productivity. Massey (1996) notes that there is not an automatic link between profitability and productivity. Some activities may be profitable but not productive (e.g. the armaments industry), some activities may be productive but not profitable (e.g. public transportation systems), and some activities may be indirectly productive and not linked to profitability at all (e.g. unpaid domestic household reproductive labour). The implication is that the conflation of the concept of

productivity with the concept of profitability contains discussions
about productivity within the (capitalist) aspect of the economy
equated with generating profits. If the concept of productivity is at
the heart of economic growth, then it is important to distinguish it
from profitability to allow for the growth contribution of diverse
economic activities.

I now turn to consider the view that economic growth occurs in
bounded spaces in the city and within particular 'spheres of (capitalist) rationality'. Against this dominant view, I hold up the analysis
developed in this chapter. In particular, if economic activities, such
as those described in Ntuzuma, have multiple meanings that emerge
from their interconnections and relations with other activities, it
follows that they have no inherent meaning or characteristics. That
an economic activity can be 'seen' or 'said' to contribute to economic
growth is dependent on its location in the networks of interdependencies, interconnections and overlaps rather than its physical location.
For example, the same activity (such as Mr B's manufacturing of
lintels in Ntuzuma) in a different network of economic relationships
(such as the capitalist, centrally located register) would conventionally
be considered to be contributing to Durban's economic growth.

That said, it is the neoliberal power to fix, immobilize, isolate and
lock in economic activities across the spaces of the city and to 'see'
these activities as contributing to economic growth that determines
the economic growth of the city. It is the spatiality of this power that
reveals the extra- or non-economic power that is brought to bear to
immobilize, fix, networks of interdependencies and interconnections
rather than the ability to be innovative (Mitchell 2002; Zein-Elabdin
2004). The involvement of extra- or non-economic power in conventional analyses of the economy alerts us to the way in which the
neoliberal concept of economic growth is reductionist. Economic
growth is what *and where* it is measured to be. 'What' and 'where'
economic growth is considered to be are in turn a function of the
power within networks to make social phenomena 'visible' and valued
(Powell, 1990; de Boeck and Plissart 2004; Simone 2004).

Thus, and alternatively, for an economic activity to be considered as productive or innovative does not only have to do with its
profitability/output or location in particular spaces in the city or

'spheres of economic rationality'. Instead, it also depends on its location in overlapping, interdependent and interconnected networks. In this new view, economic growth is based on innovation, which involves *generating multiple economic meanings*, sharing infrastructures *in new and more intensive ways*, creating *generative overlaps*, all alongside using equipment and assets more productively, intensively and sustainably.

To conclude, I return briefly to Ntuzuma to illustrate this view of productivity and innovation. In terms of generating new meanings in relation to existing economic activities, it is possible to think of Ms H's involvement in the valuation of dwellings in Ntuzuma as diversifying the aspects of the economy in which the dwelling could be perceived as an asset and creating the basis for new interconnections with financial institutions. Ms S's production of church uniforms, using sewing machines donated by a Chinese charity to her associational group, to diverse customers within and beyond the city,[7] demonstrates the initiation of new interconnections. There are a number of examples of using infrastructures more intensively. The obvious examples include the production of *iziqeda* and lintels, which both depend on the (limited) municipally supplied free water. However, another example could be the informal fruit and vegetable sellers, who until recently used the roadside to conduct their activities, or the informal traders selling small snacks to schoolchildren during their breaks on the school grounds.

However, there is a crucial distinction to be made between suggesting that economic activities are overlapping, interconnected and interdependent and the ways in which the results of these relationships distribute resources and assets. Not all overlaps or interconnections work to allocate resources, commodities and people in the same way. This underscores an earlier point in relation to the neoliberal economic processes, that they are not always dominant but that it is important to be attentive to the times and places where they are. The ability to convert innovative economic activities into a propulsive force appears to have much to do with existing inequalities in the distribution of resources as well as the extra- or non-economic power to fix spatially the reach of particular activities. As Friedland and Robertson (1990: 12) comment, 'if the determinants of state policies that shape costs and profitability, investment and growth, lie outside of the marketplace, then analyses that bracket off the market are likely to be mis-specified.'

Not all economic activities can be part of growth in the same way, simultaneously. By definition, the activities that are associated with economic growth must be randomly and unevenly distributed. This is a key feature of neoliberal representations of the economy. But, unlike these neoliberal models, the generative activities that can be considered to result in growth are no longer found solely in the capitalist aspect of the economy. Now, since the generative activities that cause growth are contingent rather than predetermined (Massey 1996; Allen et al. 1998) or, to use Gibson-Graham's (1996) terminology, overdetermined, the impetus for economic growth (and different forms of economic growth) could be located anywhere in a differentiated spatial economy. A similar point can be made for activities that transmit or sustain processes of growth. The implication of this view is that in some cases an activity could generate/transmit/sustain a growth dynamic because of the actualization of certain qualities, and in some cases the location of the activity in a network could be more important in terms of the growth dynamic. If a differentiation between diverse economic activities cannot be made within hegemonic accounts of the economy, it is necessary to direct the attention to the extra-economic power that is brought to bear on defining what is 'seen' as part of economic growth.

Conclusion

Attention to the enactment and embodiment of economic activities across different economic spaces requires attending to how activities are understood in terms of their relationships with other activities (Bathelt 2006). It becomes possible to see dominance or separation or the interdependence between activities, not because of any inherent quality attached to a particular aspect of an economy, but because of the effect of the relationships themselves. These effects are likely to have different geographies, temporalities, and will affect different people in different ways (Allen et al. 1998).

The proliferation of interconnections and interdependencies between poor people's economic activities in one of the poorest parts of the city and other economic activities start to challenge the view that the 'the economy' consists only of what are considered to be capitalist activities and that the activities that are associated with productivity and innovation are only to be found in the central parts of the city. This provides the basis upon which to begin resisting the neoliberal arguments that new investments should primarily reinforce existing investments (and economic privilege) rather than engage more diversely in redistributive public investment.

The multiplicity of the interconnections and interdependencies also point to far more diverse ways that (poor) people might make their way through economic life despite the strictures and exploitative pressures of neoliberal attempts to reorganize social relations. The recognition of this diversity requires more imaginative responses from progressive local government officials intent on achieving more socially just outcomes. Policy responses need go beyond, for example, eThekwini Municipality's small-business training programmes and micro-credit schemes that are assumed to equip marginalized people to engage with the capitalist economy in the centre of the city. Instead, support needs to be provided to poor people's economic networks and their abilities to pursue economic activities that have multiple meanings through the provision of productive and generative infrastructure that can create new interconnections and interdependencies between economic actors.

The corollary of the existence of the multiple and diverse interconnections and interdependencies between poor people's economic activities and other economic activities is that there are more diverse ways in which neoliberal attempts to extend and create new forms of exploitation can be 'transmitted' in cities. This aspect has not been explored in the chapter but is critically important to consider, because I am far from claiming that capitalism is never or even rarely dominant in a diverse economy. In this respect, what the analysis in this chapter has achieved is recognition that the relationships between poor people's economic activities and neoliberal activities are more complex than the view suggested by an understanding that neoliberalism is always dominant.

Notes

1. It is important to resist ascribing any inherent, unchanging qualities to any part of urban economies. For example, it is equally important to avoid mythologizing any qualities of an informal economy (Samers 2005).
2. Ntuzuma is a large area in the north of the city that has many smaller neighbourhoods. The research was conducted in one of the smaller neighbourhoods, but for purposes of confidentiality I refer only to the broader area.
3. The demographic profile of the participants and their households were located firmly in the grid of probabilities that increase the chances of being considered among the most burdened by a neoliberal economy in South Africa. The participants live in a peripheral location, they are mostly women, not in full-time and permanent employment, and the household heads have low education levels, low household incomes and in terms of South Africa's racial categories, are Black.
4. eThekwini Municipality is the name of the local government that covers the city of Durban and broader metropolitan area.
5. *Iziqeda* is the isiZulu word for ice lollies in small, clear plastic bags (*i* singular, *siqeda*).
6. At the time of research US$1 was equal to R6.33.
7. Ms S takes orders for church uniforms at the annual Easter celebration of her church when large numbers from all over the province congregate at Maphumulo. The orders are paid for up-front and the uniforms delivered the following Easter.

References

Allen, J., D. Massey, A. Cochrane, with J. Charlesworth, G. Court, N. Henry and P. Sarre (1998) *Rethinking the Region*, London: Routledge.

Amis, P. (2004) 'Regulating the informal sector: Voice and bad governance', in N. Devas, with P. Amis, J. Beall, U. Grant, D. Mitlin, F. Nunan and C. Rakodi (eds), *Urban Governance, Voice and Poverty in the Developing World*, London: Earthscan, pp. 145–63.

Bathelt, H. (2006) 'Geographies of production: Growth regimes in spatial perspective 3 – towards a relational view of economic action and policy' *Progress in Human Geography* 30: 223–36.

Beall, J. (2002) 'Living in the present, investing in the future – household security among the urban poor', in C. Rakodi and T. Lloyd-Jones (eds), *Urban Livelihoods: A People Centred Approach to Reducing Poverty*, London: Earthscan, pp. 71–87.

Benjamin, S. (2000) 'Governance, economic settings and poverty in Bangalore', *Environment and Urbanisation* 12: 35–56.

Boggs, J.S., and N.M. Rantisi (2003) 'The "relational turn" in economic geography', *Journal of Economic Geography* 3: 109–16.

Burt, R.S. (1995) *Structural Holes: The Social Structure of Competition*, Cambridge MA: Harvard University Press.

Callon, M. (1998) 'Introduction: The embeddedness of economic markets in economics', in M. Callon (ed.), *The Laws of the Markets*, Oxford: Blackwell, pp. 1–57.

Cameron, J., and J.K. Gibson-Graham (2003) 'Feminising the economy: Metaphors, strategies, politics', *Gender, Place and Culture* 10: 145–57.

Casale, D., and J. Thurlow (1999) *Poverty, Inequality and Human Development in the Durban Metropolitan Area*, Durban: Durban Metropolitan Council.

Castells, M., and A. Portes (1989) The world underneath: The origins, dynamics, and effects of the informal economy', in A. Portes, M. Castells and L.A. Benton (eds), *The Informal Economy: Studies in Advanced and Less Developed Countries*, Baltimore MD: Johns Hopkins University Press, pp. 11–37.

Community Economies Collective (2001) 'Imagining and enacting noncapitalist futures', *Socialist Review* 28: 93–135.

Cross, C. (2000) *Durban's Economic Future: Why Help the Invisible Economy?*, eThekwini Municipality, Durban.

Cross, C., M.T. Mngadi, T. Mbhele, P.L. Masondo and N. Zulu (2001) *Employment Issues and Opportunities in the Informal Economy: Case Studies of Home-Based Workers in Durban's Shacks and Townships*. Durban: Durban Metropolitan Council and International Labour Organisation.

de Boeck, F., and M.-F. Plissart (2004) *Kinshasa: Tales of the Invisible City*, Amsterdam: Ludion.

de Certeau, M. (1984) *The Practice of Everyday Life*, Berkeley: University of California Press.

Desai, A. (2002) *The Poors of Chatsworth*, Durban: Institute of Black Research/Madiba Publishers.

Devas, N. (2004) 'Urban poverty and governance in an era of globalisation, decentralisation and democratisation', in N. Devas with P. Amis, J. Beall, U. Grant, D. Mitlin, F. Nunan and C. Rakodi (eds), *Urban Governance, Voice and Poverty in the Developing World*, London: Earthscan, pp. 15–36.

EDD (2000) *Durban's Informal Economy Policy*, Economic Development Department, North Central and South Central local councils, Durban.

EDD (2001) *Durban Economic Review*, Economic Development Department, Durban Unicity, Durban.

eThekwini Municipality (2001) *Long Term Development Framework: An Overview of Key Developmental Challenges, Unicity Vision, Outcomes and City Strategy*, Office of the Mayor, eThekwini Municipality, Durban.

eThekwini Municipality (2002) *eThekwini Municipal Area: Development Profile. Changing Durban for Good* Urban Strategy Department, eThekwini Municipality, Durban.

Freund, B. (2002a) 'City Hall and the direction of development: The changing role of the local state as a factor in economic planning and development in Durban', in B. Freund and V. Padayachee (eds), *(D)urban Vortex*, Scottsville: University of Natal Press, pp. 11–42.

Freund, B. (2002b) 'Contrasts in urban segregation: A tale of two African cities, Durban (South Africa) and Abidjan (Côte d'Ivoire)', in A. Bouillon, B. Freund, D. Hindson and B. Lootvoet (eds), *Governance, Urban Dynamics and Economic Development: A Comparative Analysis of the Metropolitan Areas of Durban, Abidjan and Marseilles*, Durban: Plumbline Publishing, pp. 151–68.

Friedland, R., and A.F. Robertson (1990) 'Beyond the marketplace', in R. Fried-land and A.F. Robertson (eds), *Beyond the Marketplace: Rethinking Economy and Society*, New York: Aldine de Gruyter, pp. 3–49.

Gibson-Graham, J.K. (1996) *The End of Capitalism (As We Knew It): A Feminist Critique of Political Economy*, Cambridge MA: Blackwell.

Gibson-Graham, J.K. (2002) 'Beyond global vs local: Economic politics outside the binary frame', in A. Herod and M. Wright (eds), *Geographies of Power: Placing Scale*, Oxford: Blackwell , pp. 25–60.

Gibson-Graham, J.K. (2004) 'Area studies after poststructuralism', *Environment and Planning A* 36: 405–19.

Graeber, D. (2005) 'Value: Anthropological theories of value', in J.G. Carrier (ed.), *A Handbook of Economic Anthropology*, Cheltenham: Edward Elgar, pp. 439–54.

Gudeman, S. (1986) *Economics as Culture: Models and Metaphors of Livelihood*, London: Routledge & Kegan Paul.

Harrison, P., A. Todes and V. Watson (1997) 'The economic development of South Africa's urban townships: Realities and strategies', *Development Southern Africa* 14: 43–60.

Jhabvala, R., R.M. Sudarshan and J. Unni (eds) (2003) *Informal Economy Centrestage: New Structures of Employment*, New Delhi: Sage.

Jones, T. (2002) 'The Port of Durban: Lynchpin of the local economy?', in B. Freund and V. Padayachee (eds), *(D)urban Vortex*, Scottsville: University of Natal Press, pp. 69–106.

Kaneff, D. (2002) 'The shame and pride of market activity: Morality, identity and trading in post-socialist rural Bulgaria', in R. Mandel and C. Humphrey (eds), *Markets and Moralities: Ethnographies of Post-Socialism*, Oxford: Berg, pp. 33–52.

Markewicz English, M. Mander and Mbokodo (2000) *ILO Employment Issues and Opportunities Study*, Economic Development Department, Durban Metropolitan Council, Durban.

Massey, D. (1996) 'What is an economy anyway?', in J. Allen and D. Massey (eds), *The Economy in Question*, London: Sage, pp. 229–59.

Meinhof, U.H., and K. Richardson (eds) (1994) *Text, Discourse and Context: Representations of Poverty in Britain*, London: Longman.

Miller, D. (2002) 'Turning Callon the right way up', *Economy and Society* 31: 218–33.

Mitchell, T. (2002) *Rule of Experts: Egypt, Techno-Politics, and Modernity*, Berkeley: University of California Press.

Monitor Group (2000) *Durban at the Crossroads*, Durban: Durban Metropolitan Council.

Morris, M., J. Barnes and N. Dunne (2000) *Globalisation and the Restructuring of Durban's Industry*, CSDS, University of Natal, Durban.

Nicholson, J. (2000) *Quality of Life of Durban's People*, Durban Metropolitan Council, Durban.

Posel, D. (2001) *A Motivation and Guide for Strategic Action in the Informal Sector*. Economic Development Department, Durban Metropolitan Council, Durban.

Powell, W.W. (1990) 'The transformation of organizational forms: How useful is organization theory in accounting for social change?', in R. Friedland and

A.F. Robertson (eds), *Beyond the Marketplace: Rethinking Economy and Society*, New York: Aldine de Gruyter, pp. 301–30.

Rakodi, C. (1995) 'Poverty lines or household strategies: A review of conceptual issues in the study of urban poverty', *Habitat International* 19: 407–26.

Samers, M. (2005) 'The myopia of "diverse economies", or the critique of the "informal economy"', *Antipode* 37: 875–86.

Simone, A. (2004) *For the City yet to Come: Changing African Life in Four Cities*, Durham NC: Duke University Press.

Simone, A. (2005) 'Urban circulation and the everyday politics of African urban youth: The case of Douala, Cameroon', *International Journal of Urban and Regional Research* 29: 516–32.

Skinner, C. (2005) *Constraints to Growth and Employment in Durban: Evidence from the Informal Economy*, School of Development Studies, University of Kwazulu–Natal, Durban.

Skinner, C., and I. Valodia (2003) 'Globalisation and women's work in South Africa: National and local approaches to economic transformation', *Agenda* 48: 75–89.

Smith, A., and A. Stenning (2006) 'Beyond household economies: Articulations and spaces of economic practice in postsocialism', *Progress in Human Geography* 30: 190–213.

Witt, H. (2000) *Research Report for the Process of Developing an Effective and Inclusive Policy for the Informal Economy for Durban's North and South Central Councils. Subsectoral Study of the Informal Economy: Formal and Informal Economy Linkages in the Fruit and Vegetable Sector*, North and South Central Councils, Durban.

Zein-Elabdin, E.O. (2004) 'Articulating the postcolonial (with economics in mind)', in E.O. Zein-Elabdin and S. Charusheela (eds), *Postcolonialism Meets Economics*, London: Routledge, pp. 21–58.

CONCLUSION

Neoliberalization, social justice and resistance

Alison Stenning, Adrian Smith and Katie Willis

In their contributions to this volume, the authors have explored the lived experiences of neoliberalization in nine different countries – Argentina, Peru, the UK, Ghana, Turkey, Germany, Poland, Slovakia and South Africa – from the 'three worlds' and at scales from the transnational to the national, urban, rural, parish, community and household. Through the lens of social justice and neoliberalism and at, and across, all of these scales, the chapters have analysed development policies, markets, barter networks, labour markets, poverty, resistance and the making of neoliberal selves, basing their analyses and arguments on extensive and often long-standing fieldwork. In their emphasis on fieldwork grounded in communities across the world, they have pointed to the connections between many of these spheres. The chapters have also explored the ways in which individuals, communities and institutions of varying kinds have engaged with the processes of neoliberalization – the extension of the market into ever more spheres of everyday life, the 'rolling back' and remaking of the state, the promotion of enterprise and personal responsibility and the deregulation of markets – in ways which contest, negotiate, domesticate and remake the global agendas of neoliberalization. In this way, they connect their work to the growing body of theoretical work in geography and beyond which attempts to document, critique and decentre neoliberalism. The contributions have also explored how discourses of social justice can be brought into a conversation about neoliberalization. Through exploring the distributional consequences of neoliberalization, the forms of organizing and 'resistance' to the extension of the market, and the role of a range of community-based endeavours in making neoliberalization tolerable, the chapters have – in many different ways – explored how social justice and neo-liberalism can be articulated.

In this conclusion, the aim is to draw out a number of themes which not only reflect the arguments of the authors but also demon-strate the value of the particular perspective adopted in this volume. This book has aimed, in the context of evidence of persistent and growing marginalization of many individuals and communities within the ongoing marketization of social and economic life, to connect dis-cursive critiques of neoliberalism with understandings of its material impacts. It has sought, moreover, to explore those materialities and the experiences of neoliberalization in a global context. Whilst much of the work on neoliberalization has drawn attention to the global scale of the project and its adoption by powerful global institutions, far less published work had focused on the diverse engagements with neoliberalization (although see the recent edited collections by England and Ward (2007) and Leitner et al. (2007)). Much of the work that has, for example, explored neoliberalization in Africa or East-Central Europe has done so from the perspective of the assumed centres of neoliberal thought and practice (e.g. Gowan 1995). This work tends to pay little attention to the nuances of engagement on the ground, in communities and households, in both urban and rural spaces. Yet, at the same time, many geographers and other social scientists do appear to have been producing grounded, theoretically informed empirical research which made analyses of these nuances possible. The articulations between the disseminated discourses of neoliberalism and the everyday practices of negotiation, contestation and domestication have been the focus of this volume, with the hope of drawing attention to the ways in which neoliberalism is constructed not only in its global centres but also everyday, in the more marginal spaces of contemporary capitalism, whether they be the migrant labour markets of a global city, the mountainous periphery of a Latin American country, the 'hidden' garment workshops of peripheral Istanbul or a persistently marginalized town in the former GDR. Thus, to reiterate, this volume is deliberately 'global' and comparative in structure and content and brings together writers who critically explore these themes in the global South, the former 'communist' East and the West, and at a variety of scales. The authors have written from a geographical perspective, grounding their work in the experiences of communities, social and spatial, and foregrounding the spatialities of neoliberalization. The volume adopts a wider framing than the common urban focus of studies of neoliberalization in the 'advanced' capitalist world (Brenner and Theodore 2002), analysing the rural and the peri-urban too.

This particular focus draws our attention to a number of key questions, which form the focus of the remainder of this concluding chapter. The authors recognize the differential practices and experiences of neoliberalism over time and explore 'neoliberalization' as a project of becoming rather than being (cf. Larner 2003). In exploring neoliberalization on the ground and in the everyday lives of individuals and communities, the authors explore the material experience of the neoliberal in its diverse forms, and consider its failures as well as the ways in which it has provided opportunities for some. As a consequence of these first two points, the authors emphasize the way in which neoliberal capitalism 'bleeds into' and articulates with its 'constitutive outsides' (Smith 2007; Smith and Rochovská 2007), including processes of ethnicity, class formation, gender, religion and ideology, different political formations and alternative theoretical conceptualizations. This articulation includes, for many, a reiteration of the role of the state and an exploration of the ways in which the state continues to articulate with 'the neoliberal' in contradiction to notions of 'simple' models of state withdrawal and decline. In connecting to these other spheres, the authors explore how neoliberalism is imagined, practised and constructed at and between a variety of different spatial scales – from the individual to the household, the community, the region, the state and beyond – and how these spatialities shape the processes of neoliberalization. This recognition that neoliberalism is constructed and enacted in multiple spaces and spheres draws attention to the ways in 'voices from the margins' are involved in the actual material and discursive constitution of neoliberal worlds, enabling a critical focus both on the processes of translation of 'core' neoliberalisms (ideas, policies, practices) in 'marginal' spaces, and on the assumption that neoliberalism is a result of the dominance and discursive creation of powerful institutions. The authors point to ways in which neoliberalism is created and contested – in part – through local discursive formations, often of those whom we might consider marginalized. This, in turn, encourages us to rethink dominant discourses of neoliberalism and to consider the possible ways in which researching neoliberalism 'from the margins' enables us to place peripheral spaces at the heart of contemporary theorizations, questioning the dominance of 'the West'. Finally, each of the authors, in different ways, explores the value of a focus on social justice, both in the form of the social consequences of neoliberalization and in the forms of community and individual mobilization and 'resistance' to the extension of market relations and what Watts (1994) has called 'the privatization of everything'. This exploration of the value of an engagement with social justice thus enables a view of the economy which embraces considerations of vulnerability, well-being and empowerment, and connects to the kinds of political practice required to create more democratic worlds.

The diverse processes of neoliberalization

It is increasingly recognized that conceiving of processes of neo-liberalization instead of a singular neoliberalism better reflects the 'reality' of neoliberal times and enables us to document and analyse the many incarnations of these economic, social and political projects (Tickell and Peck 2003; Leitner et al. 2007; England and Ward 2007). The cases explored in this volume reinforce this perspective since they point both to the inconstant nature of neoliberalism and to temporal and spatial differentiations. In particular, a number of the authors (including Olson, North, and Smith et al.) draw attention to the wavering commitments of policymakers in different countries to, and the resultant variance in manifestations of, neoliberalism. North documents, for example, how Argentina 'moved from the status of

IMF poster child to that of problem child', whilst Smith et al. highlight how in Poland and Slovakia shifting governments, of all hues, took steps both towards and away from the full neoliberalization of labour markets. These differentiations encourage a conceptualization of neoliberalism as a diverse project, promoted by different groups and developed in articulation with other social and political formations (as we will see below).

This conceptualization is taken further by many of the volume's authors, who suggest that the diversities of neoliberalism can, in fact, only be fully documented through an exploration of its everyday material and discursive impacts. Thus, for Pattison, the key concern is to account for – and build political campaigns on the basis of – 'actually experienced neoliberalism', which he defines as 'how the global trends of textbook neoliberalism manifest themselves in the lives of individuals within a specific spatial context'. Pattison and others argue that what can often otherwise be seen as an abstracted and global concept is made real by its effects on everyday lives, especially the lives of the poor and marginalized. As we suggest further below, neoliberalism cannot simply be conceived as a top-down project created and implemented by national or transnational elites but is rather a technology for the remaking of social life, and one which is, in turn, remade every day.

The focus of Pattison's chapter – as of many other chapters, given the book's emphasis on social justice – is those households and communities that have been hit hard by the transformations wrought by neoliberalism. Yet neoliberalization also has differentiated outcomes for various classes and social groups. Of course, it is widely recognized that some elite groups, and considerable sections of the middle classes, have benefited from the neoliberalization of the economy through positive returns on investments, favourable tax regimes and the subsidization of enterprise, for example, as the segmentation of labour markets and the polarization of economic opportunity have fed growing inequalities (Harvey 2005). But some of the chapters here also indicate ways in which those at the 'sharp end' of neoliberalization have experienced more positive transformations. Some apparently marginalized groups not only perceive of some aspects of neoliberalism positively, but have also benefited materially from opportunities presented by neoliberalization. For example, Hörschelmann explores the ways in which the remaking of the East German economy has created brighter prospects for a minority of young people than those offered to their parents in previous decades. This promotion of individual opportunity is also celebrated by some in Argentina (North) and Peru (Olson) where the emphasis on enterprise, responsibility and self-sufficiency is seen as a powerful antidote to a failing state and to the inequities of long-standing clientelism, and a reflection of cultural (and/or religious) preferences for self-improvement. In their chapter, May et al. recognize that for the Ghanaian and Polish migrants at the centre of their research the freedom to migrate to jobs created in London opened up possibilities for income generation which would been unheard of at home. Yet, diminishing opportunities at home are also a result of neoliberaliza- tion, as May et al. eloquently suggest, such that, whatever the material benefits of migration, it is also often experienced as enforced, and carries significant costs too.

Yet, for all neoliberalism's diversities, the book's authors also point to its commonalities. The varied incarnations of neoliberalism do not detract from the powerful connections between the economic values and practices inculcated in policy and corporate spheres in all three 'worlds'. Indeed, the parallels drawn between the experiences of structural adjustment in Ghana and transition in Poland documented by May et al. illustrate this point – and highlight the very particular geographies of neoliberalism's development and dissemination. The accounts of structural adjustment in Peru, Turkey and Argentina reiter- ate these commonalities, as do the experiences of post-socialist east Germany, Poland and Slovakia, post-apartheid South Africa and post- industrial Manchester. Notwithstanding the many variations outlined above, in each of these diverse locations, the experience has been of ever-increasing insertion into global circuits of capital, increasing flexibility and insecurity in labour markets, and growing emphasis on the actions of individuals to respond to these pressures in the light of declining collectivities, within and beyond the state.

One further point is, however, worth making. For all the attempts to push the neoliberalization of economic and social life further, such projects do encounter failures. North's account of the desperate state of the Argentine economy and the failure of the peso is a clear example of this, but in other more mundane ways we can also identify the failure of neoliberal logics to colonize all the spaces of everyday life. Smith et al. and Marx point, for example, to the persistent presence of other economic and social logics in the communal and reciprocal labour, which is shared within social networks and is articulated with the dominant economies of neoliberalism (Smith and Stenning 2006; Smith and Rochovská 2007). Indeed, in his account of small-scale, informal sales ventures (lintels, ice lollies, socks etc.), Marx identifies a number of sectors which more formal economic actors, such as commercial firms and the state, are both unable and unwilling to enter.

Neoliberalism and its others

As this last point suggests, neoliberalism never acts alone. As Castree (2006: 5) explains, 'it is never "neoliberalism" alone that causes anything.' The effects of neoliberalism are always felt through its articulations with various subjectivities, other social and political formations, and other related technologies and projects.

A number of the chapters in *Social Justice and Neoliberalism* centre on the mediation of neoliberalism by particular subjectivities. Hörschelmann focuses on the ways in which neoliberalization transforms youth and youth transitions, but also how the varying class positions and educational backgrounds of the young people researched shape their engagements with flexibilized and insecure labour markets. Ergün explores the ways in which Turkey's insertion into global circuits rests on the development of widespread industrial subcontracting in the clothing sector, a sector almost wholly dependent on the exploitation of young women workers, but she also points to the ways in which the young women workers' shared subjectivities enable them to create some, if small, spaces of resistance and negotiation (see also Hale and Wills 2005). May et al. document the powerfully racialized immigration policies which mean that the experiences of migration and migrant labour markets vary markedly for those from Europe and from Africa. A number of authors (Pattison, Smith et al., North) examine the ways in which the processes of neoliberalization remake class subjectivities, often extending economic insecurity into previously secure classes, such that having a job or identifying as middle class appear no longer to protect individuals or households from the threat of poverty. It is these kinds of transformation, which suggest the decline of more collective subjectivities and the apparently growing analytical importance of personal subjectivities in shaping life-chances, that have led to the analysis of individualization as a social process allied with neoliberalization. As Hörschelmann suggests in her chapter, individualized discourses of the self, most especially the enterprising self, are oft-used explanations for poverty and marginalization. Hörschelmann and others, such as Olson, May et al. and Smith et al., indicate the importance of seeing neoliberalism not just as an institutional project but also as one which seeks to remake subjectivities, often through labour market transformations, to better fit the demands of neoliberal times.

We have already suggested that neoliberalism is remade, sometimes tempered, by its articulation with domestic electoral politics and the varying hues of governing parties, but the policies of neoliberalization are also articulated with the practices of other political, social and cultural institutions whose presence and activities reflect the particularities of local and national formations. Thus, for example, Olson centres her analyses on the ways in which, at different times, the Roman Catholic Church has been critical in adapting, contesting and easing the processes of neoliberalization. Other chapters identify organizations such as trade unions, community organizations, NGOs and civil society groups as ones which engage daily with neoliberal institutions. Some of these groups, as we will see below, have sought to resist neoliberalism, but all have been engaged in its remaking.

For many commentators neoliberalism's most significant other is the state (Tickell and Peck 2003). As North suggests in his chapter, the doctrines of neoliberalism were developed and disseminated as a reaction to the post-war dominance of Keynesianism and its alleged overemphasis on state-led solutions to economic crises. As a result, neoliberalism is often interpreted as a rolling back of the state, and, as we suggested above, in a number of contexts discussed here (such as east Germany and Argentina) some facets of neoliberalism are indeed celebrated because they challenge what had been seen previously as dysfunctional and suffocating states. Many of the authors do indeed indicate ways in which the state has withdrawn from prior functions – in the weakness of employment regulation in Turkey's subcontracted workshops, and in the erosion of welfare systems in Poland, Slovakia, the UK and east Germany. North focuses in his chapter, in fact, on an almost accidental withdrawal of the state in Argentina from the issuance and control of the currency. In this instance, the state's failure to secure a workable currency led to its replacement by communal currencies controlled from beyond the state.

Yet, for all these examples of state withdrawal, many of the chapters highlight examples of the state's continuing presence and authority, in ways which support the further development of neoliberal spaces, but also in ways which complicate the apparent freedoms of neoliberalism and which enable other practices. Perhaps the clearest example of the first aspect is in Ergün's chapter, in which she stresses the absolutely critical role of the Turkish state in supporting and subsidizing the development of export-oriented, industries and thus their ability to compete in global markets. It was not simply the 'invisible hand of the market' that enabled the growth of Turkey's textile and clothing industries but explicit and important support – political and fiscal – from the state. State policy also plays a critical role in the analyses of May et al. in their discussions of migration and neoliberalism. In this case, despite the apparently free flow of neoliberal policy prescriptions from the West and the emphasis within these on free markets, immigration is an area in which the state, in this case the British state, continues to play a very proactive role, limiting the freedom to move to the UK, especially for some groups. Notwithstanding the deregulation that characterizes many of the labour markets in which migrants participate, the state still manages access to them and this indicates the limits of state withdrawal. In Marx's chapter, the actions of the state are seen as critical to many of the informal economies of Durban's Ntuzuma district. In documenting the articulations between these informal activities and other economic spheres, Marx draws attention to the importance of state-provided infrastructures (water, electricity, public transport) for many of the activities highlighted. But in identifying this connection, Marx also notes that the dependence of informal activities on state infrastructures puts them at risk if the state were ever to withdraw provision. All of these examples point to ways in which the state – and analyses of it – remain central to our understandings of the spaces of neoliberalization.

The spatialities of neoliberalism

Many of the issues explored above indicate clearly the multiple spaces of neoliberalization. The articulation of neoliberalism with so many spheres of economic, social and political life suggest its extension into myriad spaces – the home, the workplace, the community, the state and the parish – and its impact on the renegotiation of relationships between the local, national and global. Equally, these multiple spaces have real effects on the form and dimensions that neoliberalization takes. Almost all of the authors suggest that one of the features of neoliberalization is indeed the collapse of scales, such that the distinctions between the local and global seem to disappear. Everyday lives are increasingly globalized and flows of capital, people and ideas prompt the emergence of both transnational and translocal spaces in which distant locations are juxtaposed and articulated. In other ways, the emphasis we have placed on the diverse incarnations of neoliberalism highlight the difference that geography makes. As a number of the chapters suggest, not only are there significant geographical variations – at every scale – in the impacts, manifestations and negotiations of neoliberalism, but there is also a consequent demand for varied responses to neoliberalism.

Above and beyond this insistence on spatial difference, the chapters have also indicated ways in which the institutions of neoliberalism employ spatial strategies. The most marked example of this is the very particular spatiality of the subcontracted workshops in peripheral Istanbul, discussed by Ergün. Despite being a key part of global circuits of value, these workshops are usually very small and find themselves not only in peripheral neighbourhoods of the city but, more particularly, hidden in residential areas, often in basements and garages with little indication of their existence (cf. Begg et al. 2005). Their size and location enable flexible and exploitative employment practices and also allow them to slip from the view of employment regulators – and also from trade unions.

The use of spatial strategies by the proponents of neoliberalism and their conflation of scales lead to similar practices on the part of those contesting neoliberalization. In Argentina, for example, whilst some barter networks valued the locality of their exchanges, others 'did not support the opposition of the local to the global, believing that the local can be small-minded and xenophobic, while globalization can imply connection, solidarity, communication and support'. In the UK, political campaigns for a 'living wage' are not only founded on widespread coalitions of local organizations but also insist on geographically varied solutions, even whilst making solidaristic connections to campaigns elsewhere.

A further point – indicated in many of the examples above but made particularly convincingly by Marx in his chapter – is the need to map not only the spaces of neoliberalism but also the spaces where other logics are dominant. For Marx, understanding the spatialities of neoliberalism and its others is politically important, since 'part of the process of resisting neoliberalism is not to presuppose that any particular economic activities are inherently confined to particular geographic areas of the city or are always necessarily dominant, but to be able to pay attention to where and when they are'.

Peripheral neoliberalisms

All of these examples highlight the spatialities of neoliberalism, both in its practices and in its manifestations. Yet one of the most important spatialities of neoliberalism is in its materialization as a mobile technology, as Olson suggests, citing Ong (2007), 'moving through and across networks to become embedded in places in different ways'. As May et al. explore in their chapter, neoliberalism's mobilities mean that policies, practices, people and myriad other neoliberal forms travel across borders, to and from cores and peripheries, and across scales.

Social Justice and Neoliberalism has focused on neoliberalism's movements to and from the margins, whether those are understood spatially or socially (and often both) and many of the book's chapters have explored the different patterns of these movements. In the chapters by May et al., Ergün, Olson, North and Smith et al.

attention was drawn to the role of key global institutions in 'exporting' neoliberalism to 'peripheral' states through the conditionalities of structural adjustment and post-socialist transition. Other chapters (such as those by Marx and North) have documented the ways in which neoliberalism's travels are assisted by many institutions and individuals in peripheral states, including political elites, certain interest groups, entrepreneurs and business leaders. Yet it is not just indigenous elites which can be seen to support neoliberalism. As we outlined above, key facets, such as the language of responsibility and enterprise, are adopted and embedded by more subaltern groups. In these ways, the book's chapters challenge any conceptualization of neoliberalism as something which is only imposed externally and only about the reinscribing of the privileges of the ruling class.

However, North's example of the ways in which subaltern groups develop their own currencies and markets, apparently mimicking the enthusiasm for market solutions promoted by neoliberal actors, raises questions about the extent to which we can automatically describe these peripheral adaptations as neoliberal. North argues that whilst a clear emphasis is placed on markets, this is tempered by rules, formal and informal, which insist that activity within the market is fair, communal and non-exploitative. Echoing Gibson-Graham (2006), North suggests we need to analyse carefully the politics of economic activities, to avoid making assumptions about their meaning and value. Similarly, Olson's account of the Surandina's reluctance to challenge the privatizations of the early 2000s could point to the Church's co-option into neoliberal structures, but in fact, Olson argues, '[p]rivatization in places where utilities are already poorly supplied and too expensive for most residents is not understood as the triumph of harsh individualism over communal compassion.' These examples, and others which could be drawn from the chapters above, all suggest that interrogating the meaning of what appear to be peripheral neoliberalisms is critical to understanding the translation of ideas and practices from the core.

Above and beyond these negotiations which allow peripheral actors to remake and revalue neoliberal forms and policies, many of the book's chapters have also focused on explicit attempts to contest neoliberalism. These forms of resistance and contestation vary from the sorts of mundane practices of other, often older economic logics (such as those discussed in Marx and in Smith et al.) to everyday activities which make neoliberal spaces liveable (such as the kinship and other collective strategies developed by Turkish clothing workers in Ergün's chapter), to more active and explicit attempts to create new, radical economic spaces, such as those of the Argentinian barter networks. Marx outlines that in addition to the need to see a rethinking of the economy as a strategy of resistance, it is necessary to make visible the many spaces of economic life, highlighted above, which have not been subsumed within neoliberal capitalism. Of course, not all of the strategies developed for coping with the predations of neoliberalism are positive – the chapters by Hörschelmann and May et al., for example, point to the ways in which some marginalized actors resort to scapegoating, in these cases through racism, to make sense of their marginalization.

North, in his chapter, suggests that not all of those who appear to be resisting neoliberalism are doing so explicitly. For many who participated in the barter networks in Argentina, their engagement was a strategy for survival rather than an act of political resistance. This meant that when economic circumstances changed, so too did the fate of these radical new economies – they 'ended in disbandment, defeat and disgrace', for all the hopes and expectations of the activists. Ergün, too, highlights the limits to resistance: 'acts of resistance and solidarity are threatened by work insecurity'. In an environment in which organized trade unions are both reluctant and unable to offer real support to these exploited workers, resistance is restricted to attempts to insist on limited rights. The relative absence of trade-union activity in this case study reflects a concern in a number of chapters for the loss of collective action: Hörschelmann argues that the east German young people she worked with are much more likely to try to develop individualized responses to the pressures of uncertain employment transitions than to seek a 'sustained political response'.

Neoliberalism and social justice

Many of the critiques that have been levelled at neoliberalism have focused on the deleterious impact that its manifestations have on social justice. This issue has been at the heart of this volume, and all of the chapters have drawn attention to the widening income inequalities and the increasing polarization of economic opportunity which have accompanied neoliberalism's travels. In every chapter, case studies have explored the ways in which less powerful and marginal social groups have become impoverished and struggled to ensure their social reproduction.

Yet each of the chapters has also drawn attention to the broader costs of the violence associated with neoliberal transformations. Repeatedly, the contributions to this book discuss the importance, and apparent erosion, of dignity and respect, pushing for an understanding of social justice which goes beyond the material to account also for the emotional costs of commodification, insecurity and individualization. The incorporation into neoliberalism of attempts at governance of the self reinforces the need to analyse these subjective experiences.

In drawing attention to these different aspects of social justice, many of the authors, and the case studies they explore, highlight movements and motivations which take responses to neoliberalism beyond the economic. These include the Green motifs of the barter networks of Argentina; the spiritual and religious spaces of the Surandina; the search, among east German youth, not only for economic stability but also for a life partner; the cultivation of other values, nurtured within social and kinship networks and derived from local cultural formations; and the demand for empowerment and the right to participate in democratic practices. It is in these variegated struggles for everyday existence that the possibilities for alternative worlds different from those of rampant marketization and commodification may begin to take shape. Most of these projects are in their infancy and their outcomes are at present indeterminate. But they do perhaps provide glimpses of present and future opportunities to imagine and enact alternative scenarios for the most marginalized of communities in a diverse but neoliberalizing world.

References

Begg, R., P. Roukova, J. Pickles and A. Smith (2005) 'Industrial districts and commodity chains: The garage firms of Emilia Romagna (Italy) and Haskovo (Bulgaria)', *Problems of Geography* 1–2: 153–65.

Brenner, R., and N. Theodore (eds) (2002) *Spaces of Neoliberalism: Urban Restructuring in North America and Western Europe*, Oxford: Blackwell.

Castree, N. (2006) 'From neoliberalism to neoliberalisation: Consolations, confusions and necessary illusions', *Environment and Planning A* 38: 1–6.

England, K., and K. Ward (eds) (2007) *Neoliberalization: States, Networks, Peoples*, Oxford: Blackwell.

Gibson-Graham, J.K. (2006) *A Postcapitalist Politics*, Minneapolis: University of Minnesota Press.

Gowan, P. (1995) 'Neo-liberal theory and practice for Eastern Europe', *New Left Review* 213: 3–60.

Hale, A., and J. Wills (eds) (2005) *Thread of Labour: Garment Industry Supply Chains from the Workers' Perspective*, Oxford: Blackwell.

Harvey, D. (2005) *A Brief History of Neoliberalism*, Oxford: Oxford University Press.

Larner, W. (2003) 'Neoliberalism?', *Environment and Planning D: Society and Space*, 21: 509–12.

Leitner, H., J. Peck and E. Sheppard (eds) (2007) *Contesting Neoliberalism: Urban Frontiers*, New York: Guilford Press.

Ong, A. (2007) 'Boundary crossings: Neoliberalism as a mobile technology', *Transactions of the Institute of British Geographers* 32: 3–8.

Smith, A. (2007) 'Articulating neoliberalism: diverse economies and urban restructuring in post-socialism', in E. Sheppard, H. Leitner and J. Peck (eds), *Contesting Neoliberalism: The Urban Frontier*, New York: Guilford Press, pp. 204–22.

Smith, A., and A. Rochovská (2007) 'Domesticating neo-liberalism: Everyday lives and the geographies of post-socialist transformations', *Geoforum* 38(6): 1163–78.

Smith, A., and A. Stenning (2006) 'Beyond household economies: Articulations and spaces of economic practice in post-socialism', *Progress in Human Geography* 30(2): 190–213.

Tickell, A., and J. Peck (2003) 'Making global rules: Globalization or neoliberalization?', in J. Peck and H. Wai-chung Yeung (eds), *Remaking the Global Economy: Economic and Geographical Perspectives*, London: Sage, pp. 163–81.

Watts, M. (1994) 'Development II: The privatization of everything', *Progress in Human Geography* 18: 371–84.

Contributors

Kavita Datta is Senior Lecturer in Human Geography at Queen Mary, University of London. Her research focuses on development, gender and migration issues. She has conducted research in Botswana, South Africa and London. Most recently, she has worked on a collaborative ESRC project with colleagues at Queen Mary examining the role and experiences of migrant labour employed in low-paid sectors of London's economy. She is currently writing a co-authored book, *Global Cities at Work: Migrant Labour in an Uneven World* (Pluto Press).

Ergül Ergün is a researcher focusing on migration, gender and employment. Her recent research projects include refugees' access to education and employment in the UK and global restructuring processes and labour flexibility in the clothing industry in Turkey. Her publications include *Making a Difference: Empowering Birmingham's Migrant Community Organisations* (JRF, 2008) and *Dynamics of Honour Killings in Turkey* (UNFPA and UNDP Turkey Branch, 2005), and papers on the integration of Istanbul's neighbourhoods into the world market.

Yara Evans is a Visiting Research Fellow in the Department of Geography at Queen Mary, University of London. Her research interests include industrial restructuring and the impacts on labour in Brazilian car manufacturing and on business responses to changing market conditions in the clothing industry in London. Between 2005 and 2007, she worked with colleagues at Queen Mary on a project investigating the role of low-paid migrant workers in London's economy. She is currently co-authoring *Global Cities at Work: Migrant Labour in an Uneven World* (Pluto Press).

Joanna Herbert is a Leverhulme Early Career Fellow in the Department of Geography, Queen Mary, University of London. Her research focuses on experiences of migration, including the South Asian diaspora and low-paid migrants in London. Her current project in on the oral histories of Ugandan Asians in Britain and she is also working with colleagues on a book entitled *Global Cities at Work: Migrant Labour in an Uneven World* (Pluto Press). She is author of *Negotiating Boundaries in the City: Migration, Ethnicity and Gender in Britain* (Ashgate, 2008).

Kathrin Hörschelmann is Lecturer in Human Geography at the University of Durham. Her research focuses on issues of identity change and marginalization in postsocialist societies as well as on globalization and young people's cultural practices. She is currently researching questions of global citizenship and young people's involvements in international politics. Forthcoming publications include the co-authored book *Children, Youth and the City* (Routledge) and the co-edited book *Contested Bodies of Childhood and Youth* (Pearson Macmillan).

Colin Marx is Lecturer in Human Geography at Kingston University, London. He has worked extensively on implementing community-based infrastructure and housing projects, mobilizing homeless communities, and feeding into South African and international urban policy debates such as the UN Global Human Settlements Report in 2003. He has researched the relationships between informal economies, poverty and urban economic growth in Durban. He is currently leading research into 'land biographies' in Johannesburg with researchers at the University of the Witwatersrand.

Jon May is Professor of Geography at Queen Mary, University of London. His research has mainly focused on the geographies of homelessness. He has also been working with colleagues on a project exploring the role of migrant labour in London's low-paid economy. He is currently working with these colleagues on a co-authored book: *Global Cities at Work: Migrant Labour in an Uneven World* (Pluto Press). He is chair of the Royal Geographical Society's Urban Geography Research Group, and an editor of *Geography Compass*.

Cathy McIlwaine is Reader in Human Geography in the Department of Geography, Queen Mary, University of London. Her research focuses on issues of gender, poverty, urban violence and migration, largely in Latin America, but also with Latin Americans in London. Her publications include *Encounters with Violence in Latin America* (with Caroline Moser, 2004). She has worked as a consultant for the Commonwealth Secretariat, the Inter-American Development Bank and the World Bank. She is currently a Trustee of CARILA Latin American Welfare Group in London.

Pete North is Senior Lecturer in the Department of Geography, University of Liverpool. Pete has a long-standing interest in social movements, utopias and alternative economic experiments. He is the author of two books on alternative currency movements, *Money and Liberation* (University of Minnesota Press) and *Alternative Currency Movements as a Challenge to Globalization?* (Ashgate). His current research focuses on radical local economic development strategies as a response to climate change and peak oil, and on local climate-change activism.

Elizabeth Olson is Lecturer in Geography at the University of Edinburgh. Her research explores emerging geographies of religion, with a particular focus on the intersections between religion and development and links with transnational processes of social differentiation. She also focuses on the influences of changing organizational culture in development, and co-edited *The Search for Empowerment* (with Anthony Bebbington, Michael Woolcock and Scott Guggenheim, Kumerian Press). Her current work examines intergenerational constructions of lived religion among young Christians in Glasgow.

Vincent Pattison is a Lewis–Gluckman Post-Doctoral Research Fellow at the Brooks World Poverty Institute (BWPI), University of Manchester. He completed his Ph.D. in 2008 in the Department of Geography at the University of Manchester on *The Living Wage and Working Poverty in Manchester*. During the research he worked closely with the public services union Unison and provided empirical evidence for the Unison submission to the Low Pay Commission in 2007. His work at the BWPI investigates poverty, social inequality and social exclusion in north-west England.

Alena Rochovská is a Lecturer of Social Geography at the Department of Human Geography and Demography, Comenius University, Bratislava. Her current research concerns poverty in Slovakia, social inequalities, household economies and feminism. She has worked on the project Social Exclusion, Spaces of Household Economic Practice and Post Socialism with Adrian Smith, Alison Stenning and Dariusz Świątek. This resulted in the preparation of the book *Domesticating Neoliberalism: Social Exclusion*

and Spaces of Economic Practice in Post Socialism for Wiley–Blackwell's
RGS–IBG book series.

Adrian Smith is Professor of Human Geography and Head of the
Department of Geography at Queen Mary, University of London. His
research focuses on the economic and social geographies of transforma-
tions from state socialism in East-Central Europe and on the restruc-
turing of global industries. Publications include *Work, Employment and
Transition* (co-edited with Al Rainnie and Adam Swain, Routledge, 2002).
He is currently working with Alison Stenning, Dariusz Świątek and Alena
Rochovská on a book entitled *Domesticating Neoliberalism: Social Exclu-
sion and Spaces of Economic Practice in Post Socialism* for Wiley–Blackwell's
RGS–IBG book series. He will be an editor of *European Urban and
Regional Studies* from 2009.

Alison Stenning is Reader in Economic and Social Geography in the
Centre for Urban and Regional Development Studies, within the School
of Geography, Politics and Sociology at Newcastle University. She has
been involved in researching household and community economies in
Poland and Slovakia, the remaking of European steel communities, the
politics of urban development in Oświęcim (Auschwitz), post-accession
labour migration from central Europe to the UK and the transformation
of gender and work in Poland. She is currently working with Adrian
Smith, Dariusz Świątek and Alena Rochovská on a book entitled *Domesticating Neoliberalism: Social Exclusion and Spaces of Economic Practice in Post
Socialism* for Wiley–Blackwell's RGS–IBG book series.

Dariusz Świątek is a Research Assistant at the Institute of Geography
and Spatial Organization, Polish Academy of Sciences, Warsaw, Poland.
His research has included work on households and community economies in Poland and Slovakia, and entrepreneurship and infrastructure
network development in suburban areas of middle-sized Polish towns.
He is currently working with Adrian Smith, Alison Stenning and Alena
Rochovská on a book entitled *Domesticating Neoliberalism: Social Exclusion and Spaces of Economic Practice in Post Socialism* for Wiley–Blackwell's
RGS–IBG book series.

Katie Willis is Reader in Development Geography at Royal Holloway,
University of London. Her research focuses on social differentiation
(particularly along class and gender lines) in processes of migration,
urbanization and health-sector reform. She has conducted research
in Mexico, China, Singapore and California. Her publications include
Theories and Practices of Development (Routledge, 2005) and *State/Nation/*

Transnation (co-edited with Brenda Yeoh, Routledge, 2004). She is editor of *Geoforum* and *International Development Planning Review.*

Jane Wills is director of *The City Centre: Researching City Lives and Connections* and Professor of Geography at Queen Mary, University of London. She has long-standing interests in political economy, labour geography and urban politics. Recent projects have focused on the future of trade unionism, looking at the development of new forms of labour internationalism, European Works Councils and community unionism; the role and significance of migrant workers in low-paid employment in London; and the development of new political identities around the London living wage campaign.

Index